*to Julus
as promised
Romy*

Over The Hills
And Far Away

Military stories from the trenches,
the desert and the jungle

Romy Wyeth

*Over the Hills and o'er the Main,
To Flanders Portugal and Spain,
The Queen commands and we'll obey
Over the Hills and Far Away.*

George Farquar The Recruiting Office

BROWN
DOG
BOOKS

Published under licence by Brown Dog Books and The Self-Publishing Partnership
7 Green Park Station, Bath BA1 1JB
www.selfpublishingpartnership.co.uk

ISBN printed book: ISBN: 978-1-78545-057-0

Cover design by Kevin Rylands

Printed and bound by CPI Group (UK) Ltd, Croydon CR0 4YY

DEDICATION

My grandfather Sidney Ernest Butt
My grandfather was born in Ryde on the Isle of Wight on 11th July 1899. He left school at the age of thirteen to become a grocer's assistant, shortly before his sixteenth birthday he lied about his age and enlisted in the 8th Hampshire Regiment as part a Pals Brigade, (The Isle of Wight Rifles, Princess Beatrice's Own) nicknamed 'The Isle of Wight Gurkhas.' He is listed on the Nominal Roll of the 8th Hampshire's on 5th July 1915 as Rifleman 1844 S. E. Butt 'A' Company IOW Rifles.

He sailed from Liverpool as part of 163 Brigade, 54th East Anglia Division, the final major reinforcements to the Gallipoli Campaign aboard the Cunard Ocean Liner 'Aquitania' to the Dardanelles. Disembarking at Suvla Bay, Gallipoli on 10th August 1915, he went into action for the first time against the Turks on the 12th August. Later he took part in the Egyptian and the Palestine Campaigns until after four years, he was 'disembodied' rather than demobilised on 24th July 1919 just thirteen days after his twentieth birthday. He re-enlisted in the Royal Engineer Corps in 1920. The following year he was posted to Larkhill Military Telephone Exchange in Wiltshire as a signalman-operator.

Later he became a civilian operator and finally the Supervisor of Bulford Military Exchange for more than thirty years. He received the British Empire Medal in the Queen's Birthday Honours on 24th September 1963, and the Imperial Service Medal possibly in 1964 the year he retired.

I grew up listening to his sanitised stories of soldiering in Egypt and Palestine, he never talked about Gallipoli. Grandad was the most significant person in my life, he taught me a great deal and it is because of him that I grew up with an abiding fascination with the military.

Egypt Sidney Butt on right

CONTENTS

INTRODUCTION

Nothing is truly gone until it is forgotten

Over the Hills and Far Away is a collection of chronological military stories that begins with an Australian soldier's journey across the sea to the Wylye Valley in the Great War and ends with the experiences of a doctor in Iraq in 2003. It takes the reader to the trenches, the desert and the jungle; to the battlefield and into the urban landscape of Northern Ireland during 'The Troubles.' It is not about any one place, or any particular war, it is a collection of fascinating individual accounts told, in the main, by men experiencing conflict in a hostile environment far from home.

When I wrote *Sterner Days*, a collection of World War Two memories published in 1995, I tapped into a treasure trove of personal information that would now be lost unless it had been recorded. Many of the people who shared their stories with me are no longer alive but their unique experiences live on the page for future generations. I am very grateful to the people over the years who have trusted me with their own or their families' stories.

This book of soldier's stories has had an incubation period of seven years. I came up with the idea in 2008, I had three complete and two part written chapters before putting it aside until eighteen months ago. By then I knew where to find some of the stories I wanted as well as discovering new sources that opened a window onto a specific period of military significance.

It is my great good fortune to know the remarkable men who have contributed to this book; they have been generous with their time, patient with my probing and willing to share personal experiences.

I am also indebted to Brian Marshall who, not for the first time, came to my rescue by altering and improving photographic images. Special thanks to David and Helen Belchamber for proof reading and correcting the text.

'Over the Hills and Far Away' is a traditional song dating back to the late 17th century. There are various versions:

Thomas D'Urfey's *'Wit and Mirth'* or *'Pills and Purge Meloncholy'*;

George Farquar *'The Recruiting Officer'*;

John Gay *'The Beggars Opera'*;

John Tam *'Sharpe' films (different verses for different episodes)*

The chorus however remains fairly constant except for the monarch.

CHAPTER 1

Training and Transit Letters from an Australian Soldier 1916

L/Cpl Henry John Hatherley
46th Battalion
Australian Imperial Force

Expeditionary Force Encampment Royal Agricultural Show Grounds, Ascot Vale 27th April 1916

Dear Mother,
You will see by the above address that I have moved from Royal Park Camp. We were sent over here as guard, about a hundred of us for a week, we came here last Tuesday and will be here until next Tuesday. We have twenty-four hours on guard and twenty-four off. I am sergeant of one guard, twelve men, and have to march them about a mile and a half to guard another camp. We go on guard at 6pm and come off guard the same time the next day, all that time we can't take our boots off. I do not have to do any guard, just sit in a tent or walk around and see if my men are at their post, at the end of the day I have to write a report out. They have two hours on and four off. We go on guard again tonight, last night I went into town to the pictures, got back about midnight.

We had three hours drill the next day and do nothing all the rest of the day- just walk about the Show grounds or play billiards etc.

You will see by this that I have no chance of coming down to Portarlington [1] I have just had my hair cut in the Show grounds.

With fondest love,

Son

Dear Ida,

Today I received three letters, one from Mother a two from yourself. I am stationed at the Show grounds now, for a week, perhaps longer. We get off every other evening but it is 7pm before we get away so you see I do not have enough time to get to Hawthorn. I had a night off last Friday from 7pm until 4pm Saturday afternoon- I went home and straight to bed. Got up at 10am the next morning.

I met Jack King *[his cousin]* on Saturday; he is on final leave, goes on the 14th of this month. I get plenty to eat here, Sundays dinner boiled mutton, boiled potatoes, onions, apples and rice, hot buttered scones, cake also bread and jam. No more news will try and meet you at the boat when you come home.

Expeditionary Force Encampment Broadmeadows 18th May 1916

A line to let you know I will be home tomorrow afternoon all being well. My cold has gone again thank goodness. We are getting pretty good at signalling, very nice officers and plenty to do, but no hard work, sitting down most of the time. This morning we all paraded off for hot

Broadmeadows Training Camp in an outer suburb of Melbourne. Harry 3rd from left Jack Laing 4th left in the third row.

showers, they are all right! Everyone must have one once a week.

The poor Infantry had had another long march today, left camp at 2pm and will not be back until midnight. I have just had a shave, had to wait nearly an hour for my turn, there are about half a dozen barber shops in camp. We had a great concert in one of the halls last night, one of the best I have ever seen. I got a letter from Colac tonight – it took nine days to reach me.

29th May 1916

Dear Ida,

We are having nice weather here now. This morning we went over for hot showers but there were so many that we came away again. I have not met that fellow Holland that you were speaking about yet but I believe he is in the school. I saw the photos today, the big one is a beauty, I am getting one of each so far, they are pretty expensive three shillings and two shillings each. They will be in one of the illustrated papers this week; I think I cannot get them until Monday. I am getting pretty good at school now; I will be a signaller before I am finished.

7th June 1916

Dear Mother,

A line to let you know I will be home tomorrow night. Are you going down to Uncle Albert's tomorrow night? If so I will go too. I will bring the photos home with me. My cold is getting on fine but far from well yet.

Two thousand left for the Front and about a thousand came in from Bendigo tonight. The Signal school is running another car Wednesday night so I should be home about 6.60.

The following letter was from one of Harry's mates, a boot maker from Colac, George Mckay. George was killed in France on the 28th August 1916 aged 30 in France. [2]

8th July 1916

Dear Jack,

Just a line hoping you are quite well as this leaves me. I received your ever welcome letter the other day and was pleased to hear from you and that you were having a good time in camp. You are having a better time than we used to have, for we had no leave only three days final leave and that very hard to get. We are having glorious weather over here and the crops are looking real well.

I don't know if you will land in Egypt, but if you do and want a good look round bring plenty of money with you, about 50 pounds will see you a good way. The time I was in Egypt a good many months cost me over 100 pounds. The best way is to get a party and hire a motorcar and they will give you some idea of all the best places to go. My Address is Geo. McKay, 7th Battalion, D Company AIF France. I am very short of news for this mail so I think I will bring this short note to a close, wishing you the best of luck.

I am your old pal,

Geo McKay

Harry left Port Melbourne at 3pm on 16th August 1916

Dear Mother, Ida and Dad,

I am having a good trip so far and the ship is rolling a treat now, I am not sick and have not been so far I think I ought to see it through now. A great crowd of the fellows including my two Jacks were down to it and are still down. I had breakfast this morning so I am pretty good. We have the full run of the ship including the upper decks and can buy eatables and soft drinks at the canteen.

We sailed down the south channel after leaving the pier. I thought it would have been light when we went through the heads but it was pitch dark and search lights from both sides playing on the water made a pretty scene. We then dropped the pilot at the pilot ship outside the heads. It is rough and very dark; I don't like his game much. We had tea before we got outside, tripe and bread and butter jam and tea, plenty of it and are crowded at the table. Two take the job of getting the meals and washing up etc. We give them a shilling each man, two men to each table (16 men at a table). They have the job until the end of the voyage so that is a good thing to miss. After tea we bought some soft drinks and went to a card table and played cards until bed time.

When I got down below they were hanging their hammocks up. The blessed place was full of them I could not stand up anywhere for them and had to go along the floor on my hands and knees they were packed so close. I got hold of a hammock; they are made of canvas and could not find anywhere to hand it. So I looked around and found a good place under the stairs, plenty of room and plenty of air. I had the pick of the lot. I did not get undressed, no one did, just my boots and overcoat off. When I got up went to the upper deck and had a good look around, we were quite close to the land at Portland. There was another ship right beside us going the same way a fine boat and she was rolling. I put the glasses on her, it was the Indiana. She is way ahead of us now, much faster than us. We expect to be in Adelaide tomorrow.

Dear Ida,
Just left Adelaide 2 hours late. We called at the outer harbour for about 6 hours but were not allowed off.

Dear Mother, Ida and Dad,
We left Durban early in the morning and all the way to Cape Town we got tossed around a treat, not rough but a very heavy swell. We were in sight of land all the way. The coastline is very mountainous. Just outside Durban we saw an old wreck, a fine big ship. It happened about 4 months ago. We rounded the Cape of Good Hope on a beautiful day just about a mile out from it. It is one mass of high mountains and with a heavy sea running made a fine picture. From the cape right up to Cape Town is one continuous range of high mountains until you come in sight of Table Mountain. You can pick it out miles ahead by the shape of it.

We got into port at 6 in the evening and were told we could not get off as we would be off first thing in the morning, but we kicked up such a fuss that they changed their mind. Before any body was let ashore we had to send a strong guard to guard certain parts of the town, the real bad parts. I was one of them. We were told it was dangerous for a soldier to walk in these parts. Five murders had taken place in these parts in the last three weeks and two Australian soldiers had been knifed as well as others robbed.

We marched about a hundred of us to the Barracks and a South African Officer took charge of us and posted us in different parts of the town. We had to go in batches of 6, as any smaller number would have been done for as the Officer told us. It was dark when he left us. We were on duty for two hours at a time. The things I saw in that short time would make any man blush. I could write a book on that two hours alone.

We were all disappointed at the place. It is a town made up of black and whites and every other breed under the sun. Not half the town speaks English, Dutch I think it must be the part I was guarding. You never heard any one speak English, unless they spoke to you, but they all seem to be able to speak it if they want to. All the blacks dress in European clothes and in the very best at that and they seem to think they are one above the whites and they like to let you see it too. When we were walking up and down these parts on guard they called us everything they could think of and young girls would come up to us and have a yarn to us and if you could have heard the talk and the carrying ons of them, it was disgusting. Of course we enjoyed it. Every time they saw some of the South African mounted soldiers riding along, (they paraded up and down to keep order) they would run and when they had passed back they would come. As usual the Australians have got a bad name here. None of the white girls in other parts of the town would speak to us.

While I was waiting outside the barracks to go on guard I stopped two young girls and asked them to post some letters for me I did not know whether I would get the chance to post them and had no stamps but as soon as I went over to them they went for their life. Any way I got them to come back and gave them a shilling to get the stamps and away they went. In about half an hour they came back with the change. I went out on one of the piers afterwards, a fine pier all lit up with coloured lights and a nice band playing, it was crowded, nearly everybody speaking Dutch. I sat down beside two girls and began speaking to them, they moved away a by then and would not look at me, so I asked them why we were all turned down. They gave us a good look up and down and seemed satisfied so we had a yarn for a good while.

Dear Mother Dad and Ida,

From now on all our letters will be censored. I had a lot of tram rides in Durban and very pretty ones at that. The suburbs are all situated on the hills surrounding the town, and if you imagine Belgrave with a few more houses, of course beautiful homes at that and change the gum trees into palms and tropical trees also the black women and boys with their bright coloured clothes on you will have some idea of a Durban suburb. The streets of the city are wide and well kept and the shops are the very latest just like our big drapers in Chappel St. Hotels everywhere, all great big buildings, oriental style all white. Durban is a great holiday resort for the heads of South Africa. It does not matter where you are whether in the city or in the hills or on the beach you see the rickshaws, no cabs. If you want to go to the hotel from the boat you hire one, if you have luggage you hire another one. You get in the first one and the other follows right behind and a way you go for three pence a mile. I think the soldiers ran them off their feet. I had a bath in the city baths just like our city baths in Melbourne but salt. On the beach they have another fine one about a hundred yards off the sea and another one in the sea. I had a go in the lot.

It was pretty warm while we were in Durban. You go into a cafe and get five courses for a shilling with blacks waiting on you. They dress in long white robes with the green sash across their shoulders and a white turban on their heads. Nearly all the white people in Durban are English the same as the Australian is. The blacks are all uncivilised and smiling at you like a lot of kids. When the ship left the people threw oranges at us in the thousand and lovely pineapples. Y.M.C.A. in the heart of the city gave us meals for two pence eggs boiled, cakes and all sorts of things, fruit as much as you wanted for nothing, cigarettes thrown in. All the toffs of the town waited on you. The tables were set out on the lawns under the palm trees. At different churches you could get meals free. Everyone was sorry when we left and we all want to see Durban again.

We had it rough after leaving Durban and rounding the Cape we got it a treat. We are all looking forward to Cape Town and another good time. I have lost my towel and have not got one now. Today we had drill with life belts on. We have to live in them when we get near England. Well Mother I am in the best of health in every way. We have finished up all the parcels. I will say goodbye for a while now.

Orontes at sea
Dear Mother,
I am sending the post card as a souvenir of Cape Town; it was the only thing I could buy there. We are going through the tropics now and it is getting very hot. Of a night the water is full of phosphorus, just like thousands of stars in the water and as far out as you can see and great flashes of it going in and out and as the nights are very dark it looks pretty. We see thousands of flying fish. They rise out of the water just like a flock of sparrows and fly about fifty yards then back into the water again. I hope Mother you are in the best of health and don't worry about me for I am having a real good time.

Royal Mail Ship Orontes left Melbourne 16th August 1916

15

S.Vicente, Cabo Verde

The town is real Spanish in appearance. For the last two weeks we have had it hot, real hot at that. I am on the last of Aunt Williams's cigars. We are about five days out from England and it is getting a bit cooler. We passed several ships today, a ship is one of the dirtiest things you can live in one gets smothered in coal dust. It is 6.30pm I had tea and a bath after, am now waiting for supper, bread and cheese. We got hold of the potatoes on board and threw them to the natives in the water to make them dive for them. We have to go without potatoes for the rest of the voyage, run out of them! Potatoes are 30 pounds per ton at St Vicente

Orontes at sea

Dear Dad,

I don't know what you think of a voyage but my idea is that it is not the best, and I am one of the best sailors in our crowd. I don't believe there was half a dozen in our boat that was not sick. It was well after Cape Town that they settled down. A trip to South Africa is just far enough, after that the time drags and with three weeks of heat in the tropics just about settles me. Durban by what they tell me has grown a lot since you were there. You did not see Cape Town and you did not miss much. From Cape Town on to Cape Verde the water is as smooth as the bay on a very calm day. Just imagine two weeks of that. From Cape Verde we are not allowed to have a light of any kind, all watertight doors are kept closed and we have to wear life belts day and night also boat drill every day. The water gets rough as you near Spain, a very heavy swell. I don't know when they get rain in these parts. I have not seen any since we left Australia. Our food was good up to a week ago, but is very crook now. There has been plenty of sickness on board but nothing serious. I have kept good right through. Will write again soon.

Orontes at sea 1916

Dear Ida,

Having nothing to do thought I would write to you. I don't know how many letters I have written home since leaving Cape Town. I just sit down and write when I feel that way. If you happened to pass our boat at sea at any time you would think it was one big laundry, washing hanging everywhere. I have a saltwater bath early every day.

On board is the Chaplain. Rev. Prof. Rentoul of RC fame. He is a very old man and very nice, he gives us a lecture on history every now and again. Nearly every evening at sun down we have a sing along on the top deck, a little organ and the YMCA man leads us, he gives a hymnbook all round then we sing. One of our favourites is " Oh Where is my wandering boy tonight ". It sounds great just as the sun is setting and some of the sunsets are beautiful, but I have seen much better in Victoria. It is ten days since we left Cape Town and I can tell you it gets monotonous, but we expect to call at an Island in the next few days

Although we are across the equator the heat was nothing to speak of, nothing to what we get in Melbourne. The ship is printing a newspaper called "The Orontes Times," sold for sixpence, all about the voyage. I am getting one and will send it home. Did Mother get the photo of me in the rickshaw?

We get news about the War every now and then by wireless it is posted all over the boat. Plenty to read on board, hundreds of magazines, great boxes full were put on at Durban. It is five weeks to the day since we left Durban. England is further away than you can imagine, you want to travel the distance to understand it. I will have to throw a lot of things away when I get to England such as socks etc., I can't possibly carry them all about with me

October 13th 1916

Dear Mother Dad and Ida,

When we were within two days of England it began to rain, that misty rain and that night a heavy fog came up and we had to go dead slow as we had no lights, we were in the danger zone and guards were posted all over the ship to watch for submarines. About this time we started to take a zigzag course about a mile each way. The next night was uncanny the water was a mass of phosphorous as far as you could see. The sea was very calm and the night very dark. The phosphorous made our ship show up like day. A sub ought to have seen us miles away. The next day our last on board we saw a destroyer coming at us full speed. She was to take us into Plymouth. She signalled to us for about half an hour giving all the orders that our ship had to do. I read the lot. She then went ahead about three hundred yards and zigzag in front of us all the way to Plymouth.

We passed about a hundred yards off a steamer that had been sunk a few hours before we came along. Just about a yard of her masts sticking above the water. Ships were coming and going all directions. We were in the English Channel. Darkness rain and fog came on again, could not see a yard in front of us. About nine that night we could see the search lights of Plymouth through the fog. We went into Plymouth sound and I could just see a hill at the entrance faintly through the fog, my first sight of England it was raining hard. We anchored out a bit and turned in for the night, slept anywhere with all our clothes on, all our blankets had been taken from us. I bought a newspaper next morning and it said that the Orontes was four days overdue and was reported missing.

We entered Plymouth Sound on Sunday 9 pm. 1st of October 1916. We awoke at daybreak next morning and ran on deck to have a look at the place. Saw nothing but fog. After a while it cleared up and we had a look around. The harbour is about a mile square and from what I could see very deep with sloping hills all around covered with green grass. The first thing that strikes you is the beautiful greenness of England. The entrance to the harbour is a mile across with a breakwater running right across it with an entrance each end. Plenty of shipping in but never saw a warship of any kind and this is a great naval base.

We went ashore in small mail boats, beautifully fitted up a bit smaller than the 'Courier', one named 'Sir Walter Raleigh' and the other 'Sir Francis Drake'. You can see the hills where these two great sailors played bowls before going out to attack the Spanish. We landed at the quay at 11am and got straight into a train, third class. I am very disappointed with their railways. This Company is the Great Western, their engines are like toys compared with ours. Their carriages are short and narrow, all corridor. Their first class cannot compare in any way with our second-class carriages and their third class is not much better than the old Hobson Bays. Their rails are about quarter the thickness of ours very light in fact they are along way behind Victoria in railways. One thing about them they can move some but if they had to pull up some of our hills, they would never get up them. Their lines run on a level track, if there is a little hill they make a cutting if a big one they go right under it

Plymouth is a large city but we did not see much of it passed through it in the train. All the houses are in terraces about five in a terrace, all two and three stories high and they all run in the one direction and face the same way not two terraces facing each other in the same street, one faces the street in the other side, that terrace faces the next street with its backyards facing the other terrace. Just a single row of houses between each street! The streets are very narrow.

They say it rains every day and twice on Sunday here. It rained all the time we were there. This city is different in every way to ours, they live differently, there houses shops and streets are all different. We left Plymouth about midday all excited. Plymouth is as you know is in Devonshire where Dad's people came from. I have been on many a train journey but that one through Devon is beyond me to describe it, it is just like fairyland. How in the world our people came to leave it I don't know. I would like Dad to see it for just a moment

Sunday 29th October 1916

A line to let you know how things are going. By what I can see the English Army is no better than ours. The Australian Army is under what they call Southern Command, which includes Canada and New Zealand, South Africa and India. The British troops are called the Imperial Army. All Australian Officers are over us except the very high Commands whom are all English Officers.

When we first landed in England we were not recognised until 48 hours after. All troops coming from Australia have to bring their own food all the way from Australia for the first 48 hours. Have to carry it along ourselves. When we arrived in this camp we remained two days doing nothing, just eating tinned meat and biscuits, which we brought with us and tons of food in the Camp. After the two days are up, we are handed over to the Australian Imperial Force and then they feed us. Red tape to start with.

All Australian troops arrive here with leather equipment on costing two pound ten each, the sort I was telling you about. When we arrived here it was taken from us and thrown in a heap to rot and we were then given webb equipment [3]. Not allowed to wear the leather at the front. This leather equipment is costing the Australian Govt millions of pounds and is given to you a week before you leave Australia and taken off you a week after you arrive here and thrown in the dust heap.

We all arrived here with two splendid pairs of boots, you saw them. When you get here they are taken off you and thrown in a heap with thousands of others to rot, I suppose, and we are then given a pair of English black boots. Not allowed to wear tan boots in France. Millions more wasted. This is only one or two of the many ways they are wasting our money.

Our fellows are getting killed in thousands, every week in the Somme battle. I have spoken to several officers I know who have come back wounded from the Somme and they told me [two of them Officers] things are in an awful mess over there. Some Officers have got no idea where they are or what they have to do half the time and its nothing for them to get a dozen different orders in as many minutes.

They say the Germans ought to be able to break through anywhere along the Somme line. The conclusion they come to is that the Germans are in a sight bigger mess that we are.

While in London and different parts of England I took particular notice and can say that every man of the fighting age in England is in the Army or the navy. Zeppelin raids in London have done no damage to speak of. London of a night is in pitch darkness and you can't see a yard in front of you, but it makes no difference, the streets are still as busy. London in many ways is disappointing although a very big city [make a dozen or more of Melbourne] is not as large as I expected. We hear of it being dirty but the streets are just as clean as Melbourne streets and all the main streets are wide and some exceptionally wide. Nearly all the London streets are wooden blocked the same as ours.

I went out to the East end to see things and you bet we looked for the worst parts, but came away disappointed. Everything very clean, the streets and lanes kept in good order. All the houses are built in one long terrace running for the full length of the streets. Some parts are bad but could be worse. Canals run in and out among the houses with barges and boats on them and the water in them is awful, they are about thirty feet wide.

St Paul's from the outside view is nothing to look at, very dirty, and if you did not know which Church it was, you would pass it without giving it a second look. Pigeon's fly all over the building and the mess they make over the buildings and the entrance is a disgrace. I don't believe it has been cleaned up for years. The pigeons are very tame. The inside of St Paul's is beautiful, the ceiling is a work of art, monuments are erected all over the floor of statesman and soldiers. Under the floor is where they are buried.

3rd October 1916

England is beautiful and so quaint and pretty, it is one great garden with little villages dotted all over it, even the big towns are not like ours just big villages and just as quaint. We landed at Plymouth, which is of course in Devonshire. England is just as I expected, in every way, but more beautiful, it is just as you read about it, the little village with the little church and the grave yard around with some of the tomb stones falling over and the little cottages with the thatched roof and little square windows, low little doors and brick floors and everything so beautiful and clean. It reminds me of that poem 'The cottage was a thatched one'. That poem describes it exactly.

The roads or lanes as they are called are past describing; they are all like fairyland. The little streams of water running through the country and villages with little rustic bridges, as you see it now so it was hundreds of years ago. The little inns with sign posts outside as it was in the coaching days of old. For 180 miles we travelled through country like this, passing hundreds of those little villages, all alike, you could not tell one from the other. The country is not flat anywhere, just a mass of rolling hills, with little dells like fairyland in between. When I walk through one of these villages of an evening I pinch myself to see if I am awake or dreaming. You may laugh but you would do the same. I realize I am in England. If I saw Pickwick walk out of one of these cottages I would not be surprised.

Harry at Codford Camp

15th October 1916

From Plymouth to Codford is about 180 miles and we were travelling by train. We had a bun and a cup of tea at Exeter. At about 5 that evening we arrived at Codford. Codford is between Salisbury and Westbury. At Westbury you can see the big white horse you read about. From the station we had to march two and a half miles to our camp, passing through Codford village about a mile from the station. Every half-mile along the road is a camp of about a thousand men, just put down amongst the trees.

We now come to the end of the early letters from the training camp near Melbourne across the world to the Wylye Valley in Wiltshire and the Codford Command Depot. Unlike many of his comrades Harry survived the Great War, alive but not unscathed. It is thanks to his son John the 16,000 words of the letters from Codford, from the battlefield and from hospitals in France and London were published in my book "Swords and Ploughshares-Codford during the Twentieth Century' in the autumn of 2007. Only after publication did I realise there were more letters, this time from the voyage across the world on the 'Orontes.'

Henry John Hatherley was born on 29th August 1888 in a suburb of Hawthorn, Melbourne. He had one sister, Ida, who ran a dress making business. His family and close cousins called him 'Son,' the rest of the world knew him as Harry or Jack. After leaving school he was apprenticed as a tailor in his home city; on completing his apprenticeship he took a position as a tailor in Colac, a country town about 80 miles from Melbourne. When he joined up he was a lot older than most of his comrades, twenty-seven years and seven months of age while most of the others were between eighteen and twenty. Being an only son the law was that he could not enlist without both his parents giving individual written consent; his father consented immediately but it took two years before his mother agreed; Harry enlisted in March 1916.

Harry met Jack Laing and Jack Box while they were at training camp in Australia; before they went overseas they were told to pick their mates, Harry told his son John "We were the three Jacks, Jack Hatherley, Jack Laing and Jack Box." Jack Box became sick in England and never recovered, so he didn't go to France with his two mates, it is likely he was repatriated to Australia. Harry's best mate was Jack Laing, the two men had trained together, shared their blankets for warmth when they were sent to Codford and their wartime adventures in the trenches and battles of the Somme. Jack disappeared in the melee of battle and was never heard of again, he is listed as killed in action on 11th April 1917 at Bullecourt aged 23 and is remembered on a panel 142 in the cemetery at Villers-Bretonneaux.

TO THE MEMORY

OF

JOHN ORD LAING

PRIVATE 46TH BATTALION

KILLED IN ACTION AT BULLECOURT, FRANCE,
APRIL 11TH, 1917,

AGED 23 YEARS.

Harry spent fifteen months on his back after being wounded by a shell at Passchendale on 19th October 1917 whilst returning to the front line with two other soldiers; he was hospitalised first in France, then in England and finally in Australia for a long period with a permanent legacy from active service, a stiff left leg. Harry returned to tailoring in the country and it was there he met his wife May Victoria Richards eleven years his junior; they had a daughter and two sons, Nancy Mary, John Evan and William Henry. In 1961 Harry revisited the battlefields and England with May; he died of a heart attack in the Repatriation Hospital in Melbourne on 17th December 1962.

Notes

1) The Hatherley family used to go to Portarlington for holidays, a tradition carried on in later years by Harry's family.

2) Private 2707B George Mckay 7th Battalion Australian Infantry was the son of

Kenneth & Martha Ann Mckay of Colac, Victoria. Joined May 1915 and embarked from Melbourne on board HMAT Ulysses 27th October 1915. George was 30 when he was killed in action on 28th August 1916 in France, he is remembered on the memorial at Villers- Bretonneaux.

3) *Webbing replaced leather that rotted in the muddy wet conditions of the trenches of the Western Front. As Harry arrived towards the end of 1916 and the war was already two years old one would have thought that the Australian Government would have been aware of the fact and saved millions of dollars. The brown boots went the same way as the Australian soldier had his two pairs of brown boots taken away on arrival and was issued with one pair of black boots.*

CHAPTER 2

Cambrai - Known Unto God 1915-1917
Douglas Aplin

The battle of Cambrai between 20th November and 4th December 1917 was the first great tank battle of WWI. The British had projected their forward line into enemy territory but had not taken advantage of the situation, so when Sir Douglas Haig ordered a withdrawal British casualties were 43,000 including 6,000 prisoners taken on the first day, a high cost without any significant gain of territory. Among those casualties, was a young West Countryman, who had been at the first Battle of the Somme 24th June –18th November 1916; Lance Corporal Douglas Aplin, newly engaged and just 18 days before his 21st birthday.

Douglas George Bartlett Aplin was born on 13th December 1895 in Durston, Somerset, the third child and first son of George and Jane Aplin. He had two older sisters, Annie and Hilda, nicknamed Hyld, and three younger brothers John, Edwin and Arthur.

In 1911 at the age of fifteen Douglas was employed as a gardeners lad, boarding with the Lye family at Stall Barton, Kingston near Taunton. His sister Hyld was a kitchen maid with the Peto family in Dorset. He enlisted with the British Army, early in the conflict, either late 1914 or early 1915; Douglas Aplin, service number 11537, served with the 15th [The King's] Hussar's as a cavalry soldier in France.

From Douglas's War Diary we learn that he left Southampton at 7pm on 8th June 1915 arriving at Rouen the next day, joining the regiment at Wormhout in Northern France on 11th June. He went to the trenches on 20th June, digging near Vlamertinghe not far from Ypres in West Flanders and returned July 2nd. He was in the trenches again when a heavy bombardment took place on 13th July and writes on the 18th that the forts they are building have not been discovered by enemy aircraft yet. At the end of July he went to Elverdinghe and Flamertinghe finding both places in ruins.

Douglas on left 2nd row

On the 2nd August when the Brigade went to Dunkirk Douglas's horse was not fit so he was unable to go with them. Two days later he was digging at Elverdinghe Chateau, on 12th August, two men of 'C' Squadron and one artillery man were killed when the position was shelled by shrapnel.

Flowers I leave you on the grass
Where my caravan has rested
All the flowers of love and memory
You will find them when you pass.

You will understand their message
Stoop to kiss them where they lie
But if other lips have loved you
Shed no tear and pass them by.

GUERRE 1914-1916. — Elverdinghe (Belgique). — Le Village et l'Eglise après le bombardment. — The Village and the Church after the bombardment. — LL

Elverdinghe

The Germans shelled the eastern side of camp and village each evening. Several men wounded and six horses killed.

Woods shelled 26th August, three officers and several men wounded of the West Yorks.

Returned from the Chateau at Elverdinghe 5th September, Douglas found the billet at Wormhoudt in an awful mess after the heavy rains.

Douglas left Wormhoudt 23rd September, 9pm and got to Blendecques at 3am 24th September, at 6pm that day he set out again on what proved to be a very uncomfortable 4 hour journey on a very wet night to Estrublanche [?]. By 7pm on 25th September he was within 2 miles of Bethune having passed the 2nd Guards Brigade on the way. On 25th and 26th September Bethune was now full of Allied wounded as well as hundreds of enemy prisoners.

Douglas now moved a few kilometre's back to the top of a hill with the Ammunition Column, he records leaving the next day in continual rain, however the billets were good. He was put on fatigue carrying the wounded at the clearing station when he reached Marles on 30th September.

His diary records:

'Went to the trenches 2nd October for two days, awful sight. We were repairing the German front line trenches. Got a few souvenirs. We were in front of Hill 70 by

Loos, came back to a billet near Flechin called Pippemont.'

He was there for two weeks then went to Rebecq where a big draft joined them. His regiment was digging near St Omer and billeted around Derves, during this time their farm was condemned so they moved to a better one.

He seems to have had a jolly Christmas- but was digging again on 26th, recalled on 28th and left his billet for the trenches on 30th December. New Year 1917 was spent outside of Bethune the regiment moved up in reserve on 2nd January and went to the front line for 4 days in the Hollenzollen redoubt on 5th. Douglas was in the saps [1] bomb throwing after which he was out of the trenches for an eight day rest period, went in again on 16th and came out on the 20th. There was a surprise turnout on the night of 26th January, the regiment had left when he returned to the billet at 8.00 so with several others he followed them up but was unable to find them until the next morning.

Douglas writes:

We stopped at VERMELLES for two days on fatigue and then took over the front line on 29th January. We had a jucit? 24 hours in sap 2, then went to OBI in reserve for 24 hours. Trench mortars have been very numerous today 31st January.

We went to BETHUNE for six days then up the ... for four days for the last time. We did not occupy the saps, until the last 24 hours. We had snow and rain. Sap 8 was the worst of all, several mines were blown up around there and the Germans had one charged under us, but didn't blow it up whilst we were there. We handed over to the Sussex on 12th January.

Went to LABOURSE/ LABONNE ? and came back to the horses on 13th. Moved to open billets at BEZINGHAN, then went to the sands below BOULOGNE for a week. Returned BEZINGHAN first week in June.

Vera Virginia Terrace, 22 Balmain Street, Knowle, Bristol
1916-July 9th in orders as L/Cpl16.1,17
Left BEZINGHAN June 23rd and tracked to the SOMME. Was at SENLIS when the attack started on 1st July. Did a lot of moving about then went to GAMACHE for a month's sports. I went in hospital at TREFONT for 10 days. Left GAMACHE and went up the line again in very wet weather and went up the line again to CARNOY valley, expecting to break through. The Guards went over on the 15th September but did not meet with success, so we had to come back. We stopped at WAIL and NAOURS for a few weeks and then tracked back to winter billets at HESDIN LE ABBE, near BOULOGNE. I went on leave 21st November, returned

1st December. Had a fine time.

Got dated back to 12th August 1916 for 1st Class Pro pay. Made Lance Corporal 16th January 1917 and put in charge of the HOTCHKISS gun.

1917

Left winter billets at 9am 5th April in fine weather and made direct for ARRAS where we were in reserve for the Canadians in the attack on VEMY RIDGE on Easter Monday [*Vimy Ridge 9th April*]. The weather had now turned very cold, with frequent snow storms. The horses had a very rough time, several dying.

We left AUBIGNY on 15th April and came back to a village near TREVENT on the CACHE RIDGE. About 17th April the fine weather set in. We moved our horses up to Brigade HQ and put them under cover at VACQUIVIE . Left VACQUIVIE 13th May and did a short march. It rained when we got to the next billet. We moved next day up behind BETHUNE, passing the villages that we stopped at after LOOS. A big digging party went up on 17th May. The digging party came back on 2nd June and we went up to ESTAIRS on 4th June and stopped a week. We got some fine swimming there in the R.Sigs. We returned again to LABOURIERE on 11th June and a digging party went up on 13th.

I went to CAMIERS on 7th June for a course of log range firing with my gun team. We came back on 4th June. Left LABOURIERE on 16th and went to ESTAIRS.

There are no further entries in the War Diary until 10th November when Douglas returns to France after a period of home leave. The story is taken up in letters to his sweetheart, his cousin, Evelyn Vera Aplin, who he called by her second name.

6th November 1917

As you can see dearest I am back in the mud once more. I sent you a PC from the rest camp last night. We had a miserable journey to here this morning. We started at 2.30am and only had about 15 miles to come it took us until almost 1pm. The French trains are awful, it took them six hours to take us about 11 miles. I had a nice trip across yesterday, I left London soon after 7.00am and got to France about 12am. I didn't like coming back, I did feel miserable. Annie and one of the girls from the Club came to see me off. I missed Hyld on Sunday, she did not get my P.C. so she waited at the Club for me and then went to Penge to see my cousin. It was no use me running around to find them so I waited at Hilda's house until she came back at a quarter to ten. I did feel miserable as I might have well have stayed with you until evening. Of course I only had half an hour with Hyld and then went and fetched Nance out of bed so as to let her know I was still alive.

Douglas with his sisters Annie & Hyld

After you making me so happy this morning, it was a shame I could not stay for a little while longer, you should have told me the week before then I could have got a ring and we could have got engaged proper and now you have not got a ring or anything to prove you are my own little girlie. It won't seem right if you get a ring and put it on would it? Although I should very much like it, I have a good mind to write to your dad and get him to get a ring and engage me to you. Do you wish me to tell our people, it just rests with you darling? I feel ever so happy that you have promised to be my little girlie, but it was miserable having to come back, I shall be able to kiss your ring goodnight every night shan't I?. But that will be awfully tame compared with your sweet goodnight kiss. You must let me know darling if you will let me write and tell your people we are engaged. I did not even tell Annie or Hyld, but it was almost the first thing H asked me, but I told her not to be so nosey.

Now darling I have to thank you very much for three lovely letters and the splendid parcel. I have not unpacked it properly yet, only to get this writing paper and pencil out. WE shall have cake for tea, as I cannot fancy army food yet. I did feel wretched this morning, we no sooner got out of town than we were up to our knees in mud, it was pouring with rain so I soon got wet through, so as to make me feel more comfortable. It is a case of "back to the army again sergeant" I have to pack my saddle now and prepare for a brigade marching order tomorrow. The regiment has not moved yet but there are rumours we shall soon. My cousin (proper) was disappointed in not seeing me on Sunday. There is a concert here tonight but I don't know if I shall go, as I am rather tired. We got up for breakfast at12am so we did not have much time for sleep, though I got a snooze on the train this morning. Well sweetheart I will have to go and seen about my saddle soon. I hope you will write before you receive this as I am just longing to get a letter from you, your letters have always been my one ray of sunshine, but what will they be now that I know you really know you really love me darling. Write soon sweetheart, I hear that we probably move at the end of the week, but I shall write before then even if I have not heard from you. Mind you tell me darling if I may write to your dad or mother, as I am longing to tell the whole world that the sweetest little girl on earth has promised to be mine. Goodbye my darling for the present. Give my love to your mother and dad, I shall never be able to thank them enough for letting me stop with you.

With all my truest love darling, I remain your own boy,

Douglas

PS How did the photos come out? I am just longing to get one. I feel sure you will be alright dear.

On 10th November Douglas makes his last entry in his War Diary as the Battle of Cambrai begins:

I have not written for a long time now. I went on leave from FRENCQ on 24th October and went across on the 26th, I go t to LONDON about 3o'clock and went to see Annie. We went to the theatre to see "Our Boy" in the evening. I left LONDON at about 1pm and Vera met me at 3.15 at BRISTOL. I had a fine time there and went down home on Monday morning. I went to CREECH and stopped the night then went back to BRISTOL Friday evening.

Went to the theatre with Vera. We got engaged on Sunday so my luck was in whilst I was on leave. I was sorry to leave BRISTOL but I had to meet Hyld as I had to go back on Monday. I did not get to see Hyld until 10pm. So I only had a very short time with her. Annie and Clarice came to Victoria to see me off on Monday morning.

I had a smooth journey across and re-joined the regiment at FRENCQ. Today, the 10th November, we left FRENCQ and we have a decent track in fine weather. We stopped the

first night at MARISQUEL. The second night at AUTHREUX in a field. The third night at FRECHENCOURT in a field. We slept in tents. Then we did two night marches. We left MORCOURT on the evening of 14th November . After that the country was laid bare by the Germans when they retired last spring.

We are now at LE MESNIL , about 4 klms from PERONNE. The horses are in the stables and we sleep in big huts, all sqdn together.

Mrs M.A. Carter
51 Newmarket Road
Brighton, Sussex

Mrs Baker
17 Victoria Terrace
Brunswick Park
New Southgate, N. London

The above addresses are my two mates in case anything happens to them. They also have mine.

We left billets at 1am and got behind the line, just as the bombardment started soon after daybreak. One brigade has just gone up and we shall probably be on our way within the next two hours. The first messages back report everything is going well.

15th November 1917
My own darling Vera,
At last we have come to the end of journey but I am not sure about the perfect day. We left civilisation at 2pm yesterday and arrived at this show at 2pm. We came all the way through absolute desolate country. The Huns have made a terrible mess of it when they retired last year, there is not a tree or a house standing, you cannot imagine the scene. Nothing but tree stumps, shell holes and ruined houses. The

thing that surprised us was the splendid road that had been made all the way. We are near the town where I thought we were going, but what for no one seems to know. Watch the papers next week and that may enlighten you.

We are sleeping in a long hut, with 120 wire netted beds in it, by lying on the wire you see we get the draft all around us, so we get nearly frozen all through. Goodness knows how we are going to exist when it gets colder. We have to finish making our stables, most of them have no roofs on. It's not safe to walk about at night as there are shell holes everywhere. There is no canteen or anything here, so if rations get short we shall starve. Some of the boys are going into town to see if they can get any cigarettes I wish them luck as my smokes are almost finished.

I am enclosing a £1 note with this, I want you to get me a good pair of gloves, lined and if possible with gauntlets. I think they are about 12/6p , then you can get me some cigs and any sort of tinned eatables with the other, I have a watch here, it is a good one it came from Australia, but the glass is broken and it has got dirty. If I can get it sent I will and then you can get it fixed up and keep it if you like.

My horse only stuck three days marching and then I had to leave him at a village, in the care of a woman. He was proper beat. I have a lively one now, I am afraid she will come to grief if we go into action, as she is too mad to do anything quietly. There are some big shell holes here, full of water. I have been of fatigues all day pumping one of them out to water the horses. We watered about 2000 horses out of one this morning and at the bottom there were thousands of frogs. I have never seen such a sight.

We are beside ruined villages so there is enough wood to last us all winter if we stop. I wish you could see this part of the country down here. I am afraid I cannot explain what it is like, as there are miles and miles of waste country, pitted with shells and trenches, like a great moor, nothing has been cultivated since the war started and then Fritz laid it bare of trees and houses when he retired.

I don't know if leave is still continuing, if there is, one of my mates may go, if he does I will send the watch ad a note by him, but I will find out before the morning and let you know. If the letter only arrives you will know the other is being sent by him.

Well darling today is Thursday; I shall expect an answer to my first letter very soon now. It ought to be an absolutely sweet love letter. I am afraid this isn't much of one, but then there is no news to tell you, later on I will be able to write a letter full of sweet nothings and sweeter memories eh? I am waiting to write a letter to your dad as soon as I hear from you. I heard from mother today; she hoped that I enjoyed myself at Knowles, as though I could have missed enjoying myself when I was with you. I am sure I was never as happy before as when I was on the last walk on Sunday morning. I kiss your ring every night and thank God for giving me the sweetest little girl in the entire world. My thoughts are always with you my sweetheart and I am always wondering what you are doing at the moment. I wish this War was over so we could come home and look forward to something definite, as everything seems so uncertain while this war lasts and we are out here. But don't worry little girlie I shall come back to you all right , however long it lasts, as the fates cannot be so unkind , as to ruin such happiness as ours. When it has started and we have everything to look forward to.

Well little sweetheart have you been and had your photograph taken again? I hope it will be a success when you do ; it seems extraordinary that you do not make a good photo and I shall be awfully pleased to get a really nice one of you. Mind you send one of us together if you get them.

Douglas with Vera Aplin

This is getting quite a long letter isn't it? There are no civilians up here so you may be sure I am being a good boy and I am quite sure that you will be a good girl, just my own little sweetheart. This seems to be almost all the news now. Did you see the king? Mother tells me dad was expecting to drive him when he went to Bath, quite an honour eh? Give my love to your mother and dad and the boys. Don't let the Sported Boyce forget me.

Goodnight my darling, all my fondest love, I remain your ever own boy,

Douglas

19th November 1917

At last your long expected letter has arrived. What a really splendid little letter writer you are. I started singing as soon as I woke up this morning and I was very happy all the morning, so I knew I was going to get a letter from you. Now darling, you explained very nicely and I am quite content to go on as we are until after the war, of course you are rather young fluffy but I feel sure you will not alter your mind. We shall be able to talk everything over when I come home, it won't be long now as with a bit of luck we go over the top in the morning then cheerio for a busy few weeks. I hope it come off alright. I feel a bit excited but not a bit frightened, as I am quite confident that I shall come through alright. If you have not sent the parcel I should leave it for a while until we know what is happening.

I say did you smoke two without being ill?

I wrote you a letter yesterday, so you will get two quite close together again, if I can get this posted. I have just bought a green envelope, [2] so I shouldn't have to trouble to get it censored.

I heard from home today and from Annie. His seems to be all the news of course we are full of what is going to happen tomorrow. I am going to have a game of football now, it may be the last kick we get for a while. Now little girlie, just wait for me as my own little sweetheart until I come and claim you. You wrote an awfully sweet letter, I am afraid this is not such a nice one in return. Remember darling, I shall always love you and you only. Goodbye my darling until I can write again. You did not mention the photo, when do you get them? You must not stay up late very often or when I come home I shall find a tired little sweetheart. Give my love to your mother and dad.

With my love and kisses I remain your loving own boy,

Douglas

This was the last letter that Douglas wrote home, he was killed in action manning his machine gun around 4.30pm in Bourlon Wood on Saturday 24th November.

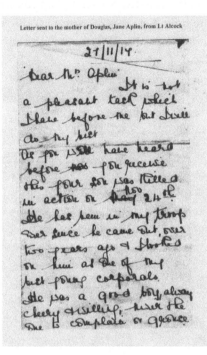

letters from Lt Alcock &Harold Baker

Lieutenant William Poyntz Alcock was the officer in command of 'A' Squadron , 15th (The Kings) Hussars . Douglas had been in his troop since arriving in France, although in his War Diary he states he was a member of 'C' Squadron it is likely that he changed soon after his arrival. For his action during the Battle of Cambrai Lt. Alcock was awarded the Military Cross. His citation reads:

"On November 24th and 25th, when the dismounted men of the Regiment with 119th brigade in Bourlon Wood , by his courage and example in very trying conditions, kept his men together and maintained a critical position, getting the men organised for attacks, and generally displayed particular courage and ability."

An extract from 'The History of 15th Hussars 1914- 1922 'by Lord Carnack M.C. describes the battle of Bourlon Wood:

'At 10am A Squadron under Lieutenant W P Alcock, and a troop of 'C' Squadron under Lieutenant W J Lowe, were ordered to advance and clear the wood as far as its northern edge. Advancing in extended order through the trees, they succeeded in reaching within one hundred and fifty yards of their objective, but were unable to advance further- the fire of the enemy was too heavy. The men began to dig themselves in, so as to hold the position they had reached. They were not able to remain where they were for very long, the troops to their right were forced to fall back owing to the pressure of the enemy and a detachment of the 15th Hussars had to retire in order to conform to this movement.

A counter attack was ordered, with the object of recovering the lost position and shortly afterwards the line moved through the wood towards the enemy. The 15th Hussars moved forward by short rushes , supported by covering fire , and eventually succeeded in getting up close to an enemy strong post in the north east edge of the wood, but at this spot they were brought to a standstill , and had great difficulty maintaining their position.

Towards evening the Germans launched a counter attack against the British positions in Bourlon Wood. The attack was prepared by a severe artillery bombardment, and covered by a heavy barrage of machine gun fire: the German infantry advanced to the attack in successive lines. The men of A Squadron fired steadily and the attack made little progress in front of them.

Unfortunately the enemy succeeded in some places elsewhere, and advanced to some depth. The detachment of the 15th Hussars was soon isolated, and it became necessary to retire in order to avoid complete envelopment.

The retirement was successfully carried out under most difficult conditions, as the enemy fire was extremely intense; the men succeeded in falling back about two hundred and fifty yards, when they turned at bay, and opened upon the advancing Germans a heavy and accurate fire from their rifles and Hotchkiss guns. This at once checked the Germans, who wavered for a short time then rapidly retreated to their original starting point. The 15th followed them up, and dug themselves in. having reached a point of one hundred and fifty yards of one of the enemy strong points. They remained in this position all night, and to the relief of all they were unmolested until the next day.'

In a letter to Vera Aplin dated 21st December 1917 Douglas's friend Harold Baker writes:

'I can't tell you a great deal about Douglas, I did not go into action myself. I only took the gun up so far for Douglas, as he went into action dismounted. I can assure you you have my greatest sympathy, for I can tell you I miss him and also our other chum that was on the gun with us, the last we heard of him he was seriously wounded. I came out from England with Douglas, and I have been with him ever since. It was the 24th November about 4.30pm when he was killed, the first day in action. But where he was buried I couldn't tell you, but should I ever come across his grave I will let you know.'

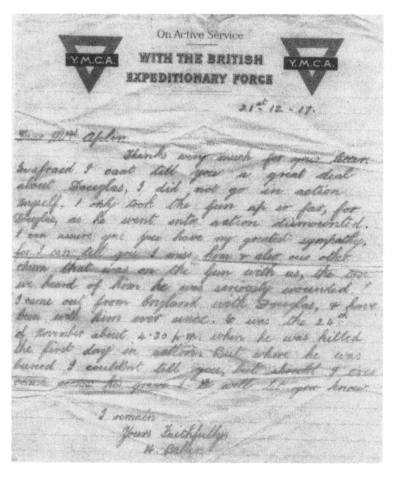

Twenty four year old Private Joseph Carter H/10938 was the other chum mentioned by Harold, these three mates had swopped addresses for just such an eventuality. Joseph was awarded the Military Medal for actions his actions during the Battle of Cambrai, in particular the action in Bourlon Wood where Douglas was killed.

The citation for the Military Medal reads:

Was acting as No2 of a Hotchkiss Gun Detachment. During a retirement the No1 of the gun was killed, and Carter immediately took charge, and, refusing to retire, worked his gun, doing great execution and covering the retirement. On receiving orders from his Officer to withdraw he extracted his gun with great coolness and skill. This was November 24th, 1917, in Bourlon Wood, with Regiment dismounted, acting with the 119th Brigade.'

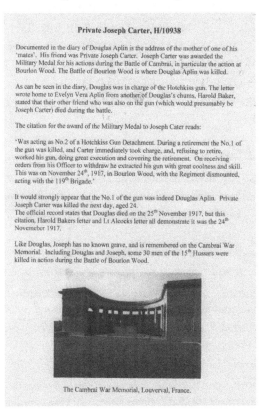

Private Joseph Carter, H/10938

Documented in the diary of Douglas Aplin is the address of the mother of one of his 'mates'. His friend was Private Joseph Carter. Joseph Carter was awarded the Military Medal for his actions during the Battle of Cambrai, in particular the action at Bourlon Wood. The Battle of Bourlon Wood is where Douglas Aplin was killed.

As can be seen in the diary, Douglas was in charge of the Hotchkiss gun. The letter wrote home to Evelyn Vera Aplin from another of Douglas's chums, Harold Baker, stated that their other friend who was also on the gun (which would presumably be Joseph Carter) died during the battle.

The citation for the award of the Military Medal to Joseph Cater reads:

'Was acting as No.2 of a Hotchkiss Gun Detachment. During a retirement the No.1 of the gun was killed, and Carter immediately took charge, and, refusing to retire, worked his gun, doing great execution and covering the retirement. On receiving orders from his Officer to withdraw he extracted his gun with great coolness and skill. This was on November 24th, 1917, in Bourlon Wood, with the Regiment dismounted, acting with the 119th Brigade.'

It would strongly appear that the No.1 of the gun was indeed Douglas Aplin. Private Joseph Carter was killed the next day, aged 24.
The official record states that Douglas died on the 25th November 1917, but this citation, Harold Bakers letter and Lt Alcocks letter all demonstrate it was the 24th Novemeber 1917.

Like Douglas, Joseph has no known grave, and is remembered on the Cambrai War Memorial. Including Douglas and Joseph, some 30 men of the 15th Hussars were killed in action during the Battle of Bourlon Wood.

The Cambrai War Memorial, Louverval, France.

We know that Douglas Aplin was No1 on a Hotchkiss Gun and it is a strong likelihood that it was he who was killed in this action. We can see from the War Diary that there were several instances where the 15th Hussars had to retire under heavy fire. The official record states Douglas Aplin died on Sunday the 25th of November, Joseph Carter's citation, and letters from both Harold Baker and Lt Alcock all demonstrate that he was killed on 24th. In fact twenty-four year old Joseph Carter was killed the following day on the 25th. .Altogether thirty men of the 15th Hussars were killed in action during the Battle of Bourlon Wood.

Neither Douglas or Joseph has a known grave, they are remembered on the Cambrai War Memorial at Louverval, 16 kilometres west of Cambrai. At the entrance of the Commonwealth War Grave Cemetery is the inscription:

TO THE GLORY OF GOD AND TO THE ENDURING MEMORY OF 7048 OFFICERS AND MEN OF THE FORCES OF THE BRITISH EMPIRE WHO FELL AT THE BATTLE OF CAMBRAI BETWEEN TO 20TH NOVEMBER AND THE 3RD DECEMBER 1917, WHOSE NAMES ARE HERE RECORDED BUT TO WHOM THE FORTUNES OF WAR DENIED THE KNOWN AND HONOURED BURIAL GIVEN TO THEIR COMRADES IN DEATH.

Notes

1) **Sap:** *Was an extension to a trench or a tunnel leading from a trench. A sapper was a private in the Royal Engineers. He was a specialist in trenches and tunnels; a military engineer who specialised in fortifications, especially tunnels dug under enemy territory or: a specialist in mines a military engineer, who lays, detects and disarms mines.*

2) **Green envelopes**: *To avoid censorship, soldiers could use a "green envelope" in which the writer would seal his letter and confirm that "the contents refer to nothing but private and family matters". While the letter was still liable to be checked by the censor, this method encouraged soldiers to write more personal communications which, invariably, contained military details that might otherwise have been suppressed.*

Lance Corporal Harold John Baker *aged twenty-five died on 30th March 1918 and is buried in St Sever Cemetery Extension, near Rouen, which contains 8,348 Commonwealth burials from the WWI. According to the Commonwealth War Grave*

Commission Commonwealth camps and hospitals were stationed on the southern outskirts of Rouen and almost all the hospitals remained for the whole of the war. This included eight general hospitals, five stationary, one British Red Cross and one labour hospital and NO2 Convalescent Depot.

I have been unable to discover whether he was killed in action, died of wounds or contracted one of the virulent strains of the early twentieth century diseases prevalent at this time. The tragic fact is that within five months the three men who had served through the war from its beginnings were all dead.

Lieutenant William Poyntz Alcock M.C. was born in 1894, at Tonbridge, the son of Stephen Poyntz (Wright) and Jane Alcock. In the 1911 Census he is residing at The School Sanatorium, Mount Park, Harrow-On-The Hill so obviously went to Harrow School.

1914 16th Dec, the undermentioned Gentlemen Cadets, from the Royal Military College at Sandhurst, to be Second Lieutenants. 15th (The Kings) Hussars. William Poyntz Wright.

1917 William changed his name by deed poll to William Poyntz Alcock, his mother's maiden name.

1918 Jan 18th Gazetted MC. Awarded the Military Cross (for action at Bourton Wood) Lt, William Poyntz Alcock HRS.

Lt Alcock survived the war, only to die in a tragic accident. He had just returned from a month's holiday in Scotland and had been transferred to the 3rd Hussars who were about to leave Aldershot for service abroad, and was on his way to Ireland to collect his kit. He was travelling aboard the SS Rowan when she was rammed from astern by the West Camak in a fog in the North Channel. Passengers mustered on deck. The sinking took place shortly after midnight on the 9th October 1921. The 1,493 ton Laird Line ROWAN, official number 128288, was on a voyage from Glasgow to Dublin. Shortly after she was rammed she was struck by the British 'Clan Malcolm.' The problem was that there was no passenger list kept and some passengers had paid for their passage on the Quay at Glasgow. In the event seventy seven passengers were accounted for and eight passengers were posted as missing. The final total of those lost from the Rowan was 34 souls, 11crew and 23 passengers.

Lt Alcock was with a representative of the 'Irish Independent' who said that he and Lt Alcock had decided to jump into the sea. Lt. Alcock drowned in the Clyde Estuary; his body was recovered and he was buried at Sedbergh in Yorkshire.

June 21st 1921 at Probate his effects totalled £35,377. 9s.

Vera Aplin

Evelyn Vera Aplin was born on 9th July 1899 in Stroud, Gloucestershire. One side of her family always called her Evelyn, while the other, including Douglas's parents, referred to her as Vera. She was baptised on 15th September 1899 in the Somerset village of Creech St Michael.

A year later her father Edwin was a twenty-nine-year old engine driver living with his wife Ellen Jane, who was a year younger, his new-born son John Thomas and Annie Cook, at thirteen a general domestic servant in Rose Cottage, Brinscombe, Minchinhampton.

By 1911 the family has grown and were living at Oaklands, Chalford Hill, Chalford. Vera was eleven, John Thomas ten and they had a four-year old brother, Leslie Charles Edwin.

On 9th March 1928 Vera married Edward T. Luen in the Holy Nativity Church, Knowle, Bristol. Little over two years later on 27th May 1930 their daughter Nancy Evelyn was born. Vera was widowed after only four years when Edward died of Hodgkinson's Disease in Pembroke on 3rd June 1932 aged thirty-three.

Seven years later, on 10th April 1939, Vera married widower Howard Hale in Wells, Somerset. Howard died on 6th October 1974 aged eighty-seven. Vera died on 27th May 1986, she is buried in St Leonards Churchyard, Rodney Stoke next to her husband of thirty-five years. Rodney Stoke is one of the nine 'Thankful Villages' in Somerset which suffered no fatalities in WWI.

Sources:
Margaret Bottomley
Andrew Frostick
Rebecca Mann
Nancy Tame

Vera in later life

CHAPTER 3

PASSCHENDAELE

Supplying the Front Line - 1917
Douglas Belchamber

Like so many other young men, my father, Douglas Foster Belchamber, enlisted in August 1914, just before the outbreak of WW1. Initially he was a Private in the Artists Rifles but then in 1916 he transferred to the Machine Gun Corps, joining the Depot Company at Grantham. By 1917 he was second in command of a service company.

'A' Company of the Machine Gun Corps (possibly 238 Company) thought to have been taken in the early part of 1917 before going out to Flanders. Douglas is the officer in the left.

On 17 July 1917, the 238th Company was sent to France to join the 41st Division in preparation for the Third Battle of Ypres. DFB eventually found time to write a number of letters home to his wife; the originals have disappeared but my mother, Doris Belchamber, carefully copied all the letters by hand that my father sent her from France. These covered a period from 11th July 1917 to 13th October 1917, when he set off from Marseille with the Company en route for Mesopotamia to join the 54th Indian Brigade, 18th Indian Division.

As my Father's writing was not easy to read (and it was made all the more difficult by the conditions under which he was writing), we are fortunate that it is my Mother's copies that we have worked from and, with the greatest respect, not his. Unfortunately page 2 is missing.

In letter Number 1, she noted: "Copies of letters sent to me by my husband when he went to France in the 1st World War."

Towards the end of his final letter, my father pointed out: "As regards my French experiences, I hope they will interest you a bit. They were not intended for, & they fall far short of, a literary effort. I merely strung down a bare outline of my movements so as to keep a record for you of what we did whilst their memory was yet fresh in my mind." For that reason I have tried to reproduce the letters exactly as they were written: he habitually used an ampersand (rather than "and") and allowed the occasional spelling mistake or grammatical solecism to creep in that would otherwise have been rigorously weeded out by a classical scholar of his eminence. David Belchamber

Letter No 1 - 14.10.17

As you know, we started off from Grantham on Thursday night the 11th (I think) of July and our train ran right through London in the early hours of the Friday morning - we got to Southampton about 6 o'clock & got on board our boat, which sailed in the evening & landed us at Havre early on Saturday morning - we marched through Havre to a rest camp. We spent a day or two here, during which time I had to go into the town & get all sorts of things, Ordnance stores, stationery etc. & then we received orders to entrain.

I forget how many days we were in the train, but we meandered about in France in a quite enjoyable way for some time. We finally began to get near the fighting & I recognized one or two places again, Bethune & so on. However we carried on & eventually finished up at a place on the borders of Belgium. We were there attached to a Division, which was then resting preparatory to going into the 31st July show.

From the station we marched about 8 miles to a village Bailleul & stayed there for one night. The next day we moved to a farm house a few miles away & billeted there. It was quite jolly little billet & we were quite comfortable.

[Page 2 is missing]

After we had been a day or so here we sent off a fair-sized party to go off with pack mules to take part in the show. Shaw & Dunton were with these, & also Bainbridge. I think it was the second night after we got there that we were sitting round our improvised mess table just at dusk, when we heard an aeroplane approaching. We listened & most of them decided that it must be one of ours. It was quite new & very low. One of the men said "If it were a Boche, our Archie's & searchlights would have been on it before now". Barely had he said this, when we heard a tremendous whistling sound, followed by the crash of a tremendous bomb. People in the field thought it had fallen on us & expected the next on them. As for us we dropped unceremoniously into the brook & lay there whilst he unloaded three more. It was unpleasant. We afterwards went to look at the hole, which was about 150m yards away & found that it was about 20ft in diameter & about 10 ft deep. That happens to be the nearest I have been to an aeroplane bomb this time, so I have been pretty lucky.

Letter No 2 - undated

I left you last time at Westoutre, where a bomb had just scared us some. I admit we did have the wind up a bit, because one feels so absolutely defenceless under canvas; & with a main road & a large ammunition dump just handy we felt somewhat in the danger zone. Every night too, a big German naval gun used to fire off a few rounds, which whizzed over us & seemed to burst about a couple of miles away.

I must try to describe our camp a bit. For shelter we had several big tarpaulin sheets, called bivouac sheets. They are about 12 ft long by 8 ft broad. Two small sticks about 3 ft long are also part of a "bivvy". These sticks are placed one at each end in the middle & cord is stretched between them & pegged to the ground. The sheet is then laid over the cord & pegged down at the sides by string which goes through eyelets in the sheet.

This may give you some idea of our little shanties, which are about 12 ft long & 6 ft wide, & open at both ends, about 3 ft high in the middle. The men then dig small trenches round in order to run off any water if it rains. The officers have bell tents. We had five tents, one of which we used as an orderly room. For the mess we stretched one tarpaulin between two trees & supported the other two corners on two pole bars from limbers. A table was improvised from broken up boxes & seats were formed of stretchers supported on ammunition boxes. This Al fresco camp was quite jolly & comfy so long as the fine weather lasted & for a day or two we quite enjoyed ourselves.

However just after we had sent away our mule convoy, which I think I mentioned in the last letter, the weather broke & it poured in torrents. One heavy shower put us in a horrible mess. The men's bivouacs were on the best ground and kept comparatively dry. Of course all the ground round them was churned into mud & they got wet & dirty crawling in. The lower part of the camp became a morass. The little river rose & flooded all that part. Where our mess was, there soon was six inches of water & mud. The roof became a big pool of water, which leaked through. The kitchen & a similar erection just by was in even worse case & my tent was almost as bad. From this time forward was a fight against water. We cut down a young tree & put it up as a pillar in the middle of the mess to raise the sheet & drain off the water. We borrowed some more sheets & walled it all round to keep out the rain which blew in from all sides. We paved the floor with tons of old tins & on top we placed big pine logs, which we managed to borrow from a dump we found. We then built clay dykes against the river & after some days we made the place a little more habitable. The men's cookhouse & store were in even worse case & we had to take the same measures there. To get from one place to another we had to wade through water & mud, knee deep in places. Under these conditions work & parades were impossible. Day after day it poured incessantly & all we could do was to lie in the dryest positions possible & pass the time away. Hitchings and I had rendered our tent quite a cosy little place & we used to repair there & lie on our beds & play two-handed bridge. I don't know how long this lasted; it seemed a long time, but I suppose it wasn't more than about 10 days really.

One Saturday (it was the 4th August, I think) Hitchings & I had just settled in for a quiet game, just after lunch, when an urgent message arrived telling him to go up & reconnoitre a position preparatory to taking the Company in.

This was just after the push of the 31st July, in which, save for our mule convoy we took no part. We had heard from our camp the tremendous bombardments for this push. It was a rotten day this Saturday & it was beastly to have to turn out, but still it had to be done; so Hitchings took four of the officers & started off. They had a look round our positions & made their dispositions & the next morning Hitchings went off with the Company & the guns & left me & Topham to look after the camp & the transport & to see to the rations going up to the line.

Letter No 3 – undated

I felt pretty fed up when the whole company departed for the line, especially the first day, because Topham had to take up his limbers to take our guns in, & also wait up there to bring out the guns of the Company we relieved, so I was alone in the Mud Patch. I decided that with the few men left behind I would endeavour to make the camp more habitable & it would also keep the men occupied.

I have mentioned the dump of pine logs. We decided to borrow these in plenty. They were of all shapes & sizes, being used for paving the muddy sides of roads to make stands for motor lorries. I came to the conclusion that we might make little houses by using these logs, or rather poles, & plenty of bivouac sheets.

I had joined the long sides of two sheets together & used the double sheet for a roof. The place was now about 5 ft high in the middle. For the sergeants' and officers' messes I built strong shanties, which were about 8 ft high & closed in on all sides when required. I had the whole lot of bivouacs etc placed in regular rows & lines & dug a complete drainage system, throwing up the banks of earth under the flaps of the "bivvies". In fact just as the Company were due to be relieved the camp was absolutely A1 & I hear that it is still used as a permanent camp.

My chief job, of course, being left behind was to ensure that everything needed up in the line got there. Of these necessaries the chief is rations. Now there are a lot of things to be considered in sending up rations. To start with the Company was in a place likely to get strafed at any time. There were a certain number of strong concrete dug outs, no trenches, but any amount of shell holes. These latter were the abode of those, who were unable to get into the dug outs. It was not a pleasant job always going from one dug out to another. Now you can see that it would not do to send up a mass of miscellaneous food stuffs to be sorted out up there, with no convenient place to put them all in & an even chance of a strong shell putting out everybody collected there, as well as the rations. To counter this we divided the whole party into gun teams & gave them numbers. We then prepared the rations by gun teams & put each team's rations in separate sand-bags & labelled them with wooden labels. We had to guard as far as possible against the food getting spoilt by the awful jolting it would have to go through. Candles must not be mixed up with bread or bacon etc etc. this meant putting in the tea say in the bottom of the bag &b then tying the bag tight & putting in the next item above that & tying that etc. It used up a great number of bags, about 80 a day for a hundred men & took a long time to get ready, but things went quite smoothly.

Each day I had to see that these rations were ready and despatched at an agreed time so as to meet a party sent by Hitchings to a pre-arranged spot. It is strictly the duty of the Transport Officer (Topham) and the Quartermaster sergeant to take up the rations. This is a rotten job, however, so I arranged that the T.O. went one day, the Q.M.S. the next and myself the next & so on. I remember very well my first time. Off we started from the Camp. Westoutre is well within civilisation & civilians go about their ordinary avocations. This lasted for about 3 miles & then about a mile short of Dickebusch civilian life ends. The whole country was now one vast camp. No cultivation, no civilians, plenty of sand bag dug outs & broken down houses, tents & bivouacs, horselines, roads with loose stones being rolled in by steam rollers, thousands of lorries, motor cars, horse-limbers, guns, troops marching etc etc, shell holes of ancient date in the fields; Kite balloons resting on the ground or overhead, but the trees still trees. This was the second belt through which we passed. Then we came to the third belt, the belt of our batteries still miles from the front line. Where they are, there will not be found a single house intact, in fact I think I would be right in saying that in front of our guns there would hardly be found anything more than a pile of rubbish anywhere where little villages used to stand.

The rearmost batteries still stand on ground where trees have leaves. When I went up for the first time I was greatly struck with the distinct line of cleavage. My road ran along in front of a wood, the wood was on the left of the road & was still a wood; on my right the country was bare. There were all the signs of ancient woods on the ridges some way away, but these consisted only in stumps scattered round in hundreds & none more than a few feet high. From behind the big batteries, or rather the longer ranged batteries, let fly over our heads; & in front & all round were guns of all shapes & sizes & pretty busy for the most part.

The road I was on skirted the belts for a time & then I came to a wooden lorry track, which plunged boldly into the old No Man's Land. Now we were surrounded by shell craters & many of these did not look old. In places the wood of the road was ominously patched or else a big hole, too recent to have been repaired, existed still & gave the limbers a problem. Guns were all round, literally hundreds of them & making the very devil of a noise. One can hardly describe the bareness of the scene & yet there was still grass. I remember that as I came up & passed successive stages I thought that each was probably the limit of war's destructiveness, but then as I passed on I found something worse & here where I was on the wooden road I thought must be the limit, but since then I have seen places far worse still. I passed within very small distance of the site of the old village, St. Eloi. I knew it was there by the map but though I have been there several times since I have never been able to discover the village to this day.

On the day I was describing the Hun was shelling when I got on to the track, but some distance away, probably a couple of miles or more. Just as I got there a huge explosion occurred about that distance away, possibly one of our dumps & that seemed to satisfy him, because I don't think he sent any more shells over while I was there. All the time, however, our guns were pouring them over in thousands.

The track led down towards rather a notoriously unhealthy spot known as the Brick Stack. This is on the Canal at the end of the Spoil Bank. Will *[his brother who had been seriously wounded in the act of throwing away a live grenade that had landed in a trench]* probably knows these places as I believe he has been at the Bluff. Just before getting to the Stack however I turned off & went parallel with the Canal & then struck for the canal again cross country. This last bit was a problem. A rough cart track had been made between the road & the canal & part of it had been paved with brick. All this bit of country was one mass of shell holes, craters overlapping each other & a gang was employed in keeping passable this track. When we got to the end of the track (i.e. the near end) we saw that it looked a bit knocked about & a gunner advised us not to take it as that was where they had been strafing just before.

However rations had to go up, so we started the limber at a gallop. About 50 yards along, however, we were stopped by a couple of craters clean in the track their edges touching. One was a huge monster (made about a quarter of an hour earlier we heard) & must have been about 20 ft deep. The limbers had sunk in more than axle deep & the mules were over their shoulders in mud. We were bogged & that in a beastly unhealthy spot. By terrific efforts we got the limber turned & then we had to pick a very tortuous way to get round these craters. Two of us reconnoitred & found a possible path. The limbers had to take small holes of 3 ft or so in depth & in one place the distance between two craters was such that the wheels both sides were in the craters. I think we were about 20 mins bogged & altogether about half an hour crossing this interesting two or three hundred yards. At the canal we met our party from the Company & issued out the rations, collected their letters & obtained news & then for the return. We sent off the limber to negotiate the bad piece of ground, while we were still talking to the men from the line & then we started ourselves. We were lucky getting across this time & once in the road we put it at a gallop & rapidly got away from the accursed spot. At Voormezeele I found a lorry going my way & left the limber.

Voormezeele is an unhealthy village of which very little but crumbled masses of bricks exist. It is now some miles behind the front line but is still considered unhealthy & is in the third belt I have mentioned. Curiously enough the lorry I had got on stopped a little short of our camp at another camp, which I discovered was that of my old regiment the 6th City of London & I went in & had tea with my old friend Mildren [?], now commanding the Battalion.

That was the end of that "Perfect Day" so I can assure you I was tired. Of course I happened on a quiet time & was therefore lucky. The Hun did not put a single shell over so far as I could see after the ones I had mentioned. Of course our guns were going hard but then they always are nowadays.

One of the features of the roads in Northern France are the vast number of Motor Lorries. They are used for all sorts of purposes. As omnibuses, ammunition carriers, stone carriers etc & one can nearly always get from any one point to any other by means of these. Officers can always stop one & take it & they make a very convenient means of transit. These lorries go right up into the lines & since being out this time I have come to the conclusion that the drivers earn their pay.

Letter No 4 - undated
In the last letter I had described, I think, my impressions more or less when I went up with the rations the first time. This trip had to be done each day the whole of the time the Company was in the line. The ration party would set out at the hour arranged whether it was day or night & would be away for about five hours during which time those in camp would be on tenterhooks, wondering whether they would get through safely. As a matter of fact we were very fortunate and except for a few chips out of a mule we had no casualties in the ration parties. The Company who relieved us had two men & a mule killed on the first day going up with rations. Apart from this my life in Camp was fairly uneventful. We carried on with our Camp making etc & looked forward to the coming out of the Company. We had nightly aeroplane visits but none of them dropped any bombs quite as near as the one I have before described.

The Company in the line was doing quite well. On the way into the position two men were wounded but these happened to be the only casualties received the whole time. The first night they were in the Hun strongly attacked Hollebeke which our guns covered & I was told by the Divisional Officer that the fire of our Machine Guns was the principle (sic) cause of the failure of the attack. I think the official communiqué mentions that that counter attack was beaten off by Machine Gun fire. If I remember rightly this was on Sunday August 5th during the night.

During the time the Company were in they were shelled at night mostly, & many gas shells were sent over. There seem to have been a great number of very narrow escapes but no casualties. In fact our luck was as much in that time as it was out in the last big push, where every misfortune, which could happen, seemed to fall on us

Nothing worth describing took place until the day following my birthday, Monday August 13th, when Hitchings sent for me to go up & see him to arrange about the relief.

On receipt of the order I just put on my oldest clothes, slung on my gas mask, donned a tin hat, made certain of my first field dressing & Iodine Ampoule were handy & started out. This time I caught a lorry up & it took me as far as the edge of the third belt, which I described. From here, it was going to another part of the line, so I reluctantly descended & as there was no other lorry going my way I set out to tramp & very lonely I felt. I could see my canal bank objective in the distance & so I decided as it had been fine for some time, to strike across country for it & avoid the roads. I suppose this reduced the distance to the bank to about 2 miles instead of three. I was still in land where grass grew, but such a litter one could hardly imagine. Guns were dotted about all over the shop with no cover of any kind. Shells were so plentiful that one could hardly understand any German shell failing to hit them. They literally pave the countryside here. Shell holes of all sizes profusely scattered about, half filled with dirty stained water. Coils of barbed wire all over the shop, old fallen in trenches, all sorts of fragments of arms, equipment, clothing etc etc. Literally fortunes on the ground for the picking up. And they are picked up because, as each bit of ground is taken it is cleared & things are salvaged as this becomes possible, but even here more than two miles behind our line there had not been time to straighten out things. Well, to get along with it. I got to that last 300 yards where we had so much trouble before & found that there were trench boards laid right across to the Canal. Of the huge crater in the track way, there was not a sign, it had been filled up (I heard that the ration party the day after my visit had found the track made up again & I thought of the difference between this, making up with little or no material of holes as much as 20 ft deep & quite as broad, under shell fire & in a few hours, and the efforts of most local Borough Councils).

Just as I got to the near end of this track our guns which had been going off pretty quickly, suddenly launched forth into what is known as drum fire. I was within a few yards of a huge great monster & no great distance from several others & I could see the flash from hundreds more if I looked. I can assure you that the wind was absolutely vertical with me. It is true that the Hun had not so far, put over a single shell as far as I could see, but I thought he was bound to take some notice of this terrific strafe, so I quite expected I might get the benefit as I crossed this rotten bit of track. However, where I was, was pretty beastly & the other end of the track was the canal bank with dug outs & tunnels & other things most comfortable to think of, so I started out & went across at a walk - but a jolly fast walk. Not a Hun shell fell anywhere near.

Letter No 6 - 25/10/17 (Narrative not continued No 5)
I left myself skeddadling over a nasty 300 yards of ground if I remember. I was extraordinarily pleased to get to the other end. There was a canal with two high banks on either side. The water looked very placid & peaceful but bore a notice "Not to be used for any purpose whatever; badly contaminated". I crossed it by a bridge & found that the opposite bank was honeycombed. I hopped into a tunnel entrance & enquired for an officer, who I knew could guide me to the Company. I wandered about for quite a long time before I hit on him & then, to use an Irishism, he wasn't there. His office happened to be a nice little cabin with table, armchair, electric light & telephone, so I sat down, phoned up the Company & asked them to send me a guide. This Hitchings agreed to do & I sat down to rest. It was an hour before he turned up & he stated that he had lost his way but was confident that he knew the way back to the Company.

I wasn't sorry for the rest because I know of nothing more tiring than wandering about over this sort of country with shells, whether your own or not, whizzing overhead & I was wet through with perspiration.

However, having got my guide, I sallied forth. We now emerged on the other side of the tunnels & into some country, which left my old 3rd belt well in the background. There was the same tremendous confusion of shell holes, but now there was no grass or vegetation of any kind. To my right was a gentle slope upwards, which hid the Boche lines & this was according to the map a WOOD. One could tell it had been a wood but now it was merely a collection of stumps, very few more than about 3 ft high. All this country round here must once have been beautifully wooded & watered country, probably quite as lovely as that round Dorking. Now it was one scene of ghastly ruin without a blade of grass.

There were any amount of men about, working or making their way to their units or on messages or something. Light railways with electric motors were puffing away & limbers even had to come up round by the brick stack way. There was any amount of activity. Further on however I got to the top of the rise & I take it, was now in view of the German lines. I was supposed to be in a wood but not even stumps could I now see.

The ground here as far as I could see was churned like a stormy sea. Not a thing was left to guide anyone. An indescribable litter of things lay about. I might have sent you some German souvenirs if I had the time & energy to collect & carry them. You know the jumble of rocks at Tryfaen. Imagine that blown up from the base & levelled with the ground & you may have some idea of what this ground was like & yet a report might mention this place as a "wood". I followed my guide, leaping from one dry spot to another, making detours where the drowned shell holes were impossible; tearing my things on the barbed wire which lay all over the shop, and all the while our guns were making a terrific row & shells were shrieking overhead. I began to wonder whether we had lost our way, & I shouldn't have been at all surprised if we had, when happening to look about 50 yds on I saw Hitchings apparently taking the air & watching us. When we got to him I saw he was in front of his dug out. This was an old German concrete dug out about 5 ft high 7 ft long x 6 ft broad. From a few yards away one would not know that there was a dug out there, it mixed with the rest of the jumble so well I was very pleased to see it & dived in with some satisfaction as I felt sure that the Hun must soon retaliate for the strafing we were giving him.

Dug out life is quite an existence of its own with its proper codes of etiquette etc. The main occupation is eating or getting things ready to eat. You may practically say that except when killing or being killed is the main proposition, eating or preparations for it are certain to be going on in any dug out. When I dived into Hitchings' home I found myself surrounded by the smaller implements of food preparation & by countless tons of foodstuffs. I have told you the size of the place. Lengthways there were two bunks made of boards & across one end there was a bench. When I came in the top bunk was the repository of all the good things & the

Sgt Major was busy boiling water over a primus. Hitchings was connected by phone to the other officers & phoned to them to tell them I had arrived & that refreshments were being served. Newell & Shaw subsequently dropped in. I forget what I had but I think I had tea & coffee & sardines, bully beef & chocolate & biscuits & a few other things whilst the others had whisky & hot water or coffee & rum as their tastes led them. All this time our guns were steadily going on, occasionally increasing to the violence of drumfire but the Hun was taking it all lying down. I must have stayed there an hour receiving instructions about the relief & talking over things in general & it was about 3.30 when Hitchings said "Well I don't want to hurry you, but Fritz has a habit of strafing round here about 4 o'clock & I should get (away) right now if I were you". Enough said; I got (up), & after a very lonely tramp I eventually boarded a motor lorry & got back to camp. I had heard unofficially that we were to have a month's rest after we came out & I was feeling very happy about it, especially as I hoped that a month might see peace within comfortable hail. The Company were not coming back to the camp which I had laboriously prepared, but to the farmhouse which we had occupied before moving up, so the next morning I prepared for the move. I sent a lot of the transport & baggage on to the farm & I rode over myself to make arrangements. I found it would be better for some people to stay at the camp for the night, so I arranged to go on to the farm myself with the cooks & officers' baggage & leave Topham to bring on the transport next day. Having fixed this up I returned to the Camp & lay down waiting for tea. I hadn't been back very long when Hitchings turned up, looking very draggled in his collarless shirt & torn clothing & unshaven face. He broached the subject quickly by telling me that the Coy would not be back that evening. They had come out at a place not far from Voormezeele (& which lay just on the boundary between the 2nd & 3rd belts) & had got to remain there until 4 o'clock on the next day & then make their way to where Motor Lorries would be waiting. There were no shelters there & no food & I was to go up & look after the Coy. So much for my anticipation of a comfortable night. The Coy did not know this yet as they expected to get Lorries at once. I managed to get to them by Motor Lorry & found them in what must have been the grounds of an old Chateau. The gate posts of what must have been a drive still looked something like gateposts but very little else of the building survived. I broke the news to them & you may be able to imagine what was said & felt for the next few minutes.

18/11/17 Letter No 9 Narrative not continued in No 8

I left off in my last letter where I had to go for the Company to Elzenwalle near Ridge Wood & stay with them for a day.

Once we had thoroughly appreciated the fact that we had to stay we looked round to make ourselves as comfortable as possible. We were fortunate enough to find quite near a number of bivouac sheets & tents & we appropriated the little camp to our own needs. There was no grub, so we had to turn in & wait for the morning when rations were promised. The night was uneventful except that our guns just in the vicinity kept up a hideous din & an occasional German long range shell whined overhead on the way to disturb the slumbers of Reninghelst or some other place further back. I believe a little long range shrapnel burst somewhere overhead but none dropped among us. The next morning I let the men lie in bed (?) until rations turned up & then we arose & performed great deeds of skill in cooking etc & prepared breakfast. We had nothing to do until the time came to move off so Dunton & I took a stroll. We thought we would go down to Dickebusch lake & started off. Suddenly we noticed that all our guns had stopped & looking up we saw 7 Bosches (sic) aeroplanes overhead. They were absolutely plum (sic) over us & quite low. Archies, machine guns & rifles were turned on them & they turned back. They dropped a few bombs just to cheer us up & one of them killed a horse quite near to us. After the interlude we continued our stroll & reached the banks of the Lake. There we lay down in the long grass & everything seemed to be at peace. We could hear the guns but where we were we could only see the lake & the wild bird life & no sign of war or destruction. I thoroughly enjoyed that half hr or so.

The rest of the day was uneventful. We started off from Ridge Wood about 3 & arrived at Hallebast corner at 4. There we caught lorries which were to convey us back to Berthen . You cannot imagine how happy we all felt. We heard that we were for a month's rest right away back & we all felt like kids on a Sunday school treat. We thoroughly enjoyed that ride & when we arrived back at the Farm (Piebrouck farm) where we were to rest for a day or two we found Hitchings waiting for us & a slap up dinner. Weren't we happy? We spent a few days here resting & getting a few things made up which had got lost & then the long expected orders came to move back to the St Omer district. All this time we had had aeroplanes over each evening & though they didn't do much damage as a rule, yet in the last evening they managed to hit a camp near us & one bomb killed about 60 & wounded as many more.

I think it was about the 19th August that we started off back. We went by road

& the first evening arrived in the neighbourhood of Hazebrouck. We camped here for the night & though aeroplanes visited us about twice I for one did not worry because I happened to be very ill during the night & nothing else seemed to worry me. The next day we marched again & finished up at Withuis near St Omer where we found billets & settled down. The men went into a big paper factory, which I had previously visited with Frank Friend & Fred Bone, whilst the officers settled down in the town in various houses. I was very comfortable in a small grocers' place.

Letter No 10 23.11.17.

We got to Withuis on about 22nd August or thereabouts & remained there until the 8th September. We had quite a jolly time there. I was pretty busy but managed to get a bathe in the river most days & some games of football (*DFB was later to be selected to play (amateur) football for England but unfortunately he suffered a serious injury before the match and did not play.*) Sir Douglas Haig inspected our division while we were there. There is nothing much else to report.

Just before the 8th September we got wind of approaching operations and as the Divisional Machine Gun Officer was on leave Hitchings was sent up to reconnoitre & draw up the plans for the Machine Guns etc. As a result of this I was left in charge of the Coy & I got wind to move on Saturday 8th. Seven motor lorries were sent for us & about noon we started off by road. We had a very jolly journey with nothing remarkable except that my lorry stuck in a ditch on the side of the road & it took us half an hour to pull it out. Just as it was getting dark we arrived at our destination which was the end of Dickebusch Village nearest to Ypres. We found a field here & as well as we could in the dark put up bivouacs for the men & tents for the officers. We were near the main road & the traffic was enormous. Motor lorries, cars, horse transport & tremendous caterpillars passed in a never ceasing stream. In addition to this was the noise of our guns & every now & again the tremendous belch of one of our monster naval guns which fired somewhere near. A few Fritz shells sailed over at intervals & burst somewhere near. As, in looking over the field I had seen quite a number of fresh craters of considerable size, I didn't feel particularly happy. Neither Newell (who shared my tent) or I got much sleep that night. Only half the Coy was with me at this time as half were at Abeele doing anti-aircraft work & didn't turn up until Monday but I had 2 sections from the other companies with me.

The next morning as no orders had come in I told my men to dig their bivouacs in i.e. dig a trench for themselves to lie in & pile up sandbags round them. I looked into the ruined houses of the village & found one which had a roof more or less whole & a cellar well covered with sandbags. The plan was something like the sketch and I allocated one room as a mess room, one as a kitchen, slept in another room and gave the cellar to the mess staff & officers' servants. I found another similar cellar next door for other officers & a little shed on the other side of the road was selected as the Orderly Room. I had made up my mind that sleeping in a tent was very unpleasant.

Sunday was comparatively uneventful. Towards midday a fleet of Bosch aeroplanes came overhead & dropped about 20 bombs, the nearest about 100 yds away. The damage was practically nil.

Shortly afterwards the D.M.G.O. & Hitchings came in & I got my orders.

The job I had to do before the show was twofold. 1) To get up ammunition 2) To prepare our positions. They were both big jobs & would take about 10 days. 1) could be done in the day time & 2) only at night. We were to start on the Monday 10th & half our numbers worked all day & half all night. I arranged to go up & look at the positions myself on Monday with Hitchings & the D.M.G.O.

For the purpose of job No 1 we got a couple of motor lorries allotted to us & they picked up the ammunition from the dump & carried it up to a point near Verrandenmolen which is well in the 3rd belt, I have before described.. Here it was unloaded & put in trucks which went on a tram line for about a mile & a half across country. A big dump was made here & the ammunition had to be manhandled into the positions i.e. anything from 800 yds to a mile across most awful country.

On the morning of Monday I met Hitchings & the Major at the Dump & we got on the first lorry, having previously despatched an officer & fatigue party to the Lorry terminus. The way we took was the same way that I went up before, but we passed the brickstack this time & skirted Hill 60 on its left & so arrived near our destination (This was on the road leading from Ypres through Zillebeke on the far side of the latter place.) In trying to cross a bad piece of road our lorry got stuck & broke its springs & we had to get out to unload it & get it towed back. After some trouble we found our fatigue party & got some trucks & directed them on their way. We then struck off for our destination which took us about 3/4 hr. The country was absolutely indescribable We came to the place where our ammunition had to be taken off the tracks & there we found some trench boards running off at right angles up to our position. This trench board track ran through what used to be a wood which had been pounded by our guns. Every inch was ploughed up & it was just like a nutmeg grater with every depression half full of stinking water. This wood was in a depression, there being quite high land all round it except from the rear towards our own country. All these hills round it are honeycombed with deep galleries & our position was on top of one of the hills. I got there & investigated & sat for some time in a shallow trench looking at the spires of churches well behind the German lines. I also investigated the galleries & felt safe, if not comfortable in them. Fritz was putting over a little heavy stuff at a stranded tank nearby & was also bursting a few "woolly bears" overhead.

Nothing came very near us however & this first trip was not too bad. On the way back we saw him quite busy round Hill 60 just South of us & on the path I should have been on if I had been on the way back from the old positions, but we were not walking We very luckily picked up by a staff car & whizzed back to Dickebusch in quick time.

Pillbox Hill 60

Bomb Crater Hill 60

I now had to organise the Company into day shifts & night shifts. The day shift started off about 7 in the morning & the night shift about 5 in the evening. The former used to return about 5 o'clock & the latter at about 7 in the morning. I cannot describe to you all the difficulties which arose such as ammunition not being at the dump when required, lorries not turning up to time, the nights being so dark that the work was hindered, the difficulty of finding the way etc etc, ad infinitum. When once a party had gone out I knew no peace till it came back. I did not know how the work might have been hindered or whether any casualties had occurred. I barely got any sleep at all.

On the Tuesday my other half company arrived & I took Shaw & Dunton up to see the position. This time there was plenty of shelling & we had to pick our way more carefully. We went up well to the right of where I went up before as they were shelling the other path. (They knocked our tramway about, one of the difficulties I refer to above.) & then we started back they started shelling the other path & we had to change again. Both Dunton & I got scratched with a piece of shrapnel but nothing serious happened. I must say I did not like it at all & was glad to get back. After this it was the same old job day & night with all sorts of unforeseen difficulties cropping up & I began to feel really worried & run down.

We used to be shelled regularly each night now & I did not think that my room was up to much, besides which there was too much row from the traffic. I therefore found a cellar on the other side of the road just near the orderly room. This cellar was absolutely all that remained of its particular house, but it was covered with sandbags & brick debris & although it would have caved in at once to a 4.7 shell it felt safer & more comfortable so four of us established ourselves therein. Although this cellar was on the road practically the sound of the traffic was deadened a bit & I got a few hours sleep there. About the third night after we had changed, we had all just got to bed (i.e. all not on duty) when a shell burst very near us. Another followed soon after & we then got one every 3 minutes all pretty close. It was beastly nerve racking & we all put on our boots & coats to sally forth if necessary.

After about the fourth shell the Sgt-Major & my clerk appeared as they didn't feel very happy in the Orderly room. We told them to come in but very soon after there was a terrific crash & the whole place was filled with smoke & dust. This was too much for us, so we all sallied out & walked up the road for a bit. The shelling continued for about 2 hrs & then ceased. Two of us walked round our field to see that the animals & men were alright, but the shells were well away from them. After the shelling had stopped for the night we hopped back to the dugout & found it none the worse for wear & so snatched a few hours sleep. The nearest shell had hit about 3 yds away on the other side of a wall in the road & had made a bit of a mess.

Letter No 11 - 3.12.17.

I was telling you last time about our experiences at Dickebusch & I think I ended up with a night when they shelled us rather badly. As I told you, one or two shells hit very close to us without doing any actual damage. this was before the Company actually went into the line. All this while Hitchings was back at La Clytte & I used to jump on a motor lorry each day & run back & see him. I found this trip such a relief. It seemed like running back into civilisation for a while. On the 18th the Company went into the line. At the last minute Hitchings decided to leave me at Dickebusch to keep house. I felt awfully lonely when the Company went up. Topham (the Transport Officer) was left with me and a few men. We had previously sent up a lot of rations as we knew it would be very difficult or impossible to get them up during the show itself; so for about 48 hrs I had no news of the Company. I used to run down to Divisional Headquarters & try to get news from them, but they had none. In their grounds was a large scale clay model of the ground over which we were operating & flags indicated our progress. On the day of the stunt I went down there and found that all was going well except on the right of our division, which was where our lads were & there we were held up. (The newspapers had this in quite correctly). Everything on the left was going swimmingly but just at this point we were getting hell. This naturally increased my anxiety tenfold & I was half prepared for the next message I got from the Company. They had had a lot of casualties & Hitchings just gave me the names of the killed & asked me to write to their relatives. I had to send up all the men I could spare & another officer who had since turned up & then I tried to write to the relatives. This was almost the last straw. I could not help thinking of the letter being received & pictured such a one arriving home. I knew most of the lads & the job was simply heartbreaking. I knew that the condition when they were killed was such that it was often impossible to collect any of his effects or even to secure his burial or in fact know that he was buried at all. One man I heard afterwards was simply blown away & was first reported missing. Two men with him were killed The first man was found quite by chance a day later, hundreds of yards away. Our Company had had to move forward & apparently were most unfortunate as the attack was held up & they got most heavily shelled. they had to come back again after losing a lot of men. Newell was wounded & two other officers. You may imagine how I felt when I read this note from Hitchings.

Meanwhile at Dickebusch things were not too happy. We didn't fortunately get too many aeroplanes right over us dropping bombs, but most days & nights they passed over us & the "Archies" let fly. The worst night however was the one just before the stunt. We (i.e. Topham, Bainbridge, who had just rejoined, and I) retired to roost in our cellar, when just about 10 o'clock there was a tremendous bang just near. This was a high velocity shell from one of Fritz's naval guns. Bainbridge immediately went to the door to see where the next pitched. After 3 minutes it came

& pitched just about 100 yards away. Thereafter they plugged away with two guns about once every two minutes. There was a third gun shelling right over us too. The shells were dropping all on our side of the road & most unpleasantly near. We stood it for about an hr & a half & then we dashed out across the road & looked round the lines. No shells had dropped on this side so we dropped in on the Sergt-Major & the Mess staff, who were in the cellar which I before described as being in the house we had appropriated as a mess. We stayed here for about 2 hrs listening to the crashes. One very loud one was succeeded by the sound of splintering in our house & in the morning we discovered that a fragment of H.E. had come through the front wall & landed on the place where I used to sleep, when I slept in that house. After 2 hrs there was a break & thinking that it was over we returned to our own cellar which was still undamaged. The shelling then started again & went on for another 3 hrs. We stopped where we were but none of us got any sleep that night. In the morning we found dozens of huge craters all round. The road had escaped but the side on which we were was badly mauled about. A Church Army hut which was, so to speak, in our back garden had one end blown to smithereens & two men sleeping in it had miraculous escapes. So far as we could find out however no real damage had been done & no casualties were caused. Fritz must have wasted a few thousand pounds here without result except that, as I suppose he intended, he kept a lot of us awake who badly needed sleep. Topham and I decided that sleep was essential so we prospected round for quieter quarters & eventually pitched on the banks of Dickebusch lake. Here we burrowed into the bank & fixed up a sort of wig-wam & furnished it with sandbags stuffed with hay & a few blankets &, to anticipate, here we managed to sleep in peace.

Other little alarms at Dickebusch were caused by Fritz sniping at Kite balloons with long range guns. He would do this at all sorts of odd times & a "woolly bear" explosion just overhead, though very harmless as a rule, makes the deuce of a clatter. Sometimes his aeroplanes would dash over & attack the balloons & I have seen two on fire & more than a dozen balloonists dropping out in their parachutes.

To be truthful, I never want to see Dickebusch anymore.

Letter No 12 - 10.12.17.
I forget where I got to in my last letter about France, but I think it was about the end of our stay at Dickebusch.

Our Division was relieved & went back soon after the show, about the 22nd I believe; but the poor old Company was left in & we thought it was going to be left in for the next show, which came off on the 26th. The Company had had a very trying time & wasn't fit for it but it was left in until the 25th when they took pity on us & ordered us out. You cannot conceive how overjoyed I was to be awakened late in the night of the 24th to hear that the Company was coming out next day. I had to make various arrangements for them such as sending up limbers to take the guns etc & this I did only too thankfully. I then prepared to give the officers & men a good meal & make them as comfortable as possible. In the afternoon the men started to trickle in. They were a war-worn looking lot, dirty, unshaven, covered with dust, clothes torn etc. As they came in, each man was given tea & bread & told to lie down. Later on came the officers in similar plight & these were also given tea etc. Then was the roll call. That was a sad business. What a lot of men did not answer. We had been unlucky to the last. As they assembled in a trench to come out a shell burst & killed five & wounded another five. Three of the officers' servants who were seen coming down with various articles were not there & nobody knew what had become of them. We made every enquiry from the men as to what had happened to all the absentees & collected all the evidence we could. It was very sad. After this we got the survivors a good hot meal & I ordered a first class dinner for the officers. That evening we sat down in a ruined house in Dickebusch, which we had patched with any old thing to make wind & light proof & had a dinner (cooked by an ex 1st class London chef.) of six courses with champagne & wine. All had bathed & shaved & changed & felt new life. After dinner as the three missing servants hadn't arrived I borrowed a car (a colonel was dining with us who had a car) & went to three hospitals where they might have been taken if hit. I found trace of two. One had been killed & the same shell had very seriously wounded another. The latter was a very great favourite with us all & one of the nicest men, well-educated & a good soldier. I could not see him as he had already been moved but I heard sufficient to know that he would in all probability recover. (He is now in England & has had to have his foot amputated. As he was on the stage his career is gone.) Of the third I could find no trace. When I returned, Shaw & Dunton, whose servants were concerned determined to try & see them altho' it was already late. So they borrowed the car & went to Bailleul where they might have been taken. Unfortunately they didn't find them & returned very disappointed at about 1 o'clock in the morning. We subsequently received information that the third man had been hit & died of wounds.

The next morning we were up early & prepared to move. Motor lorries were sent to us & with the greatest relief we packed up & started off from Dickebusch where we had been now about two & a half weeks. That day we went to a place called Borre near Hazebrouck & settled for the night. We received some reinforcements here including two officers and stayed for one day. The next day we started again & went by lorry to Ghyvelde up near Dunkirk. As we stopped, a staff officer drove up & spoke to Hitchings. Hitchings then came back to me and said "I have some awfully bad news for you". I thought "Hallo, I suppose we have got to go back to the line", but he went on "We have to be ready to entrain for service overseas on the 30th". This was late on the 28th. I could have jumped for joy. At first the wild idea crossed my mind "perhaps England first & leave". In any case I felt overpoweringly relieved to be leaving France, no matter where I went. I felt that another three weeks like the last would be more than I could stand & often at Dickebusch I had prayed & prayed that we might be chosen to go to Mesopotamia or to the farthest part of the world from France where we might be sent. My mind had been so full of this thought that it was really not so much of a surprise when I heard Hutchings as otherwise it might have been.

Letter No 13 - 16.12.17.
I think in my last letter I nearly completed my story of my life in France. I think I told you how we arrived at Ghyvelde & were met by news that we should have to get ready for service overseas. I can remember that evening well. We seemed so far from that beastly Ypres salient & we felt jolly at being so much nearer the sea & England. I had no kit with me that evening so that I didn't relish sleeping in a tent & I went into town to see whether the Town Mayor could allot me a billet. On the way in the searchlights started & we heard the well known song of Fritz aloft. Then the "Archies" started & we knew a raid was in progress. All of a sudden there was a deuce of a crash nearby & we ducked into a ruined house. Four more bombs dropped just near & then Fritz departed & we went on our way to the Town Mayor's. He was out & we waited. When he came we heard that the first bomb had killed two officers & wounded two more so we felt that even yet we were well in the war zone. He gave us rooms in his own house & we slept in peace. I think we were at Ghyvelde for three nights. All the time we were there, we were hard at work trying to get ready for overseas. Each evening Fritz came over but he did not drop any more bombs on us. He usually went on to Dunkirk. One evening our searchlights were extra good.

As Fritz returned from Dunkirk each of his machines was picked up & our Archies shot awfully well. Three were successively driven out to sea in this way, though whether any were brought down, I don't know. On the 1st October we entrained at Ghyvelde & how we bucked up at leaving France. Next to going home this was our dearest wish. We forgot the horrors of the last show & felt great compassion for the unfortunate devils who were left. I think we were three nights in the train. The second night two bombs fell just in front & men had to go & see that the line was alright before we could proceed. After that we left the war zone behind. We skirted Paris & I found a nice look out on the top of our truck from which I could view the country in comfort as we passed through. Ever as we went South the country seemed to grow prettier & war became more remote. At Marseilles itself we found nothing of war but a rather large number of troops about. Everything otherwise was in peace. We arrived at Marseilles on the 4th October & we left on the 13th. Of the voyage there is little to tell. It was simply day after day a peaceful progress in lovely weather. We touched at Malta, Port Said, Suez & then to Basra. I read a lot of books, wrote letters & played Bridge & thoroughly enjoyed my time. We didn't seem to worry about submarines except for the last night in the Mediterranean, when everyone seemed a little windy. Don't ever believe a man again who tells you he wants to get back to France. If he says so he is either a "base wallah" or a liar. In France for fighting troops it is real red hell, with varying intervals of semi-disturbed peace & comfort, always with the certainty that you are being fattened up for Hell again. If only our Tommies had not been so plucky that they would not let their real feelings appear in the their letters home, I don't suppose we should have so many politicians & others who so self-resignedly consign their fellow countrymen to this hell. Remember the German has had hell & has it now & they feel as we do, but so long as politicians etc can persuade us that the German meditates untold evil against us & the German politicians persuade their people that we mean the same to them & more also, so long will the poor soldier on either side be put up as cannon fodder. .....Well I really must stop grumbling. I am feeling very homesick so I suppose that is the reason I have let myself go this time.

....As regards my French experiences, I hope they will interest you a bit. They were not intended for, & they fall far short of a literary effort. I merely strung down a bare outline of my movements so as to keep a record for you of what we did whilst their memory was yet fresh in my mind. If I could have kept a record of my thoughts &

conversation during that time I flatter myself that there might have been something worth recording from time to time, but then I had neither time nor inclination to write or do anything. We all used to talk things over & I guarantee that if people who cull their views from the average piffle written in the newspapers had been present they would have thought either that we were a pretty despicable selection of British officers or that it would be a good plan to hang a few die-in-the-last-ditch comfortableurs (sic) in England. Two of the despicable British officers in question did magnificent work in that last butchery & have most nobly earned the M.C. to which they have since been gazetted. You know them both, Dunton & Shaw. I have never met men who were braver than these two but I should like the selected die-in the last ditch etcs to hear them talk honestly about this war.

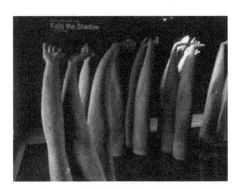

Falls the Shadow sculpture

Passchendaele site from Tyne Cot

ACKNOWLEDGEMENTS

Christopher Fry once wrote:

*I have always found
Her handwriting to be her way, not
Of giving but of withholding information.
She has taken some pains with this
One guesses almost at once that words are meant.*

It is not out of filial disrespect that I quote these lines with reference to my father's handwriting in the diary that he kept from 1 January 1918 to its final entry on 30 April

1919 but rather to serve as a fitting testament to the enormous patience and skill that my wife Helen displayed in the long labour of love that she undertook when transcribing the text. Let us say that it was not easy but, with the exception of a handful of words, she has managed to crack the code, for which she deserves sincere thanks.

I am also very grateful to Colonel Sir William Mahon LVO for translating some army acronyms my father used; to Anthony Richards from the Imperial War Museum for revealing the meaning of others, to Majid for telling me the meanings of a number of Indian and Arabic words and finally to Graham Sacker who very kindly researched father's service.

CHAPTER 4

Service in Mesopotamia 1918
Douglas Foster Belchamber

Excerpts from the War Diary of Lt-Colonel D.F. Belchamber M.B.E. with 54th Indian Brigade, 18th Indian Division working with the Department of Local Resources in Mesopotamia 1918-1919.
Edited by David Belchamber May 2012

Mesopotamia – January 1918

I have long felt tempted to keep some sort of a diary so that I may in after days be able to reconstruct my life during this eventful period but up to the present laziness has withheld me so it is that I open the enterprise now after nearly 3 ½ years of war when it is to be hoped that the end is in sight.

I have in a series of letters endeavoured to portray our moments generally from our landing in France in July 1917 up to the present day but such a record is incomplete & the events narrated were in many cases already several months old. Later on if my industry still serves me I will endeavour to jot down the principle (sic) events which have happened to me since that never to be forgotten date the 4th August 1914 before they fade totally away into oblivion.

In the meantime I have made a resolution to note day by day anything which may strike me as worthy of record although I shall probably find it impossible to adhere eternally to such a noble purpose I think that the result may ultimately prove of interest to at least one person who I think will deserve that amount of recompense for his trouble.

Nominally my diary commences from New Year's day 1918. Actually I am writing these lines in my tent which is pitched in the comfort of the 54th Brigade, 18th Division, about 3 miles NW of Bagdad (sic), the time being 8.35 pm on the 5th Jan 1918.

Hinaidi Camp nr Bagdad (sic)
Jan 1 1918
On this date I formally took over command of a section and gave up my Orderly room duties and the duties of the P M C (*President of the Mess Committee*). It is with a regret that I think is natural that I abandon these posts which I have held since the formation of the company but I can see very considerable compensations. In both of my former capacities I had considerable opportunity for falling foul of certain officers. I believe I can claim in fairness to myself that I endeavoured not to outrage their feelings more than I needed and yet several unfortunate contretemps had occurred from time to time. I hope that when I retire into comparative obscurity I shall be able to avoid much of this unpleasantness. In thinking over the whole matter I often feel tempted to reduce to writing an analysis of the characters of my colleagues but I doubt if ever I shall summon up sufficient energy. One advantage I shall get from my change is that I shall have a far less busy time especially during moves and other disturbed periods. Now my little tussles with the Ordnance Dept will have to be undertaken in future by Bainbridge *[Lieutenant L P Bainbridge, MGC]* my successor and he will have no enviable task in this country.

I spent most of the morning in going through Ordnance Indents with Bainbridge. We were mainly concerned about clothing for the men. We managed to get in our Indent at one place and just as they are beginning to think about supplying our wants, we move and have to start all over again. Meanwhile our men are in rags. But still Ordnance don't mind, which is considerate of them.

While I am wrestling with these indents my new command together with the whole company is parking limbers and preparing for a G.O.C.'s (*General Officer Commanding*) inspection for to-morrow. Later on however we hear that we shall have to move on the 3rd and that an advance party is to go off on the 2nd with all the stuff which we can spare. Hitchings *[Captain F B Hitchings, M.C]* and Topham *[Lieutenant H Topham]* were riding to Bagdad in the afternoon and at first I thought I would go too. I finally decided not to then Hitchings asked me to call on the Staff

Captain to ascertain a few details about the move. It was agreed that I should take my section on the following day as the advance party.

My visit to the S.C. was unproductive as he was out but I spent a pleasant hour with McCormitis 2nd in command chatting over various points. I returned to camp to find that orders for the move had been received and I then considered the necessaries to be taken by our small party. It was agreed that we should take over all the fighting kit and as much other stuff as we could and dump them at the new camp and then send the transport back while we remained and guarded the dump. An early start was necessary as we had to get through Bagdad and cross a very difficult pontoon bridge before 10 a.m.

Owing to my change of command I had to relinquish the services of Harper (my batman) who was a signaller. I found his successor in a man named Hodder and so far he appears to be a real treasure. I managed to have Harper added to my party as a signaller and this was sufficient to make me feel comfortable in anticipation.

The evening closed in with a high wind, squalls of rain and I retired to bed at an early hour with the uncomfortable feeling that when I was called at 5 o'c it might be to find a sea of mud under torrents of rain, in which conditions shifting camp would have been a most uncomfortable operation

Jan 2nd 1918

I awoke at 4.30am and lighting my lamp smoked a cigarette in bed. At 5.0 am Hodder punctually called me and in that miraculous way which batmen have produced some hot water for shaving. To my great relief he reported the ground dry though there was still a high wind. I am a slow dresser and it was not far off 6 o'c when I wandered out and went into our subterranean mess to see if breakfast was in sight. The cheering news of breakfast at 6.30 more than reconciled me to my early '*levee*' and I felt quite bucked as I went round the dark but already busy camp. A long string of A.T. *[Animal Transport]* carts (25 in number) had arrived and as it grew light these were packed with all sorts of material.

After breakfast we were ready to start. The party consisted of my section (1 Off 2 Sgts 21 O.Rs.(*other ranks*) and Harper attached - the other officer Harrap *[Lieutenant W G Harrap]* is in hospital) and Topham and Henson *[Lieutenant H Henson]* accompanied me with 33 men as brakemen etc. We were quite an imposing cavalcade as we set off with over 11 limbers and 25 carts and made for Bagdad. It was strange to ride through Bagdad at the head of this column. A few years back the idea would have seemed fantastic, today it is all in the day's work.

Crossing the bridge was a long job. The bridge seems to be constructed with the idea of testing the skills of the drivers and the strength of the animals. To get on to it we had to descend a very steep sharp bend to the left and after a few yards an equally sharp bend to the right. The bridge itself is about 200 yards long & is composed of planks on pontoons at the further end the way is straight but immensely steep. As I neared the bridge I halted the column and seeing some notices prominently displayed I went up and perused them. They purported to be Bridge Rules and in the simplicity of my heart I determined to act on them. One rule was that if a column was likely to take more than 15 minutes getting across the Bridge Officer should be informed so I promptly sought for him. It was now about 9.15 and he was breakfasting. His surprise at being summoned was great and when I told him why I had reported to him he showed me that these Bridge Rules have much the same force here as the 'Drive slowly to avoid raising dust which draws shell fire' notices have in the Ypres district. I had also had the leaders unhooked and sent across separately which undoubtedly delayed us as they had to be hooked in to get the limbers up the opposite bank. The bridge officer was very affable and quite ornamental though one must conclude that these two qualifications are not the sole requisites for his post. There must be others and possibly if we had waited long enough we should have discovered them. We took an hour to cross. The next day by discreetly disregarding the orders the Company passed in under half that time.

During our crossing when the bridge was blocked more than half way by limbers waiting to be hauled up the opposite bank and about 20 more carts were on our side of the river an excited policeman asked me whether I minded the Political Governor's car coming through our column I graciously gave permission and was rewarded by being able to salute the Brigadier who fulfils this important office as he passed on the bridge. Had I wished to I could have saluted him again many a time and oft as his car could not pass our limbers on the bridge as there he sat in state till they were hauled up the further bank.

After this obstacle was passed we had a fairly easy task getting to the site of our camp. We had to cross over a canal (I don't know its name yet) by an iron bridge built I believe by the Turks and then we found our site on the bank of the canal. We arrived about 12 o'c and found a patch of rough desert land covered with a dried up thorny species of plant and this was to form our future home. We must have been lunatics, lovers or poets because out of this airy nothing our imagination figured forth habitations and homes. When we arrived our imagination was assisted solely by lines scratched with a pick axe. These lines enclosed the spaces reserved for Officers' lines, mess lines, cook lines, horse lines, incinerators etc etc and all the things which one day would be but to-day were not. Roads were designated between various lines and as I was shown over the camp site our imagination pictured forth the wonderful town which should soon spring up. This marking out of the camps is called *spitlicking* it.

To return to our arrival. Having ascertained the exact locations we dumped all our material and covered the dumps as well as we could with waterproofs and horse rugs. The party now naturally divided into two, those who were staying and those who were not. For the former I found a master cook in my second sergeant Sgt Hay and he soon had a camp fire going and tea in the offing. The latter party settled down after their work to a cold lunch.

Meanwhile with my section sergeant I marked out the sites for my sections, his tents and also for my own. This seems easy but when it is realised that we were on the left of a brigade front and that every tent to the right must be dressed exactly on our tents on pain of having to move them all or lose the row it may be imagined what a lot measuring and re-measuring and checking was necessary before we ventured to erect the tents. Having selected the sites the rest was easy. Up went the tents & then tea was ready. Unfortunately I had been misled into thinking that I should be able to mess with a M.G. *[Machine Gun]* company reported to be next door to us, but as it needed half an hour's stout walking to reach my next door neighbour I had resigned myself to a lunch less day. However I found that my section had determined that their officer should not fast and my servant soon appeared with plate, knife and fork and mug of tea and I fed with considerable zest on the men's rations.

Just before this the transport had departed and we were left in the middle of the desert having as near neighbours the advance party of the West Kents on our right.

In the afternoon Harper & Hodder made of my tent the beautiful little snuggery that it now is whilst the men levelled the ground inside their tents and made them weather proof. In the meantime Sgt Weir and I marked the exact sites for all our other tents which should save a lot of time to-morrow. Tea came to me in the same gratifying manner as lunch. I decided to visit my near neighbours for dinner and at 6 I started out taking careful bearings by the stars to guide my return.

On the way I met the O.C. *[Officer Commanding]* of another company which had formed in India and accepted a very kind invitation by him to breakfast next morning. I got back without any trouble and went to bed in my little tent. It was somewhat weird lying like this in the middle of the desert and I awoke once with a jackal crunching something just outside my tent.

Jan 3rd

This morning we were all hard a work after 8.30. The company arrived in at about 10.30 and tents were soon pitched. There is plenty to do in getting the first necessary things done but we are getting used to it and by the evening we have more or less settled down.

I am reading 'The Voyage of the Discovery' by Capt. Scott and find it very interesting. The hardships that he and his men underwent must have been tremendous and I cannot help admiring them. I happened to mention this book at Mess and it led to a short argument. Dunton *[Lieutenant A W Dunton, M.C.]* stated that he looked with nothing but contempt on all people like Scott who tried Arctic and Antarctic exploration. Whilst Henson characterised them as notoriety hunters. I am afraid I am rude enough never to think that the latter's opinion on such matters as those of any value though he is excellent at the common sense of daily routine, but Dunton I can never quite understand. He is undoubtedly clever but there is a curious something about him which can almost be termed narrowness. I have often noticed an entire lack of sympathy with anything or anybody which do not immediately concern him. I don't think that he was joking when he made the above remark and yet it is difficult to conceive that a man of his age and intelligence can have made it seriously. If he knew that I was writing like this he would probably dub it impertinence on my part and yet I find that when books run short I can best pass long spells of time thinking of the phases of human nature with which I am in contact. I once thought that in Dunton I could find a spirit somewhat akin to dear old Bunny's *[E N Makeham, a close friend at Battersea GS]* and God alone knows what a Godsend such companionship would be now to me. But I feel that a man like Bunny only exists now and again as a miracle and it is only when some others that I have met are at their best that they can compare with him. His was a nature as pure and unselfish that you could praise others to him without raising in him any jealous feeling of comparison with himself, whilst I find here that very seldom is it wise to praise anybody at all in front of some members of the mess for fear of making them think that there is some invidious comparison being made to themselves. I am afraid I get very misanthropic sometimes and I must confess that at times I miss most keenly the society of some of those old idealistic friends whom I possessed before this devastating war turned the earth upside down. As a matter of fact I blame myself as much as anyone because I realise that if I possessed a little more of the character I so much admired in Bunny I should always find out the best side of everybody I met instead of so frequently hitting up against the worst side as I do.

Jan 4th

Today we dug. That sums it up. We had to weatherproof our camp so we dug trenches round the tents. After lunch it poured and we had to put all our stores under cover. Towards evening it came on to blow very hard and during the night it rose to a gale. Some tent poles broke and many tents were only saved by the occupants putting in some overtime during the night. My tent was safe and sound and I slept like a top.

Jan 5th

It was lovely morning and the whole camp was in good humour when we fell in for our various tasks at 8.30. All sorts of jobs had to be tackled, pits and trenches to be dug an incinerator erected and various shelters devised. At 10 a.m. the Brigadier visited us to inspect the sanitary arrangements.

These were not yet complete but in their unfinished state they managed to pass muster. The General (*Probably Brig-General M R W Nightingale, C.M.G., D.S.O., 5th Gurkha Rifles*) was very interested in our guns mounted for anti -aircraft duty. It got very hot toward the middle of the day and it became quite fatiguing digging. At lunch one of the officers bought in a local paper which has just begun to appear. The most interesting item in this is the announcement that the mails from England are expected at Basra tomorrow. If we are lucky we shall get some more news from home in about a fortnight's time. After Mess this evening I returned to my cosy tent and started writing up this diary. The tent is rather populated with spiders, crickets and one ferocious looking beetle but is nevertheless a little oasis of peace and comfort. I got to sleep about 10.30

Jan 6th

Today I am orderly officer so I am called at 6.30. The morning is dull and misty though not very cold. Digging and constructional work proceeded this morning as usual. I took the men down across the iron bridge at 11 o'c to wash their clothes and took a photo of the bridge trying the Bulb stop at about 1/5th second. After lunch the sky cleared and I went into my tent to write home. I wrote to Doris (*his wife*) and then turned in to snooze and read until time for inspecting the guard at 3.45. At 3.30 I heard somebody say "I am going round with a mallet as it is going to pour" and I looked out to find heavy storm clouds rolling up from the south.

I called my servant in to take a few extra precautions and then went out to inspect the guard. I had scarcely finished this when the storm burst on us. For some minutes previously the air had been full of noise and suddenly the hail started with a tremendous wind.

The hailstones must have been quite half an inch in diameter and the wind was of the utmost violence. I raced to my tent and Hodder and I stayed within whilst it strained madly at its moorings. The storm subsided as rapidly as it started and we congratulated ourselves on a happy ending. The camp was in a shocking state and in many places ice was standing inches deep. Some tents were badly flooded and I felt awfully sorry for the men.

Meanwhile news was brought that our animals were all stampeding over the plain. They were being taken to water when the storm burst and immediately bolted. A lot of them jumped into some trenches and one unfortunate horse was killed breaking its neck.

It was now getting dark and I returned to the mess and had tea. After tea we had another heavy shower but not quite as bad as the first one and later on I thought I would retire to my tent till Mess time. I stepped into my tent and found myself in 3 inches of water. This was unfortunate and I could not divine the cause on looking round. We spent some time in draining the water away from the trench around the trench (*tent?*) and then bailed the water out. The walls of the well in the tent showed no sign of leaking and the whole thing seemed a mystery. As a last resort, it being now five we emptied the tent and moved out my box and could still see no entrance. On feeling the floor however the ground was found to be very soft on one corner and it appeared that this must be the spot where water percolated through and gradually filled the tent. While I had dinner Hodder and Topham's servant gallantly struggled with the tent and when I returned I found it restored nearly to its normal condition again.

Great excitement however was caused by the discovery of a long snake amongst the earth which had been shovelled out and I should imagine the soft piece of ground must be caused by the existence of a snake's nest there. The snake was promptly dispatched by the interested officers of the mess. I feel a bit damp tonight as my boots are wet through and alas my spare pair which were on the floor. My valise was also under water and its contents are soaked but they don't matter much. I have had to have the tarpaulin sheet out as it was covered in mud and very wet so I shall feel a bit muddy as to the feet when I crawl into bed. However, it might have been much worse and I oughtn't to complain.

It is now 9.15 and in a few minutes I shall receive the reports as to the Company being present and then will turn out the guard. After that to bed to dream I hope of home and roofs and peace. I hope it will be a fine day tomorrow. If so everything will be ship shape again if not, I may be drowned out. Altogether to a certain extent my feelings are like those depicted by Scott in his Antarctic Voyage.

Jan 7th

I awoke this morning to find the sky still threatening and the wind changed to the N.W. Digging was the order of the day and just after I had started operations round my tent I was hauled into the Orderly room and told by the O.C. that I should be President of a Court of Enquiry assembled to enquire into the loss of one of our tents on the move and also into the circumstances of the death of the horse which I mentioned as occurring yesterday. About 10.30 it started to pour with rain and the wind changed to the West. I gave a hand to Hodder around my tent and got wet through in the process. Everything was very damp and uncomfortable. After lunch I sat on the Court of Enquiry, Wright (*2/Lieutenant L V W Wright*) and Shaw (*Lieutenant W G Shaw, M.C.*) being the other members. We sat in the Officers Mess tent as the only convenient spot. This was a wretched 160 lbs tent leaking like a sieve and the ground inside was a morass. However it stopped raining and we got the first enquiry practically completed. About 3 o'clock the joyful news was received that the Garhwalis (*an Indian regiment*) would lend us an E.P. (*English Privates*) tent for a mess and as this tent arrived shortly after, we set to work and put it up and now it stands proudly next to our mess kitchen and is trimbed (*put in good order?*) round, the ground inside levelled, matting on the floor and all is peace and joy. We are going to discuss at Mess this evening ways and means for furnishing the Mess in style.

My tent is quite alright this evening and I am in hopes that it will now weather the rain. Yesterday the GOC (*General Nightingale*) had our water tank moved down nearly on a level with the canal to save the pumps. Today the canal rose several feet and the tank is in the middle thereof.

I had another little unpleasantness with Shaw today. I can trace all my little worries like this to the unfortunate fact that in point of date I am junior to two officers in the Company. This fact has been accentuated by my reverting from the rank of Captain (*from Acting Captain to Lieutenant*) since I came out. The position is beastly difficult for me and I would gladly cut and run but I am loth to leave the Coy. Hitchings has been very decent to me and all my worry really comes from Shaw though I am inclined to think this is more due to the ignorance of his youth than to malice aforethought. I know I am hypersensitive on these points but I try to avoid all occasions of dissension as much as possible. Thinking over the whole subject raises to my mind one which will be prominent after the war. I expect everyone has noticed how much side a lot of men who have been out give themselves. I know that I have fallen into this vice sometimes (to be honest, frequently) and that I admit without much cause but since I have been with this company I have been sickened to such an extent by this that I hope I shall never again fall into it myself. This is not general and several members of the mess speak but little of their previous experiences and are charitable to others who have not been through the same. At quite the opposite extreme is Shaw. To do him justice he is a capable officer and undoubtedly did well in the line when he earnt his MC. The unfortunate thing is that the fact that he previously spent 15 months in France and went through the Somme is so omnipresent in his mind that he will obtrude it into every conversation if possible and if any opposition is received to any statement made by him on such incontrovertible authority the unfortunate opponent will be treated to one of Shaw's frequent outbursts of temper. The other day I ventured to state that the general opinion of the troops at the front in October 1914 was that Peace would be declared before Xmas 1914. I thought I might safely venture thus far as I happened to have been in the ranks in France just behind the line at the time and my guard duties brought me into contact with men of the old 7th Division who were billeted in the same place and from them and ASC (*Army Service Corps*) men etc. I gathered that the above view was held. At that time Shaw was in England, at School, I believe, but apparently he had had a conversation with a wounded Colonel from the front and he promptly informed me that my view was certainly wrong, referred pointedly to the fact that I was behind the lines. In fear of the Somme being produced to my utter discomfiture I promptly abandoned the argument.

Dunton is the only other officer who seems to feel his position and he again is a very good officer. From these two I am continually getting the sly digs that are so irritating. They can be passed off as leg-pulling but they are not intended as such I firmly believe. Today the Brigadier inspected the lines and I passed their party and saluted. Hitchings stopped me to ask a question and then told me to come along with them. At lunch I had remarks from both Dunton and Shaw about the way I managed to be in the way when the Brigadier was about.

Again when I assembled the Court this afternoon Shaw was obviously preoccupied and I guessed why. I was therefore ready when after taking evidence he said 'Now, hadn't we better see whether I am qualified to sit on the Court'. I referred to the paragraph in K.R. (*King's Regulations*) which says that after a President has been appointed no member must be appointed who is Senior in rank to the President. I pointed out that he was not Senior in rank and we proceeded in apparent harmony. These are a few incidents during the last few days but there have been whole series of incidents before this. I don't suppose I am blameless but I feel certain that Shaw and possibly Dunton have some feeling against my occupying my present position. Shaw of course is a spoilt youngster and I feel that in many ways a sharp lesson would do him good but Dunton's case is different. If any man in the company is fitted to holding my post it is Dunton and yet he has curious streaks in his character. He once said that when he was younger he was considered to be a very fiery customer. He doesn't look one and yet he is and every now and again he strikes me as completely loosing (sic) his balance and behaving like a man 15 years younger than he is. It is a mixed problem and I should like it ended. Shaw is the thorn in my flesh. I feel that after what has gone on for months I can no longer serve with him. If I commanded the Coy it would be different as I know what to do when my position is clearly defined. As it is with a vague and nebulous authority I can do nothing.

On resuming after Mess I read through the foregoing and it struck me, as it might strike anyone who happened to read these lines how insufficient must appear the grounds for writing my last reflections. This is true but had I kept a diary from the formation of the Company I should, if I kept it fully, have had it full of these trivial incidents, which in sum make up a mighty mess of unpleasantness.

We had quite a merry mess this evening though I began to get very cold as my boots and socks are wet through and I am generally damp. As at present I have not dry change I decided to go to bed and so I left the Mess at 8.30 and am just writing these four lines before turning in.

I have not said much in this diary about my thoughts of home but it is really incomplete if I don't mention them. I am a terribly homesick person and my thoughts are constantly in my own little corner of London. I always specially devote my thoughts after turning in before I sleep to all at home and night and morning I long for peace and an early return.

Jan 8th
Today it was fine though cold with a brisk breeze from the N.W. My servant was unfortunately in the Mess as a waiter but in spite of this everything has been cleared out of my tent and aired in the sun so tonight I am again sitting within in comfort as before the deluge. I sat on the Court of Enquiry again this morning and after this was finished I busied myself with my tent. A subscription of 15 Rupees per officer was called for the furnishing of the Mess and tonight we rejoice in a brilliant lamp, a warm looking table cloth and many chairs and cushions; altogether a little home from home but sadly needing a stove as the temperature has fallen very low tonight. It is unfortunate that our Mess tent will have to be uprooted and put in line with some other tents some hundred of yards away but if it is fine the alteration will not take us very long.

We are beginning now to expect the Mail every day but I am afraid it will be a week or more yet. I must write home again tomorrow. Although I constantly think of them all it is wonderful how easy it is to forget how to write.

Jan 9th
It froze hard during the night and this morning the ground was covered with hoar frost. It has been a lovely day however and Hodder was able to get all my sodden garments washed and dried so that I am now really comfortable again. Digging was again the order of the day as far as the men were concerned and they were paid out at the end of the morning parade. Our mess tent and kitchen were successfully moved and tonight we entertained two guests from 207 Coy at Mess. A few minor additions have greatly embellished the Mess tent and if we manage to get a stove we shall be extraordinarily comfortable.

I went for a topping ride with Hitchings this afternoon and Cuthbert (*his horse*) was on great form. Our destination was on the river bank and at this point it is a charming view. The river is about half a mile wide and the banks are fringed with trees amongst which some quite decently built houses are attractively set. I must knock off now because I really feel that I ought to write home and 10 o'clock has just sounded.

Jan 10th

It was not so cold this morning but the sky began to cloud over about 7 o'clock. I inspected the Sections rifles at 9 o'clock and after this digging was proceeded with. I was occupied in writing down a list of books for my servant to try to get in Baghdad when Hitchings came over and told me he wanted to speak to me. We walked apart and then he said that he had recommended me for a staff job. It would be on probation at first with the possibility of a good staff billet later. I was naturally astonished at the news and I fear I did not show the gratitude I felt, but I think Hitchings understands me alright.

We paraded for cleaning guns and equipment this afternoon and I took the opportunity of taking down a roll of the section and allotting them their various tasks. At 3.30 or rather later we started footer, Officers & Sergeants v Company. It was a most pleasant game with plenty of good rough and tumble in which the Sergeants played a heroic part. I hurt my ankle and retired a little before the end with the score 0 all but after I left one of the Sergeants scored the winning goal.

The day had kept fine though overcast and there was a magnificent sunset this evening. I had tea and was playing with Wright in the Mess when the Brigade Major (*Major J C Gretton, 126th Baluchis*) came in and asked to see Hitchings who was in his tent. After his conversation with the O.C. he came in again and took me out and told me that if I cared for the job I was to understudy the Staff Captain for a month at the end of which time I should be reported on and there might be a possibility of a good job. I am to start this tomorrow by accompanying the General to visit one of the Battalions which is arriving. While he was telling me this Hitchings was telling the other officers and when I returned it was amid an ominous silence and I could see that Dunton & Shaw were very perturbed. I thought this might be my imagination but Hitchings also noticed it and it continued throughout Mess. I hardly said a word and there was not much conversation. Shaw made the remark 'I suppose they'll be wanting a groom in the Brigade staff soon'. I think I was discreet in refraining from standing drinks round. It is rather heartrending after being with a Company for so long that when a piece of good fortune comes along like this, one's natural pleasure should be damped by the jealousy of one or two others. Hitchings and I both returned early and talked this matter over.

I found that his observations coincided with mine and that both Shaw and Dunton were obviously consumed with jealousy. If it hadn't been for their attitude my time in 238 Coy would have been such a happy one. Perhaps when I have gone they will be able to settle down though I fear that if Shaw is made acting Second in Command he will be at loggerheads with Dunton very soon. He decidedly has no balance.

My writing so far doesn't seem to have much of interest in it. I think the difficulty is in really laying bare one's mind upon paper. Every Englishman in reported to be reserved and this is undoubtedly true. If a diary would be kept showing the exact state of mind of the individual keeping it at the time of the events narrated it would most certainly form a very interesting if not instructive record for future perusal. Besides this natural reserve there is another hindrance to free writing. Unfortunately there are several points in the character of some of my colleagues which I at any rate privately criticise consumedly. In committing such faults to writing I feel restricted in two ways. Firstly it seems like saying things behind a man's back and secondly there are always two sides to a question and I can only fairly put one side as it appears to me. If therefore at any time these rough jottings were to be seen by any third person he would either realise these latter points, especially if he had read these last few lines, in which case no injustice would be done or he would read my account in an uncritical spirit and would condemn the objects of my criticism unheard.

One of the many things which really strikes me as amusing are the customs used in drinking. I may admit at the start that I am here a prejudiced observer as I seldom drink anything but tea. I can remember an old argument we once had in the Mess on the subject that Drinkers are of more generous disposition than non-drinkers. The main plea in favour being that a man did not like to drink by himself but invariably asked his neighbour 'What's yours?' I believe that the majority of us condemned the hypothesis as absurd which to my mind is to the credit of the Mess. Since then I have watched the habits of the drinking members with some interest. Originally we went on the plan that the mess generally paid for a certain proportion of the drink consumed and the drinkers themselves paid the remainder equally. Later on we have adopted the plan of the drinks being paid for as in ordinary messes. There are two members of the mess who are very generous in standing drinks all round and who certainly pay for a good bit more than they themselves consume. There are four more who generally give and take amongst themselves and it works out evenly. The other two provide the fun. One of them is as reckless with his money as is to be expected from a youngster who has never handled much before and he stands drinks in a lordly manner, but his peculiarity is that he is well on the look out to see that the standee (to coin a word) also stands in turn. The other man is I suppose the second biggest if not the biggest drinker in the mess but his drinks bill is quite frequently less than the modest bills of the two of us who are teetotallers. I have often watched him in mess. Whenever a drink is broached it is 'Oh, I'll have one with you Bill' in a grand way. He does it in the most jovial way in the world so that an outsider would think he had just merely desisted from treating so as to let someone else at long length have his turn. He condescends to drink with all and then sometimes as the Mess is fast emptying it will be 'Well what about a nightcap?' or something equally breezy and he escapes with one or two drinks. The night I watched him he had two whiskeys, a beer, a glass of port, Italian Vermouth and a Kummel and at that point he was debited with none. At the end of the week his bill will be 3 chips or thereabouts 'Is that all?' says he in his grand manner 'I'm practically on the water tap lately ' and up he pays without any fuss.

I have quite come to the conclusion that as a general rule treating is ridiculous. The majority of treaters simply pay for two or more drinks at one time for different people, because these in turn by the rule of the game must pay for the same number and Treater No. 1 will eventually have the same amount of drinks as he originally paid for. So far, so good, but when there are, as I have seen in some messes, about 6 people together having an appetiser before mess and this benighted custom leads them all to have six appetisers instead of the one which is all they really want the custom becomes, at least to my mind, a vicious one.

I should divide drinkers into four classes.

I. The generous who don't worry if they drink as does everybody all round at their expense and they don't expect the return. These are a fair minority.

II. The Just drinkers. These drink according to treaty rules and must not be done. I should say these are almost an absolute majority in messes.

III. The Spongers who drink largely at the expense of No. 1 Class. A comparatively small minority.

IV. The Sensible who drink when they feel thirsty and don't worry about treating at all. The last class is very rare. I have dubbed them the sensible because I think logically this way of drinking is the most sensible though I don't propose to write a treatise here to prove it. It would need a strong minded man not afraid of hostile public opinion to belong to this class.

Jan 11th

This morning I started on my new job. It has been a lovely day again. My principle (sic) care was to dress moderately decently which is not as easy as I have practically no decent clothing left and cannot buy any here. At 8.45 I walked over and reported to the General. I was given a packet of papers to deliver to the Adjt (*Adjutant*) 52nd Sikhs and then I rode down with the General and the Bgde (*Brigade*) Major to see this Regiment. They have just arrived at Hinaidi and were to start again for Aziziya to mend the railway or some similar job. We had a fine drive through Baghdad and I must find time one day to describe this place.

The Sikhs had to go off in two parties and the general left just before the first party went and told me to remain behind and see the second lot off. He said he would arrange to have my horse sent to the bridge to meet me. I eventually got away at 4.o'c and found my horse (at the wrong bridge) and got back at 5.30. I then put in a few minutes with the Staff Captain in his office and dressed for Mess. Mess was quite interesting and the General talked with some authority about the ancient history of this region. He seems to be well read on the historical side and I quite enjoyed the evening. I am just jotting these few lines down at 9.30. I shall then go to bed. My things were in an awful muddle as my servant has packed everything ready for my move to the Brigade quarters. I think if I can find my notepaper I shall just write home before turning in.

Jan 12th

After Breakfast I went over to Ordnance with Capt Gore (*Captain F L Gore, 113th Infantry*) and spent the morning drawing stuff. In the afternoon I remained in the office and dealt with one or two minor matters. Tonight the General told me to meet the 25 Punjabis who are marching over here tomorrow and I have to start before 7 a.m. so I must get to bed early. It has been a lovely day as far as weather is concerned. My tent has been transferred and is now pitched in the Brigade lines. Tomorrow Hodder will complete it as it was before the transfer.

Jan 13th

Up at 5.45 a.m. and after breakfast set out to meet the 25th. Met them at Hinaidi and conducted them to Camp. Col Hunt the C.O. (*Lieut.-Colonel H.R.A. Hunt, D.S.O., 1/25th Punjabis*) seems to be a very cheery man who has seen much service on the Staff in France which he left last July. I am going to try to make arrangement to learn Hindustani from a man in his regiment.

Spent the afternoon and most of the evening in the office indexing G.R.O. (*General Routine Orders*). The General and Major Gretton dined with the 23rd Coy this evening and only Capt Gore, MacLeod (*Lieutenant K MacLeod, Seaforth Highlanders*) and I were in mess. We had quite a jolly time and spent till near 11 o'c conversing on various matters. I wrote a very short note to Doris last night and must try to write at fuller length tomorrow.

Jan 14th

Accompanied the General round the lines in the morning and noted down various points on which I afterwards wrote to Units concerned. The Company had an unpleasant experience as they discovered before breakfast that all the bread had been stolen. No trace of the thieves has been found as yet.

This afternoon I borrowed the Staff Captain's horse and rode over to inspect the S & T (*Signals and Transport*) Section. When dismissed from this I returned and had tea with Hitchings and did a few odd jobs in the office. I have fixed up with the 25th Punjabis to send me a man to teach me Hindustani and I hope he will turn up to-morrow. Rumours of the mail become more and more prevalent and I do hope it will really arrive to-morrow. I don't know how I am getting on with my new work. I am trying to make myself useful but I am afraid that up to the present I have not sufficient definite knowledge to make myself an efficient Staff Captain. Everything in my mind is rather vague and nebulous and I shall have to set myself a kind of programme of study.

Jan 15th

Another very fine day today. This morning I spent in the office and I had an early lunch. During lunch I started reading a book in five volumes on Mesopotamia. It is very interesting and I think I shall quite enjoy reading it as I mean to do after going to bed each night. It contains a fairly large vocabulary of words in Turkish, Arabic, Armenian, Persian and Syrian as I hope to pick up just a smattering of these languages in time. This afternoon I spent in Baghdad. When I get time I must describe this place more fully. I fixed up for a delivery in camp of the new local paper the Baghdad Times and had a look round the Editor's premises. It is extraordinarily comfortable. He also issues a sheet in the vernacular.

I did a few jobs at Ordnance and returned to camp about 5.10. My Hindustani teacher did not turn up today but I was really too busy to see him so it did not make very much difference. I have just finished mess and in a few minutes I am going to join Capt Gore in indexing a few general routine Orders. I found three letters from home here when I came back this afternoon so that that (sic) is the event of the day. One from Doris with interpolations by Christine (*his younger sister*). One from the Pater (*his father*) and one from Will (*his brother, seriously wounded in France*). I mean to write a few notes as soon as I get time on the different things I see here. The method of transport is one which will be quite interesting. The little oriental shops reminiscent of Chu Chin Chou, cultivation, etc., etc. Meanwhile time presses and I must stop for to-night.

Jan 16th

Today has been as fine as its predecessors and I spent the morning marking out a Camp site for the Veterinary Section when it shall arrive. An unfortunate accident occurred during the morning, one of the R.W.K. (*Royal West Kents*) being accidentally shot by a Lewis Gun and killed.

I did nothing in particular during the afternoon except to have a bath. I was again disappointed in my Hindustani teacher in the evening but I managed to borrow a book from McLeod the F.T.C.O. which I shall endeavour to swot up.

Jan 17th

I spent the morning going to Ordnance and Stationery. I had four men of the 25th Punjabis sent down to help me and as they could speak no English I had to do my best with signs. I picked up a few words from one of them who seemed to be fairly intelligent. It was really quite an amusing experience. I am just going to write to Doris.

Jan 18th

I got up early and rode over to Hinaidi to meet our Signal Section. In Baghdad I bought an Arab primer which I want to study if I get time. On return to camp I did nothing much. Marwood the Signals Officer seems a very decent fellow. He was at Oxford and new (sic) the Rev. W.J. Carey (*Co-founder in 1890 and first President of the Barbarians RFC, he later became the Anglican Bishop of Bloemfontein*). It was a ripping day.

Jan 19th

I spent the morning marking out sites for camps for the Veterinary Section and for the Field Ambulance. The former turned up in the afternoon. In the evening Gore and I dined with the Coy and had a game of bridge. It was hotter today.

Jan 20th

I went to Church parade this morning, the first for many months. The padre was good but the whole thing was spoilt by the lamentable singing of the men. The Field Ambulance came in afterwards and I showed them round. This afternoon I came to my tent and began to read the Volume on Mesopotamia. Unfortunately the day being warm, and I being tired, I fell asleep and therefore in the Words of Tory MP "Work done Nil". I wrote to Doris this evening. On the corresponding Sunday last year I had just rolled up unexpectedly at home having left Clipstine on my way to Grantham. It was the first time we had together after the end of our honeymoon. So far my Hindustani has made little progress as no teacher has yet arrived. I have just heard of an officer of the 39 Garhwalis who might help me. I should like to make a start I must confess.

Jan 21st

The weather still keeps beautifully fine, though very cold at nights. This morning I spent in the office doing odd jobs. This afternoon there was a lecture by Col Hunt (*Lieut-Colonel H R A Hunt, D.S.O.*) of the 25th Punjabis. He was originally on the Staff of the 2nd London (Territorial) Division, mobilised with them and came out with them. My old regiment was attached to that division. Col Hunt was in France till July last and then came out to India and from thence to here in command of the 25th. His lecture traced the development of the present platoon system in the Infantry and he probably will continue on Wednesday.

I read Hindustani last night after going to bed but in the absence of a teacher I got on beastly slowly. As yet I haven't even opened the Arabic book. I find my time is split up by frequent odd little jobs that it is very difficult to sit down to anything quietly. I have tons of things I want to study and I could comfortably do with the day clear off after 2.0 pm. If I had that I could lay in vast stores of knowledge which might ultimately qualify me for a staff appointment.

Jan 22nd

Last night orders arrived that the 25th and 39th were to go off digging bunds (*walls to prevent inundation*) and as is usual in this country the notice was only given a few hours before the duty was to be performed. Consequently there was much panicking last night arranging details etc. Eventually matters assumed a final shape and I was detailed to accompany Col Hunt to Hinaidi this morning to complete arrangements. We had a fine ride in ripping weather and Col Hunt's conversation on France was very interesting to me. We got to camp again at 2 o'clock and I have been most of the time since fixing up the thousand and one details that crop up in connexion with a move.

A mail came in last night, letters 85 and 86 from Doris and one each from the Mater (*his mother*) and pater. I need hardly write how overjoyed I was to get them. I can see that living in England gets harder and harder and it makes one long all the more ardently for peace. I find Baghdad quite an interesting place to pass through and I must try to describe it in a few days.

Jan 23rd

I saw the Punjabis off today. The General and I rode down in a car and saw the entraining at Hinaidi and then the General returned leaving me behind to see the second train off. This went off punctually at 2 and I returned to Baghdad where my horse was waiting for me. On the way back I took a couple of photos both from the Kotah Bridge. The second one included a 'gufa' or coracle. This evening I had a very interesting talk to the General. He developed his views on the way in which Agriculture should be run in this country and declared himself frankly in favour of a 'Souahotu' form of organisation, claiming that this was essential for the development of any oriental country. We also discussed the difficulties experienced by a civilian joining at the outbreak of war, in settling down to Army discipline. The General is a most interesting conversationalist and I quite enjoy the little discussions that take place after Mess. It is a great treat as we don't often have these in our own Mess where, if any serious subjects of conversation crop up, they rather lead to displays of feeling from certain members or are resented by others as an attempt to talk above their heads. Well I must stop now without adding anything of any worth as I have left the writing till past 10 o'clock and I want to put in a little time at Hindustani.

Jan 24th

I spent today in the office doing odd jobs. Dunton went off to Hospital sick this afternoon and Hitchings was seedy and in bed this afternoon. The weather has been brilliant now for some time though it is very cold at nights. There is always ice on the water in the mornings.

Jan 25th

Last night after Mess I fancied I heard the familiar sound of a Boche 'plane and mentioned this to Neame (*Major L V Neame, 1/5th RWK*). We were both incredulous but as the noise continued we started out of the tent to look round. Barely had we emerged when a bomb exploded in the Baghdad direction. Soon after an antiquated Archie (*anti-aircraft gun*) started operations at random and we even had bits of shrapnel and nose cones in the camp. The alarm had been given and all the men were in the Aeroplane trenches. I don't know how many bombs were dropped. After the excitement had subsided we turned in but at 1 o'c I was lugged out for another plane. This time also Archie had a go without any rhyme or reason as far as I could see. Directly I heard his beastly bark I put on my steel hat because I realised there might be real danger from him. This morning all the talk was about the raid. The vast majority had never been in one before. We have received all sorts of reports as to damage and casualties and they nearly all contradict each other. It is not clear whether there was actually any damage done at all.

I did nothing in particular all day except office work and indexing Orders.

It is the Pater's and Will's birthday today and I have just written them a line and also a short letter to Doris. The weather is still brilliantly fine though it was rather cold all day.

Jan 26th

Another beautifully fine day. This morning I spent in the office. This afternoon Hitchings gave a lecture on Machine Guns and after that I turned out for the Company against the West Kents at football. It was quite a good game and we won 2-1.

Tonight after mess the talk turned on various subjects including the weights carried by Coolies.

Some marvellous stories were told of carriers in Indian Hills and a few of the Kurds of this country. I myself have seen some extraordinary performances. The way in which a weight is carried is by putting it on the back and then passing a strap right round the weight and over the head, the front of the strap lying across the forehead. In this way the local Arab carries bales at which an English Porter would strike. On the day we disembarked at Hinaidi I watched coolies loading a mahda with oats. The average load was four 80 lb sacks but the most interesting item was a small boy about the size of an average child of 9 or ten carrying three of these sacks. It is one of the sights which is most strange to the new arrival seeing these carriers. In the streets of Baghdad and out in the country one sees patriachal old gentlemen with huge loads - great piles of Camel Skins or huge nail studded boxes - and women to carry these huge loads. Lighter loads seem generally to be carried on the head and it is interesting to see. Arab women balancing a pitcher or tin full of water going along in a smooth trot. Possibly their upright carriage is due to this practice.

During the day I took a photo of the Brigade Major, Major Gretton.

Jan 27th

The General and Gore went off to see the Punjabis today at Bhawi so I had to look after the place. I was moderately busy all day in the office. Several reports were sent in of hostile aeroplanes seen flying about near the front but none materialised. I attended Church parade this morning and the singing was much better, due no doubt largely to the presence of the Middlesex (53rd Brigade) Band.

The wind changed to the South this morning and is now blowing quite strongly. The sky is very overcast and I expect we shall have some rain. I hope the post comes in to-morrow as I am feeling very homesick again.

Jan 28th

It rained and blew terrifically during the night and I was in fear and trembling for my tent. The foot of one of the end poles was dangerously near to the edge of the dugout and I was afraid it might slip in and let one end of the tent down. I think that sub-consciously I must have been thinking of that all night long. At 5 in the morning I woke up with a loud flapping noise in my ears and discovered that one of the pegs at the other end of the tent had come out and I was forced to rise and set matters right in case worse might befall. I was luckier than others. Marwood's (*Lieutenant S L Marwood, I.A.R.O., 18th Divisional Signal Company*) tent came down on top of him at 7.30 o'c and the wretched Postal people also were in the same plight.

(I have just had the switch over to pencil as the ink is so bad.)

During the morning I had to ride over to see the Garhwalis at their digging camp. The message I went on was totally unimportant (it usually is) and the weather of course was abominable. In spite of this I am glad I went because the ride was quite an interesting one. It fortunately did not rain hard while I was out though the weather was very wild. I started off on Cuthbert across fairly normal country and crossed lines of railway; at this point I left the Musinjit road which I had been following and kept near the river. My road, if such it can be called, was the top of a bund which was broken every now and again by cuttings made for irrigation purposes. The way was very muddy and slippery and the road was so bad that progress was very slow. The country round was cultivated in parts and was liberally sprinkled with bones of various animals, sometimes whole skeletons and other times just a skull and a few old bones.

My way led through several Arab Villages or settlements of the most primitive type. They looked something like decrepit farmyards surrounded with mud walls and little mud cabins. Generally there was a species of shallow shelving moat all round and all garbage and refuse appeared to be shovelled through holes in the wall into this moat. Huge bundles of camel thorn were scattered about on the mud roofs and on the surrounding ground. The farmyard interior generally contained a selection of fowls, dogs and asses and occasionally calves.

Amongst these villages I discovered a camp of the Madras Gardeners. These came from India about May last and have been cultivating the land round here producing vegetables. I don't know what success they have had but just past their camp I noticed a good deal of cultivation. I arrived at the Garhwalis camp at about 12.30 and had Tiffin (*lunch*) there. The Quartermaster, Tresham (*Captain B F Tresham, 1/39th Garhwal Rifles*) and I had a little talk which turned mostly on the great possibilities of this country after the war. If the government were to take over all produce and ensure good communication and the development of irrigation there is no doubt that this country would be able to produce immense quantities of wheat. I returned to camp by a slightly different route and arrived back at 4o'c.

I heard that the RW Kents had to go off digging to a camp just on the other side of Baghdad and naturally enough I fell into the job of going over in the morning to see the new camp. That means rising at 5.30 and clearing from camp at 6.30.

I got two letters from Doris this evening written on 26th and 27th November. All is still well at home.

Jan 29th

I got up this morning at about 10 minutes to six and sallied forth at a quarter to seven with Capt Carvosso of the 1/5th RWK. We rode down to Baghdad and through the city and out on to its North eastern side. We passed the mounds which I presume are the remnants of the old city walls and found all the ground thereabouts was one mass of tombs. It was evidently a cemetery. Just outside the city perimeter was the site of the camp, and Carvosso and I fixed up the details for the Regiment to come in. I then rode back to camp. On the way I managed to get some Hypo from Victors. In the afternoon I kept house whilst the General and Gore rode over to see the West Kents at their new camp. I managed in that time to print a few photos from my last completed film. Unfortunately the film had been spoilt somewhat by my sticking them in the book before they were thoroughly dry. In the evening I got three more letters, one from the pater and two from Doris. I can see how Doris feels the time very long but I am sure she cannot wish more for the end of the war than I do. I was pleased to get some few more details about dear Bunny. Will must be a great acquisition at home. I was always tremendously fond and proud of him and he is certainly turning out trumps now.

My Hindustani does not get very much forwarder I am sorry to say though I always do a bit each night before I turn in.

The other day I bought a lottery ticket for Rs5. If I win the first prize I may get a lakh (*100,000*) or thereabouts. I could well do with it I am sure.

Jan 30th

This morning all the staff went out and left me to look after things. I spent the morning doing odd jobs and indexing orders. Before lunch I took the photos of Gore, the General and Neame, I developed them with Hodder's help after lunch and I think some of them will be fairly good. I spent the rest of the time in the Office and to-morrow I go out early to see the 38th C.F.A. (*Combined Field Ambulance*) into camp. I am jotting this down just before Mess and I shall turn in soon after and hope to read some Hindustani. I am quite looking forward to getting back to the Company at the end of my spell here, as here I am continually lazing around doing nothing in particular. If I were with the Company I should have a definite job and should be able to spend my spare time quite profitably.

Jan 31st

I had quite a nice ride this morning over to the 38th C.F.A. and arrived at their camp soon after 8.30. Their transport was very late arriving and it was about 11 o'c before we were ready to start. I piloted them into camp being accompanied by a Bubu (*native*) medico with whom I exchanged views on the possibilities of this Country. I surprised him by some of my descriptions of London.

In the afternoon I printed some of my films and they are all fairly good though unfortunately a bit blurred. I was just going into tea when Hodder asked me if I would play football for the Brigade Staff against Signals. I agreed and sallied out to find that the staff by mustering everybody had just got eight men together. We had quite a jolly game without a ref and were beaten 3-0 before the ball showed ominous signs of bursting and the game ended. I went an awful purler early on and bashed my left knee, left thigh and left elbow. It took Hodder an hour or so to bandage me up afterwards.

My thoughts turned somewhat to Doris's letter in which she suggested that when I come home I should bring with me some oriental stuff for our dug out. The General was talking about Japanese work in the evening and I gathered that (1) if I were a connoisseur I should get good stuff by paying a small fortune, and that (2) if I were not a connoisseur I should not even see good stuff, but might get some less good stuff for a decent price.

It always seems good to talk of what one will do when one gets home, but that day sometimes seems to be a mere vision of impossibility. News came in Reuters of another Air raid on London with a lot of casualties. I always feel worried after learning of a raid in London until I have heard again from home. If only wishes could kill there would not be a single Hun, man, women or child alive.

Having just reached the age of 26 at the outbreak of WW1, my father, like so many hundreds of thousands of other young men, lost some of the best years of his life to a bloody and brutal war. At least he emerged physically unscathed in 1919, though his younger brother Harry was killed in France in April 1917 and his other brother, Will, was seriously injured in the trenches in France by a grenade blast.

The three brothers had all enlisted shortly after the outbreak of war in 1914, my father as a private in the Artists Rifles, having held a Territorial Army commission since 1910. In October 1914, he was sent to St Omer in France and soon after was appointed (a "temporary") Sergeant Instructor; as he noted four years later in his diary, he helped form the French Machine Gun School. After about a year, he returned to England and was attached to the Machine Gun Training Centre at Grantham, having been appointed to a commission ("on probation") in the Artists Rifles.

The Belchamber family December 1916.
Standing (L to R) Christine Sophie, Ernest Henry (Harry),
Douglas Foster, Winifred Mary.
Sitting (L to R) Christina, Sidney William (Will), Sidney Charlie.

In 1917, he became an acting Captain and possibly Adjutant of the 238th Machine Gun Company. In July, the Company was sent out to Passchendaele, where he was second in command of the service company responsible for supplying the troops in the front line. His letters to my mother, Doris, make for very interesting reading for the few months that they were there, but in October the company was then sent out to Mesopotamia (modern Iraq) as part of the 54th Brigade, the 18th (Indian) Division.

In the middle of February, he was seconded to the Department of Local Resources (DLR), first in Baghdad and later in Hillah, to help with the logistics of feeding the military and the civilian population.

During his time in Mespot (as it was familiarly called) he kept a diary, as so many people did. This was not intended for publication and was more a series of jottings. He made no attempt to correct, edit or improve the text, so, even for such a highly educated person, there are mistakes of punctuation, spelling and grammar that I have made no attempt to correct on his behalf.

The diary is of particular interest, as it operates on several levels. There is the day-by-day record of what his work entailed and his interaction with his colleagues and subordinates.

Underlying this main thread is his concern for those at home and his bouts of homesickness: his partially blind father (or the Pater, as this classically educated scholar was wont to call him) trying to maintain the boiler and laundry machinery, which his parents operated as a business and his mother's (or the Mater) courage and resolution in keeping the family afloat, despite all the trials and tribulations of the war. For her, especially, the loss of one son and the grievous wounding of another must have been hard to bear, while trying to run a business and having a partially disabled husband to look after and two young daughters to bring up.

And then of course a major concern was his wife, Doris, whom he had not seen since their wedding when he was home on leave in December 1916. Doris lived initially with her parents-in-law in Clapham and, as a labour of love, she transcribed all the letters that father wrote to her while he was serving in Flanders. This was very convenient, since her writing was very legible, which his was not, and it is her transcriptions that have survived.

Apart from his home concerns about food shortages and the air raids, his constant anxiety was about the way the war was going in France; even until quite late in 1918, the Germans (or 'the Boche' or 'the Hun') seemed to be holding their own and even gaining back ground that the Allies had won, which is why he found it difficult to understand why the Americans were so long in entering the fray.

For relaxation, he was fortunate in that there were excellent sporting facilities at 'the Club' and he played a lot of tennis and football (or 'footer', as he invariably called it). He captained a side (presumably the Department of Local Resources' side) which lost 1 – 0 against the Advanced M T Depot in the final of a knock out cup the day before he left for England. Father was an excellent sportsman, who, after the war, played amateur football to a high standard and reputedly would have played for England had he not been injured.

Before the war he had also been a very good club cricketer but he took up tennis so that he would be able to play with Doris, who was already a good player (and a future England international at hockey); both later played county tennis for Derbyshire.

It so happened that Norman Brookes, the Australian tennis player who had become the first non-English player to win the Men's' Singles at Wimbledon was also in Baghdad and my father watched him play quite frequently but doesn't appear to have played with or against him himself.

Finally, we see the scholar. Father had received an excellent education at Battersea Grammar School but, as his parents could not afford to send him to university, he had already obtained an external BA from London University before the war and then passed out first in the testing Civil Service examination. In Mespot, he did not allow his mind to stagnate; he started to learn Hindi and Arabic and brushed up on his maths. Above all, he read voraciously and quickly. His taste was catholic to say the least: Dickens, Austen, the Bronte's, Zola, Hugo, Sven Hedin, Borrow, various Lives and Biographies among others.

As a mathematician, it is hardly surprising to read that he was delighted to find some kindred spirits in the Mess to play Bridge with and he even recorded the details of the four hands of one especially memorable game.

Not the least interesting matter in the diary is the question of father's army rank; one is never quite certain what his substantive rank was at any given moment. Before enlisting, he had held a Territorial commission, which he resigned on enlistment. He rose from a Private in the Artists Rifles to a Lieutenant Colonel with an MBE but the passage from the one to the other was a bit of a roller coaster.

In December 1914 he was appointed a 'Temporary' Sergeant Instructor, in March 1916 he was appointed to a commission 'on probation' in the Artists Rifles and attached to the Machine Gun Training Centre in Grantham. In 1917 he became a 'temporary' Lieutenant, than an 'acting' Captain until February 1918, when in Mesopotamia he reverted to 'temporary' Lieutenant with the Department of Local Resources.

In March, he again became a 'temporary' Captain and in May he was given the 'temporary' rank of Lieutenant Colonel. Having reached England at the beginning of May 1919 he relinquished his rank of Lieutenant Colonel and so presumably went back to where he started nearly five years earlier, a humble Private.

The one commissioned rank below Colonel that he hadn't held was Major but two years after the war he had the satisfaction of being granted the rank of Lieutenant Colonel.

Finally, as my father became a senior civil servant, it must have given him real satisfaction to read General Dickson's final report on him:

"Hard working and of exceptional administrative capability. His handling of the many problems connected with the Euphrates Development were most successful and of very great service to the Department."

DAVID BELCHAMBER

CHAPTER 5

Mohawk – the Mystery Aircraft of the Wylye Valley
John Edgar Dutton

My first contact with Aviation Archaeology was when two young men from the Marches Aviation Society knocked on my door in August 2004. Ian Hodgkiss and Gareth Jones were searching for a Spitfire that crashed near Codford on 6th November 1943. The American pilot had bailed out at 7,000 feet over the village and survived the crash site was undetermined. Local publicity pinpointed the crash site and the remains of the Spitfire were excavated in September of 2005.

The press coverage of the search for the Spitfire generated more information, this time of a mystery aircraft that crashed in Hanging Langford in the Wylye Valley. Aviation Archaeology were contacted by Mrs Twigg of Andover, who said her father-in–law had witnessed an aircraft crash during WWII. Over the coming months Mrs Twigg returned to the small village of Hanging Langford to refresh her memory, identified the spot where the plane had come down, contacted the landowner and obtained permission to investigate the site. All that was left was to find what this mystery aircraft was. There were two ways forward; the first was to examine the records of every one of the many hundreds of aircraft that came down in Wiltshire to check for mention of Hanging Langford. The second, less time consuming, was to identify the aircraft from the small parts left behind at the crash site.

A morning spent with a metal detector found a surprising amount of aircraft debris lying just under the soil; however the finds just deepened the mystery as to the type of aircraft buried beneath the meadow. A shiny black push rod suggested an

American aircraft with a radial engine, while yellow painted aluminium from the skin of the aircraft pointed to a British training aircraft. During WW II British training aircraft had yellow painted on their undersides as an aid to visibility and to warn other pilots that there was a learner in the air. The recoil buffer from a British .303 machine gun showed that the plane was armed and a stainless steel ammunition track again pointed to American manufacture. This suggested that the plane was either a Miles Master III, or, more likely, a Harvard. A long trawl through the Air Britain logs drew a blank. It was only when cleaning a rather unpromising looking access panel that the yellow paint washed away to reveal the legend 'Vidanger de......' (to empty or drain down) possibly referring to the cover for a drain plug! Unmistakably French!

Now Ian and Gareth had a clue, they knew what they were looking for. They discovered that on 1st March 1941 a Curtiss Mohawk fighter aircraft took off from Boscombe Down airfield near Amesbury. Its pilot was Squadron Leader John Edgar Dutton AFC, aged 30, an experienced test pilot who had been awarded the Air Force Cross earlier in the year for making a skilful wheels up landing without flaps. The purpose of the flight was to test a staggered layout and heating equipment for the aircraft's six Brownings. During the flight a fire started on board. At 10.30 in the morning the Mohawk was seen to dive, burning, out of the cloud base and bury itself in a large crater. The accident record reads 'Gun-heating test flight involving a high altitude climb. The aircraft was seen to dive out of low cloud on fire. It was presumed that engine failure occurred at altitude and the pilot had been overcome by fumes. The aircraft crashed at Hanging Langford Wilts. 1 killed. Cat5.' (Category 5 = Damaged beyond repair, missing or is not worth repairing.)

Mr Edmond Tibbotts, a dairyman working on the water meadow next to the Wylye, witnessed the crash. His witness testimony was called on in the following Air Force investigation and the event made such an impression on him that he passed the story on to his daughter-in- law.

With war clouds looming in the late 1930s the French Government realised they did not have enough modern fighters to defend themselves. They turned to America and ordered large numbers of Curtiss H75 Hawk fighters, [the Curtiss sales brochure was apparently a joy to behold.] By the time the Nazi Blitzkrieg struck in 1940 the French had several squadrons of Hawks in service but this was still only a small part of their order. French Hawks shot down the first Luftwaffe aircraft of the campaign and accounted for more Germans than any of the home produced Morane Saulnier or Dewotine fighters, but they could not stem the tide of the forthcoming invasion.

With the surrender of France some pilots flew their planes to Britain, although more sided with the Vichy government in the south of France. Vichy Hawks were later flown against the Allies in North Africa, one of only a few types to serve on both sides during the war. The US Air Force was still flying Hawks in 1941 and it was one of these which shot down a Japanese dive-bomber during the attack on Pearl Harbour. The remaining French Hawks were shipped directly to Britain, still in French camouflage, with French instrumentation and equipment. One of these was tested at Boscombe Down against a Spitfire, but due to its higher speed the Spitfire could break off combat quicker than the Mohawk, so as a result the type was deemed unfit for service in Europe. The remaining Hawks, or Mohawks as they were named in RAF service, were issued to the South African Air Force for use in East Africa, shipped to Asia to fight the Japanese and used extensively in India.

With the knowledge that the Hanging Langford plane was an American Aircraft built for the French it was quickly identified as a Mohawk III, Serial No BK877, of the Aircraft Armament Experimental Establishment at Boscombe Down. It had been excavated in 1980 by the London Air Museum who had removed the engine, propeller and cockpit. [Ian remembers being very impressed by a display of the wreckage at Tangmere as a child.] The only mystery left was whether the aircraft was one of those which served in the Battle of France or one of the later batches shipped to the UK.

The indispensable Forster bomb locator showed there was a lot of wreckage remaining on the site despite the previous dig, so with the landowner's permission a licence to excavate was obtained from the Ministry of Defence.

Mohawk Excavation Hanging Langford, Wylye Valley, Wiltshire

The dig started smoothly with topsoil removed and pieces of aluminium structure quickly appeared. The JCB driver, whose father had carried out the London Air Museum dig, was impressed that all the wreckage was being recovered. The previous group 'only wanted the engine' and discarded most of the rest. Amongst the first identifiable pieces of the plane were the magneto, the British throttle quadrant [a replacement for the French unit which worked backwards] and the label from the fire extinguisher, manufactured in Detroit but

American throttle control substituted for a French throttle control which worked backwards and confused RAF pilots.

Label from the Mohawk's undercarriage with aircraft type and instructions in French

with the operating instructions in French. With the excavation down 5" the low water table took over and the hole quickly filled up nearly to ground level. From then on the JCB gave the impression of fishing in soup, pulling out buckets of mud and water with fragments of aircraft mixed amongst it. This made it very difficult to identify pieces and the wreckage was simply loaded into trailers to be cleaned and identified later. One section recognised had a label showing that the Mohawk was the 99th A-4 model and had been completed in May 1940. This meant it could not have been shipped across the Atlantic in time to take part in the Battle of France.

Big pieces included a self-sealing fuel tank from the wing and some large pieces of the cockpit floor. Some of the items were in a perfect state of preservation, still shining after 65 years underground, whereas other sections had corroded away almost to nothing. It was clear which pieces had previously been exposed to the air. Amongst the mud encrusted items were the pedals and seat of a bicycle and a garden hoe. Not standard RAF equipment!

The last and slightly alarming find were four of the aircraft's six .303 Browning machine guns, one sticking out of the digger bucket like a cocktail stick. These were located with the aid of the Forster by dangling precariously over the hole, the most deeply buried items being with the Curtiss prop boss. Three of the Brownings were wing mounted and one was a hand-charged from the fuselage. All four had been deactivated to comply with the law.

Ammunition Empties Box

In all about a ton of wreckage was recovered and pressure washing over the following days revealed more of its history. A flattened stainless steel emptie's box contained fired bullet cases, dated 1940, the results of the gun testing on the final flight. Painted panels had more French instructions on them as well as showing parts of the French camouflage pattern the plane was delivered in. It could be seen where the RAF fitters had masked the underside of the aircraft before spraying it, with over sprays of yellow paint on the silver wheel rims. Most telling of all was the blackening on some of the structure where it had been touched by fire, particularly on the cockpit floor and wing root. One of the wing ribs had melted through leaving a blob of once liquid metal. A large proportion of the canopy frame was found showing the hood had not been jettisoned. The pilot was probably overcome by the fumes at high altitude.

Test pilots would always try to bring an aircraft back for analysis rather than abandon it and lose the results of their work. It seems that 30 year old Squadron Leader Dutton died in a valiant attempt to bring his burning aircraft back to base. He was buried in Hooton Roberts (St John the Baptist) churchyard in his parents' hometown of Rotherham.

There is now a large private museum next to Old Sarum Airfield, Salisbury and it is fitting that some of the larger pieces have been returned there so many years after the fateful flight left on a fine spring morning in 1941.

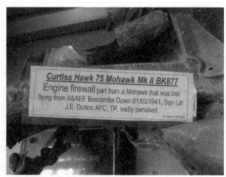

Engine Firewall

Additional info from Chris Green

UK Flight Testing Accidents 1940-71
Derek Collier Webb, An Air Britain Publication
1st March 1941 Mohawk IV BK877
Sqn Ldr J.E.Dutton AFC, 'A'Flt Armament Test Sqn, A&AEE. Gun-heating test flight involving a high altitude climb. The aircraft was seen to dive out of low cloud on fire. It was presumed that engine failure occurred at altitude and the pilot had been overcome by fumes. The aircraft crashed at Hanging Langford Wilts [refs 195]. 1 killed . Cat5. Took off 10.30   Killed
Damage categories:
Cat 1= Damage repairable on site by established first line servicing personnel.
Cat 2 = Damage repairable on site by established second line service personnel.
Cat 3= Damage is repairable on site but external assistance is required.
Cat 4= Damage not repairable on site. Aircraft must be removed to a repair depot or civilian repair organisation.
Cat 5= Damaged beyond repair, missing or is not worth repairing.
Cat 5 =slang =write off.

Squadron Leader John Edgar Dutton A.F.C.
John Edgar Dutton was born in the last quarter of 1910, the first child of newspaper clerk Edgar Dutton and his wife of one year Kate ('Kitty' nee Bryars.) In 1911 the new family were living at his grandfather James Charles Edgar Dutton's home at 17 Mansfield Road, Rotherham in South Yorkshire. Later Edgar and Kitty lived at 8 Summerfield, Chatham Street.

Jack, as he was known was a pupil at Rotherham Grammar School on Moorgate. He was married in Rotherham in the first quarter of 1937, and was living at 100 Earls Road in Amesbury, Wiltshire when he died.

Jack joined the Royal Air Force as an Aircraft Apprentice at the age of sixteen in 1926; he did well to be accepted for a three year apprenticeship, with many more rejected than accepted. His initial service number was 560751. He would have graduated in 1929 and became a mechanic on the aircraft of the day. The normal entrance method for airmen was (at the age of eighteen) to undergo recruit training followed by trade training at a basic level, several years' experience on squadrons and then advanced training to become an engineer or an airframe fitter. Apprentices covered all this ground in three years.

1st Photo taken from Christmas & New Year Card
In Iraq while he was still a sergeant.

Six years later, he trained as an airman-pilot, again a feather in his cap as there was a lot of competition from serving airmen as well as civilians, for places at a Flying Training School. Jack took the entry exam and passed at RAF Halton. He became an airman pilot, and between 8th September 1932 and 31st August 1933 he completed his Basic Flying Training (BFT) at No 4 Flying Training School formed in April 1921 at Abu Suier in Egypt. Its role was primarily to train pilots for squadrons based in the Middle East operating the improved, redesigned radial engine models of the Avro 504Ns, a WWI biplane with a new undercarriage, powered by the Armstrong-Siddeley Lynx engine.

When his training as a pilot in Egypt was complete Jack was posted to 70th (BT-Bomber Transport) Squadron, the Royal Air Force Station Hinaidi near Baghdad in the Kingdom of Iraq. This was established under British Army command as the main British base in Iraq after WW I until 1922 when the RAF took over. There were extensive barracks, recreational facilities, a large hospital, Air Headquarters, communication facilities, maintenance units, aeroplane squadron hangars, RAF Armoured Car Company lines and a Civil Cantonment. After completing BFT

Jack flew various planes around the Middle East including the freighter and troop transporter the Vickers Victoria; as well as moving military personnel it was used for long range training flights. The Victoria was a twin engine biplane with an enclosed cabin that had room for twenty- four troops on collapsible canvas seats arranged along the side of the fuselage.

On 31st March 1936 Jack was posted to the Home Establishment as a result of receiving a permanent commission (giving him employment until the age of fifty-five) as a Pilot Officer on 21st May that year and his service number became 36071.

From 25th May until 31st August 1936 he was with No 215 (B) Squadron at Upper Heyford, when the Squadron moved to newly opened (July 1936) expanded airfield and camp at Driffield. In the early 1930s Driffield had been selected as one of the RAF's expansion airfields with construction work beginning in 1935 and was to become the home of a number of bomber squadrons. Jack was obviously an exceptional pilot as evidenced when he was posted eight months later, on 19th April 1937, to Aeroplane and Armament Experimental Establishment (A & A. E. E.) at Martlesham Heath The A & A. E. E. carried out the testing and evaluation of many aircraft types and much of the armament and other equipment that would be used during WW II. Test Pilots were, and still are, the best of the best; Jack Dutton's quality is further enhanced by his rapid promotions. On 21st November 1937 he was promoted again to Flying Officer. After the outbreak of war on 21st November 1939, Jack became a Flight Lieutenant, and on 10th December 1940 the London Gazette announced his promotion to Squadron Leader.

The recommendation for The Air Force Cross for Flight Lieutenant John Edgar Dutton, No 3 (Training) Group, Aeroplane and Armament Experimental Establishment is dated 2nd September 1940 and signed by the Group Captain commanding Boscombe Down in Wiltshire.

An Extract from the London Gazette dated January 1941
THE KING has been graciously pleased to approve the following award:
Air Force Cross
Flight Lieutenant John Edgar Dutton RAF

'This officer has been a test pilot at this Establishment since April 1937 during which time he has carried out considerable flying in connection with Bomb Ballistic experiments and the trial of flares. The work he has been doing calls for numerous experimental flights both by day and night, often at altitudes reaching 30,000 feet. He has also for various periods commanded the Experimental Bombing Flight most successfully. He recently skilfully landed an aircraft whose undercarriage and flap gear he was unable to lower, without injury to the crew and with minimum damage to the aircraft.

He at all times carries out his duties most conscientiously and willingly and I consider that the hard work that he has carried out in armament testing during the last three years well merits the award recommended. '

Between 3rd September 1939 except for a period of approx. 6 weeks at 10 OTU (Operational Training Unit) Abingdon (*opened in 1932, initially as a training station for RAF Bomber Command – a role it continued through WWII*) in Oxfordshire until his death in March 1941 Jack Dutton was stationed Boscombe Down on Salisbury Plain in Wiltshire. In August 1939 as WW II hostilities commenced the A. & A.E.E. moved from RAF Martlesham Heath to RAF Boscombe Down near Amesbury.

Jack's log book shows during the months of May 1940 and February 1941 he flew twelve different aircraft: Blenheim, Beaufort, Whitley, Botha, Hampden, Virginia, Wellington, Havoc, Valentia, Harrow, Battle Boston DB7 and Heyford.

In May 1940 Jack's duties included bombing and flare trials at Lyme Bay, gunnery trials, air test with 4 passengers, bombing wall at Porton , turret test, local formation flying with 3 passengers, night flying test, automatic gunsight trials, local flying, and low level bombing (incendiaries). In each instance Jack was the Captain with a second pilot; passengers not involved in flying could include moving personnel around the country or observers for flight testing and trial duties.

In February 1941 the record shows he flew Blenheims five times for a variety of bombing trials including for incendiary bombing at Porton, inspecting locality for bombs .... "SAM" container trials @ 175mph, "SAM" on L.S. carrier @250mph, a Havoc to test of a 12 gun installation and a Botha turret trials diving @240knots . At the end of the month he had flown an ongoing total of 2,143 hours 50 minutes throughout his career.

Mohawk temperature gauge

On entering service with the RAF the Mohawk armament was changed to 6 x .303 Browning machine guns and an English throttle. The purpose of the test on the day of the Curtiss Mohawk crash was to test the heating equipment as the aircrafts six Browning machine guns had often been frozen in the cold air above 20,000 feet. The Mohawk was either fitted with straight (in line) or staggered machine guns. It is believed (not proven) that BK877 had staggered machine guns. BK877 was the 99th A4 model off the production line and was completed in May 1940. It is known the aircraft was employed on gun heating system trials that included high altitude climbs. It was painted in camouflage colours, with large amounts of yellow paint applied over the top of the camouflage.

On the 1st March 1941 Jack Dutton took off from Boscombe Down in the

Mohawk IV that had replaced a similar aircraft that had previously crashed, for gun heating trials. The Operations Log Book for that day records that the morning was fine to fair, becoming cloudy occasional showers: rain commencing about 220BST. [British Summer Time] It also mentions Air Marshall L.A. Pattinson, CB, DSO, DFC, C in C visited the station.

At 10.30 that morning the burning Mohawk was seen to dive out of the cloud base and crash in flames impacting the ground into a large crater at Hanging Langford. The aircraft was not recovered to A.& A.E.E. and there does not appear to be any kind of official accident report, possibly none was done due to the large number of crashes in Wiltshire during the war.

Bomb Carrier Sea Harrier Boscombe Down Historic Aircraft Collection. Carrier situated under the wing and above the bomb

Bomb Carriers

Jack's Air Force Cross was presented to his widow Florence Mary Dutton by the King at Buckingham Palace. Her father in law Edgar Dutton accompanied her.

John Dutton Record of Service as a pilot:

No 4 Flying Training School 8/9/ 32 – 31/8/33
70th (BT) Squadron Hinaidi Iraq 31/8/33- 31/3/36
Posted to Home Estb on being commissioned 21/5/36
No 215 (B) Squadron Upper Heyford 25/5/36-31/8/36
No 215 (B) Squadron Driffield 31/8/36 – 19/4/37

A & A. E. E. Martlesham Heath 19/4/37 -3/9/39
A & A. E. E Boscombe Down 3/9/39 – 2/6/40
10 OTU Abingdon 2/6/40 -22/7/40
A & A. E. E Boscombe Down 22/7/40

From Log
May 1940

11th	Blenheim L8669	flare trials at Lyme Bay.
12th	Beaufort L4473	gunnery trials
14th	Blenheim L8671	to Warmwell?
	Blenheim	bombing Lyme Bay
	Whitley	N1346 air test4 passengers
15th	Blenheim 8671	bombing wall at Porton
17th	Botha L6209	turret test
18th	Blenheim L8669	flare trials at Lyme Bay 2 passengers
19th	Blenheimlocal formation flying 3 passengers	
	Hampden L4035	night flying test
	Hampden	automatic gunsight trials
20th	Virginia J7130	local flying
21st	Blenheim L8669	low level bombing (incendiaries)

1941
February

24th	Blenheim L8689	incendiary bombing at Porton
	Wellington W5389	country & 400lb (dummy) Sidmouth Bay
25th	Blenheim L8689	inspecting locality for bombs from ....
	Wellingotn W5389	400lb (dummy)
26th	Havoc AH433	test of 12 gun installation @ S.......... Bay
	Blenheim	bombing p......4x450lb
	Havoc AH433	test of 12 gun installation @ S.......... Bay
28th	Blenheim L8689	"SAM" container trials @ 175mph
	Blenheim"SAM" on L.S. carrier @250mph	
	Blenheim	" " " @260mph
	Botha L6133	trials diving @240mph

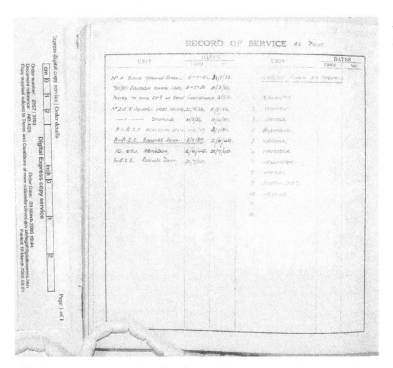

Record of Service

Log book 1940

Final flight log book

OPERATIONS RECORD BOOK

of (Unit or Formation) _No. 8, A.E.A., Boscombe Down_

Date	Time	Summary of Events	References to Appendices

Operations Log Book

Notes from Log

- [BT] Bomber Transport
- [B] Bomber
- *[OTU] 10 Operational Training Unit, Abingdon between 2nd June and 22nd July1940 - Andrew Dennis at the RAF Museum in London believes that given his experience Jack Dutton would have been acting as an instructor.*
- *Log on 24th February Wellington W5389 country & 400lb (dummy) Sidmouth Bay refers to a cross country navigational exercise*
- *"SAM" does not appear in any RAF terminology of this period. Pilots often used their own abbreviations in their log books that would be recognisable within their squadrons. 1941 is too early for 'Surface to Air Missiles'; 'Simulated Attack Mode' is language not used during this period. Having accessed two months of log book entries almost all the tests were simulated attacks - yet this abbreviation only appears in relation to the Blenheim L8689 which was a gunnery trials aircraft; in this instance carrying out container trials and tests of the Light Series Carriers. The Air Historical Branch (RAF) having consulted widely has been unable to reach a conclusion as to what this particular abbreviation would have referred to at this time.*
- *[SBC] Small Bomb Container, a rectangular, re-usable alloy container winched directly to the bomb-bay. The SBC commonly used in Blenheims, is listed as a potentially*

*dangerous solution to the armourer's problems of bombing up [loading] with small
ordnance and their safe release or retrieval. As Boscombe Down was an experimental
establishment the reference to 'container trials' possibly involved conducting tests of a new
type/ sort of bomb container.*
• *LSC refers to a Light Stores Carrier, 'stores' being an RAF term for bombs. In the Mark
1 Blenheim there were mountings for 2 LSC's under the fuselage installed fore and aft
just aft of the bomb-bay.*

Sources

Ian Hodgkiss & Gareth Jones of the Marches Aviation Society for the Aviation
Archaeology Report in its entirety.
Tony Dyer
Richard Brown
Christopher Green
Major Don Bartlett
Norman Hibberd
Imperial War Museum
Andrew Dennis RAF Museum, London
Gordon Morris & Norman Parker Boscombe Down Historic Aircraft Collection
Alan Thomas Air Historical Branch (RAF)
211 squadron.org/blenheim armament

CHAPTER 6

Market Garden and the Bridge at Arnhem 1944
John Bosley

In April 1944 I joined 11th Battalion, The Parachute Regiment almost directly from parachute training at Ringway. Prior to this I had served in a young soldiers' training regiment in the Royal Artillery, where I learnt everything to do with this arm of the service but knew very little about Infantry work. I could drive a motor vehicle as well as knowing all about the mechanical side, ride a motor cycle, operate a wireless set, fire a 25 pounder gun, was a Specialist in R.A., Signaller, map reader, aircraft and tank recognition expert, morse code operator, observation post and range expert. The course I attended was for potential Officers and NCOs, but all that ended when most young gunners were sent to the Infantry where there was a great shortage, so being keen on aeroplanes I applied for the Para's and soon found myself doing the tough course where they weed out the men from the boys prior to parachute training.

On arriving at 11th Battalion the Parachute Regiment in a pleasant little town called Melton Mowbray, I was placed in the Intelligence Section, probably because of my previous experience and also because I knew a lad in this section whom I had been with from Ringway. He was a German Jew called Gustav Sander, a very well educated lad whose father managed to get out of Germany just prior to the outbreak of War in 1939. Gus was later commissioned in the Middlesex Regiment but was killed in action in Korea. The Intelligence Section comprised of an Officer Lt Crawford, Sergeant Michael Elliott MM, a real gentleman and a fine soldier, Corporal Rocky Knight, L/Cpl J. Prout, Ptes John Latz, a chap called Jack, an older man of about 35 and a fine draughtsman, Ptes Jerrard, Harry Liston the IO's batman and Jim Bourne, all of whom wore the Africa Star, and of course us two youngsters, Gus and me.

I was issued a queer little gun called a Sten, which when fired always stopped after a round or two. We trained quite a lot with the 38 wireless set, a small two-way radio with a fishing rod type aerial, but found that its range was only a couple of miles and the battery only lasted about four hours.

John Bosley

Early on June 1944 we were suddenly placed on standby and expected to become part of an invasion force. We were shocked to learn that the 6th Airborne Division had landed in Normandy as we regarded that our Division, 1st Airborne was much more experienced and was the best for the job. Later that day, 6th June 1944, we were briefed to land at Caen in Normandy but this was soon cancelled owing to German Panzers being on the Drop Zone [DZ].

From then on we were stood to and stood down for various operations ahead of the Invasion Force but all were cancelled until the second week in September when we were briefed to go to Arnhem in Holland to capture a huge bridge over the River Rhine. Everybody though this operation would be cancelled again and did not take it too seriously, however on Sunday 17th September we heard that the first lift had gone and realised that we were going into action at last.

John Bosley 1944

Very early the next day the battalion went to an airfield at Saltby where there were hundreds of US Air Force Dakota aircraft. I took the 38 set and other Intelligence Section equipment in a kit bag attached to my right leg. At the airfield we were told that the take-off was delayed by fog so we sat under the wing of our allotted aircraft drinking tea, a great mistake as there were no loos in the Dakota's.

We finally took off about four hours late, the flight to Holland was uneventful until about 20 minutes before we reached the DZ. Suddenly the aircraft started to rock and weave and I heard explosions close by above the noise of the engines. I could even smell cordite from explosions and heard flak striking the aircraft. We were stood waiting for the green light ordering us to exit from the aircraft; with all the rocking and weaving I found it hard to keep my feet. I was thankful when the green light came on and for the first time was glad to jump because I felt sure that we were going to be shot down. I had great difficulty reaching the door with the kit bag on my right leg, but a fine RAF Dispatcher sent me out before I had time to think twice.

When my parachute opened I released the kit bag that was on a piece of rope 20 feet long, I heard shooting and saw that below there was a lot of smoke. I hit the ground heavily and on releasing my harness and going for my kit bag I saw that the aerials of my 38 set were snapped in two. I recovered the set and equipment and started to head for the rendezvous. I heard bullets whizzing close to my head and saw many of my pals holding entrenching spades around their heads for protection. I followed the rest into some woods out of the shooting and found the Intelligence

Officer and Gustav interrogating a large group of tough soldiers in German uniform, dressed in camouflage smocks. I stayed on guard with Gus who was speaking to the prisoners in German and found they were Waffen SS that came as a shock as they weren't supposed to be in the area. At that time I learned that my friend Sgt Elliott had been killed just after jumping from the aircraft and that Jeb Prout had been hit as he was about to jump and had been taken back to the UK. This was a bad start- two men lost already out of our section of ten.

We were told that our role had been changed and that the 11th Battalion was to proceed to Arnhem Bridge as quickly as possible at about 5 pm: my company thankfully in the rear as there were a lot of bloody Germans waiting for us in the woods, ambushing when they could. After a lot of stops and starts we finally got right down into Arnhem, about 8 miles from our DZ at midnight.

We came to a halt about 2 miles from our objective and our CO went off to confer with other Battalion commanders on how and when to resume our advance. There was very heavy firing ahead, coming in our direction and I wondered where the Germans got all their ammunition from as they appeared to be firing just so we would keep our heads down. We moved off again slowly in columns each side of the road about 4am as the firing increased, when daylight came all hell was let loose, mortars, shells, and bullets rained down on us and we took to the houses for cover. I went to the top floor of our house, on looking out of the window I saw the River Rhine, in front and to my left about a mile away, covered in smoke I saw the huge Arnhem Bridge. There was a lot of shooting from across the river, well out of range for us to reply with our little Sten guns as they only had a range of about 50 yards.

I remained in the house for some time, waiting for orders to resume the advance but the barrage became more intense and it was suicide to leave cover. About midday a cry went out for the Projectile Infantry Anti-Tank [P IAT] men to go forward and we were told later that groups of men were being put on jeeps and were making a dash for the bridge. About an hour later I was ordered by an NCO to board a jeep outside, as I boarded the jeep along with 5 or 6 other chaps, all heavily laden with our equipment, expecting to go to the bridge, I saw a lot of anxious faces including Major Webber our company CO. To my surprise, instead of heading for the bridge into the firing, we headed back in the direction we had come from, coming to a halt in the relative peace and quiet by a railway bridge in open country. We disembarked and the jeep headed back into Arnhem. We stood around, all alone, wondering what to do- no one was in charge and we had no orders. On the railway line was a stationary electric or diesel train, which appeared abandoned.

The peace was shattered suddenly when a group of aircraft appeared overhead, I immediately recognised German ME 109's. The others did not believe me when I told them they were German planes, they soon changed their minds when the planes dived on the train and started machine- gunning it. We all scattered in different directions, when all became quiet again I looked around but could find no one. I was all-alone, loaded down with all sorts of equipment, miles out into enemy country, feeling very scared and wondering what to do. I saw a house in the middle of a field so I went over and looked inside. The house was deserted, the occupants had obviously left in a hurry, so I waited hoping to see some of our men, after a while I heard voices and saw a group of Airborne soldiers heading across the field. I headed in their direction making my way to a small town, which turned out to be Oosterbeek. I found some of our Division dug in around a small church in gun positions so I set about looking for any of our 11th Division, without success. I dug in around the gun position and spent an uncomfortable night getting hardly any sleep because of shelling in the area.

The next day, Wednesday, I set out with a party of mixed units, armed with anti-tank bombs [Gammon bombs] searching for tanks reported in the area, we had none so they were obviously enemy. These bombs were name after their inventor Lt. Gammon, they consisted of plastic inside a velvet bag, stuffed with explosives with the detonator in the small handle. We had to throw the bombs so would have to get close, I had never seen these bombs before so didn't know how to use them. Luckily I didn't see any tanks but some were in the vicinity as 2 were destroyed by men of the South Stafford's manning anti-tank guns and a VC was won. The rest of the day was spent dug in around the church at Oosterbeek, I remember seeing a re supply mission come over and a Stirling bomber fly over my slit trench on fire. The pilot was obviously trying to pancake in the River Rhine but he failed, he crashed and exploded on the riverbank.

It was during the re-supply mission when a lot of shrapnel was coming down that I took cover in a nearby house when a shell came through the roof, landed about 4 feet behind me and did not explode. I got out of the house pretty quickly. I remained around the church that night and the following day was picked up by RQMS Dave Morris from my unit HQ company 11th Parachute Battalion and with others from the unit, [this was Thursday] we fortified a house at Weeverstraat, just the Arnhem side of the church. We held this house all day against a great deal of shelling and mortaring. I was put on guard for most of the night in the attic, keeping a look out for Germans who luckily went to sleep. I was later relieved and got some sleep in the cellar of the house.

The following morning, Friday 22nd September 1944 Cpl Rocky Knight came to the house and ordered me to go with him, he took several others from my unit together with an officer with the rank of Captain, also Harry Liston, the IO's batman who had been badly wounded in the attack on Arnhem bridge. We patrolled and searched an area towards the railway line at Nijmegen, attracting a lot of enemy fire, I can remember diving into a dyke, which was partially filled with water and getting quite wet. During the afternoon Rocky Knight again took us out on patrol to an area a few hundred yards west of the church, for what purpose I was not told, but snipers were firing at the gun site near the church. As we were going through some woods we came under a terrific barrage of mortar bombs or shells, and I felt a blow to my right leg. I sat down, rolled up my right trouser leg and saw a neat, round hole in the left side of my right calf, blood was pouring out at a fast rate. Harry Liston saw my plight, came over and put a huge shell dressing around the wound in an effort to stem the flow of blood. I also felt very damp and sticky under my left armpit and putting my right hand into my smock and under the armpit I found it very wet, I withdrew my hand and found it covered in blood. In the meantime Harry Liston was also hit and needed help.

The barrage continued all around us, I remembered passing over a small dip in the ground so I ran to this and took cover until the barrage passed over. When things quietened down I looked around and found myself all alone once again. I staggered back to the church feeling very shaky and dazed, I stripped off my equipment, smock and battle dress blouse and asked a couple of chaps to look at my back. My shirt, vest and blouse were very blood stained but one of the chaps said it was only a scratch and put as field dressing on it. Later a piece of shrapnel the size of a shilling was found in my back and it is still there to this day. The two chaps took me to a first aid station but on the way we were heavily shelled and shot at so I was dumped in the road while they took cover.

When I took cover in a nearby house still under heavy shelling I saw Major Lonsdale, heavily bandaged, who said "You better go next door son, " which I did. I found the Regimental First Aid Post in the church vicarage, the home of Kate and Jan Ter Horst [a], was overflowing with wounded Arnhem men, they were lying everywhere, I found a place in a corridor where I was thankful to lie down. I placed my right leg in the air to stop the bleeding, there were so many wounded in the house and only one doctor with a few orderlies and no one came to me. As men died in the house they were simply put in the garden, after the war a total of 57 graves were found in the garden. Putting my right leg up seemed to work as the bleeding stopped. I was thankful I was out of the battle and in the safety of the Red Cross, but I soon found that this was as bad as being in action as the shells and mortar bombs came raining down, some hitting the house and further wounding the men inside. Wounded were constantly being brought in and some were even put in the attic.

The next morning, Saturday, I felt a little better and wanted to visit the toilet, however on trying to get up I found I couldn't bend my left knee. On investigation I found a lump of shrapnel about 2 inches long embedded behind the back of my left kneecap. The doctor and orderlies were still very busy with more wounded coming in so I set about extracting the piece of shrapnel, which I did with some difficulty. There was no blood! The day went on with a terrific barrage, more shells hitting the house and killing and injuring more men.

By Sunday I felt a lot better but found it difficult to walk. I saw Jack from our section lying close by, he was in a bad way and Jim Bourne who was shot in the face. The next day water had run out so the doctor asked for a volunteer to try and get to the pump in the garden. I was dying for a drink and very hungry, no food since Monday, so I volunteered. In the outhouse I found a walking stick and managed to get to the pump with a bucket, but the effort completely exhausted me and I passed out. The next morning I woke to complete silence to find the men able to get away had gone across the river, the wounded and the medical staff were left behind. The Germans were outside and I tried to hide in the attic but found 2 dead men there, so I tried a cupboard but couldn't shut the door, the Germans spotted me and I was hauled out.

Outside the garden was littered with dead Airborne. The wounded were lined up against a wall and searched, a German soldier actually gave me an apple and he was a very tough SS man. I thought he was going to shoot me. We were then marched to Arnhem , a distance of 2 miles, which took all day carrying each other. We arrived at a hospital [St Elizabeth's], which was overflowing with British, German, Dutch and Polish wounded and we were sorted out. I was put in a German ambulance and taken to a place about 11 miles away called Apeldoorn, along with other wounded men. The next day I was taken under guard to a nearby hospital where my wounds were checked and dressed. I was also given a shave. After about 4 days I was issued with a piece of black bread, about 4 slices, loaded into a cattle wagon with approximately 60 men per wagon, bound for Germany. The journey took about a week with no food or water or sanitation, as men died they were just thrown out at the next station. We finally got to a transit POW camp at Limburg on Lahn Stalag XIIA in a terrible state. I was put in the camp hospital but had to lie on the floor as no beds were available. Food consisted of ½ pint of watery soup and a slice of bread once a day No washing facilities existed except for a tap left on for about 30 minutes a day.

After three weeks of this with only the clothes I had on when first I went into action, we were moved to a huge POW camp, Stalag 4B at Muhlberg, 60 miles south of Berlin. The journey took 4 days in a cattle wagon with no food or water.

At Stalag 4B I was in a hut with about 100 others on bunk beds with only one small blanket. Food consisted of 1/7 loaf of bread and ½ pint of watery soup. I had to attend the camp hospital twice a week for dressings. There were 14,000 men of all nationalities in this camp and conditions were terrible, in a short time we were all full of lice. Christmas 1944 was a nightmare with no extra food, we did get the odd Red Cross parcels, 7 men to share each one, which gave us a little extra.

Early in 1945 I was sent to a small working camp near Leipzig, Stalag 4G in a small town called Borna. Food was a little better but still very short, just a bowl of soup and a slice of bread per day, and you had to work 10 hours a day on an open cast coal surface. We did have a better hut to live in with running water so we managed to clean up a bit. My legs were again playing up so I had to clean the camp instead of going out to work!

Early in April 1945 we were ordered to pack up and evacuate the camp, we were going to southern Bavaria to be held as hostages. I could not march so I hid in the camp hospital, when the men were marched away I came out, found 3 or 4 others and hid in a coal mine shaft. Four days later the Yanks arrived and I was free. I was down to 8 stone, normally 12½ , full of ulcers and boils, very weak but still alive! A week later I was at home on double rations. Three months later I was ready to fight the Japs- but that is another story.

Notes

*a] Jan was in the Dutch Resistance and was away from home during this period.
Kate was awarded the OBE after the war for her efforts.*

*John Bosley was issued with jungle kit but he never got to the Far East- the bombing of
Hiroshima and Nagasaki ended the war with Japan before he was deployed. Instead he
was posted to Palestine and was in Jerusalem on 22nd July 1946 when the King David
Hotel was bombed. In civilian life he joined the Wiltshire Constabulary. I first met him
in the early 1970's he was a sergeant at Warminster Police Station.*

CHAPTER 7

WWII and Occupation 1939- 1945
Michael Elcomb

In the summer of 2000 retired Colonel Michael Elcomb received the following letter having been forwarded after being sent to his brother who was a fellow officer in the same regiment, it was from Roselies Kerkhoff living in Pocking, Bavaria and was dated 26th March.

Dear Mr. Elcombs! (is the name correct written ?)
You will be astonished, to receive a letter from me, but sometimes funny things happen in the world, so I will explain you the story.

I was invited by my neighbour and there I came to know a gentleman, who is living in England. During the conversation I told him, I am coming from the eastern part of Germany and that we had much luck, to leave the Russian Zone the night before the Russian s occupied my home place at the end of June 1945. I said, that I will never forget, whom we thank for this

Major Elcombs from the Yorkshire Light Infantry.

The name of my home- village is Hotensleben, situated between East and West Germany. When the war was over, the Americans occupied our district and got in contact with my father , because they knew, that he belonged to the circle, who was against Hitler and that the Nazis therefore put him several times into prison in Magdeburg.

After the Americans the British forces took over the command and they informed us, that after them the Russians will take over the district.

Because we were 4 young girls, my father decided, to give up all our property and to go to the western part , as there was no difference between Kommunisten and Nazis. A great decision, not light but right. So we prepared 3 great carts with furniture and valuable things. At midnight of I think 30th June 1945 you were standing in front of our door and said "The frontier is closed, its curfew, you must go, we help you." We also took 6 horses and 3 German prisoners of war were allowed to drive the car. This night changed our life. We found a flat in the house of friends near Göttingen University, who were also British, immediately found a job for me. For 2 years I was working as interpreter for Special Investigation Office and 3 years for Public Safety in Göttingen. So I earned enough for me and the family and even food was spended for me and my family by the British.

Can you understand, why I cannot forget you after 55 years? Now I am 77 years old, my husband is dead, my daughter married with a Frenchman and I live in wonderful Bavaria at the Starnbeg Lake. I would be very glad, to get in contact with you.

Excuse my bad English, I have no practice. I would be glad, to hear from you and I remain with many greetings

Your thankful

R Kerkhoff [1]

Michael Elcomb was born in the Spa town of Buxton in the Peak District of Derbyshire, the son of an officer in the Royal Artillery. Until he was eight he lived in India. His father eventually left the army because promotion prospects were poor and the pay abominable- he then began a career in engineering. Michael was eighteen and still at school when war was declared. He listened with his parents, brother and sister to the famous announcement by Neville Chamberlain; they all stood to attention whilst the National Anthem was being played. His mother wept but both the boys were very excited, Michael enlisted as a potential officer candidate two days after the declaration of war. During the months awaiting his call up papers Michael joined the newly formed Local Defence Volunteers (LDV) later the Home Guard.

Being assessed as potential officer material he had to wait some time until the 163 OCTU (Officer Cadet Training Unit) was formed at Pwllhieli. Michael was eventually called to the Colours on 15th August 1940. He spent time in North

Wales before being commissioned into the 1st Battalion Kings Own Yorkshire Light Infantry, part of the 5th Division, on 1st March 1941. The other two battalions in the Brigade were the 1st Battalion the Green Howards and the 1st Battalion the York and Lancaster Regiment. After basic training Michael joined the 1st Battalion in Rochdale where the Battalion was accommodated in one of the mills.

Captain Mike Elcomb

In April 1941 the Division moved to Northern Ireland for intensive training, returning to England and billets in Surrey in January 1942, well trained, physically fit and combat ready for operations in North West Europe. The next few weeks the Battalion were re-equipped with vehicles including Bren Carriers, with weapons such as the PIAT [Projector Infantry Anti-Tank] (2) and issued with new uniforms including solar (Wolseley) helmets (3).

The Battalion embarked on the Cunard Liner S.S. Samaria from Liverpool, sailing to Glasgow to join one of the largest convoys to leave Britain, with escorting warships it headed for Singapore. However in February 1942 the Imperial Japanese Army under General Tomoyuki Yamashita got there first, so the convoy diverted for South Africa, en route they stopped at the natural harbour of Freetown in Sierra Leone, where the troops were not allowed ashore but were entertained by locals in their canoes, nicknamed 'bumboats'. From here they sailed to Cape Town where they spent a few days. Michael remembers the hospitality of the white South Africans who met them at the docks, took them into their homes and entertained them. Then on to the lush green tropical landscape of Mombasa where the soldiers were able to leave their arms and equipment aboard ship and go on a route march enjoying the sights and smells of an exotic new country.

From Kenya they sailed past HMS Warspite (4) to Bombay arriving on 21st May

1942, nine weeks and three days after leaving Liverpool. Their destination was Poona, the largest garrison town for the British Army in India, sixty two miles south- east of Bombay on the Deccan Plateau. They were accommodated in the native cavalry lines, the officers had good quarters but for the other ranks it was different. Billeted in native barracks with mutti (earthen) floors and sleeping on charpoys, the traditional woven beds consisting of wooden frames strung with light ropes. After the comparative luxury billets of pre-war India, in proper barrack blocks with such conveniences as fans and toilets one old soldier complained "This is not the way British soldiers should be treated!" The troops eventually cheered up with the thought this was just a temporary station and things would get better. They were wrong!

Moving on by rail to the next camp at Ranchi they were met at the railway station by trucks from the Royal Indian Army Service Corps and taken to the campsite. On arrival the men did not even have a water truck as the Road party with vehicles and equipment had yet to arrive. The conditions were more primitive than in Poona; - there were no buildings of any sort on the scrub land, officers and men slept on the ground until eventually they were provided with tents.

The Battalion was now due to go to Burma but once again there was a change of plan, they were deployed to Persia as there was a perceived threat that the Germans would come through the Caucasus to take the oil fields. Michael found this a fascinating country with wonderful mountains but very harsh winters with strong winds. They were stationed near Kermanshah in a tented camp close to Taq-e-Bostan (5) in the Zargos Mountains, then later onto another tented camp near the Holy City of Qum. (6)

In the event the Russians defeated the Germans in a series of battles over the oilfields, so the Division went into Palestine then on to Egypt for combined operational training for the invasion of Europe. Looking back Michael remembers the experience as tremendous fun- messing about in boats! Join the army and see the world was certainly true- mountain training near Damascus in Syria, back to Egypt to embark on landing craft ship, 'Reina del Pacifico"(7) to sail around Arabia into the Persian Gulf and practise assault landings. Dummy mines would be laid on the beach, anyone stepping on one would send up a puff of smoke. One Naval officer was a source of merriment for the men, every time he set foot on the beach he would set off a succession of the mines. When Michael was wounded in Sicily and in hospital in North Africa he met the same naval officer- who had stepped on a mine!

At last the training was over and Michael was on the Reina Del Pacifico with assault landing craft hanging on davits. Using aerial photos of their beach the men had practised landing at an unknown location where Michael was to lead an assault on an enemy pill box. They had no idea whether they were destined for Sicily, Italy or Greece, as they set sail they turned north towards Greece then later west to Sicily. Seventy years later, in a typical understated comment he did admit he was "quite excited."

The night before the landings the padre held a service that attracted a much larger congregation than normal. Afterwards the officers, who had lived on the ship like paying passengers- thanked the steward then emptied their pockets of loose change and offered it to him. The steward was horrified- he said he couldn't take their money as they were about to go into battle but the officers pointed out the money would be no use to them in Sicily.

On 9th July 1943 as the blue lights dimmed, the men filed onto the deck and got into the assault landing craft to be lowered into the sea. The wind was strong, the seas heavy and the boats were bobbing up and down - everyone had been given sick bags and these proved invaluable. Michael's memory tells him he was one of the few who didn't suffer - but in a letter to his mother discovered many years later he had written that he was very sick.

As the assault craft headed for their destination there was a slight navigational hiccup- they didn't know where they were so they asked a passing ship, the Destroyer HMS Eskimo for directions. On the way in the landing craft lost way and stopped further out than planned, not quite reaching the beach. Michael jumped off to lead his men and measured his length in the water which was much deeper than expected. Ready to lead an attack on a pillbox - a pillbox that wasn't where it should be! They had an easy landing on the wrong beach which was undefended. As they cleared the beachhead and went inland towards the Coast Road there was some confusion as many of the assault troops had landed on the wrong beach and were attempting to reach their assigned objective. The young officer who led the attack on the pillbox assigned to Michael on his intended target beach was killed.

As they moved inland to establish the beach head they encountered little resistance until they moved further up the coast near Melilli. Three days after landing Michael sustained a chest wound during an attack and was shipped to a hospital in North Africa, re-joining his unit as they travelled up the toe of Italy, moving by road past the airfields at Foggia to the Central Sector for active patrolling into the mountainous high ground that is the Spine of Italy.

Michael was sent behind the lines to instruct at the Divisional Tactical School close to Salerno so was not with the Battalion when it was pulled out of Central Sector in January 1944 for the assault across the deep and swift flowing Garigligiano River.

On January 22nd 1944 the Allies carried out the successful amphibious Anzio landings, by the end of the day 36,000 men with 3,200 vehicles had landed - the Allied casualties were 13 killed, 97 wounded and 44 missing. The Germans had been unprepared, not expecting a winter landing. By 25th they were able to organise a strong defence, by the end of January the Germans were reinforced and had almost 70,000 soldiers in the area. This was to be one of the most fiercely fought and bloodiest battles of WW II. Michael had re-joined his unit at the Anzio beachhead; he and his men lay in slit trenches, waddies and deep gullies under heavy mortar fire. The situation was a stalemate- neither were able to move far, there was little patrolling on either side as it was necessary to crawl on hands and knees. After the Allied breakout in May 1944 the 5th Division were deemed no longer a fighting formation having taken heavy casualties, so they were relocated to Palestine to be reformed and refitted. When the D. Day landings took place the Battalion was south of Rome

After leaving Palestine they became part of 'Operation Goldflake', a plan to move and conceal the movement of troops from one theatre of war to another, allowing the reinforcing of Allied troops in Germany. Since the invasion of Sicily in July 1943 British led forces had been fighting in Italy, in the spring of 1945 the Allied Commanders decided to move British and Canadian troops to fight in North West Europe. This was a logistical nightmare as troops and materials were dispersed all over Southern Italy and the vulnerable front lines still had to be defended.

Michael arrived from Palestine for 'Operation Goldflake' travelling right across Italy to Naples by train, before embarking on an American troopship to Marseilles in the South of France. Most crossings took two days, and then military convoys took approximately five days to drive the 674 miles through France to the Belgian frontier. By the end of April over 60,000 troops and support personnel had been relocated in North Western Europe. When they reached Belgium the men were granted a brief respite, going home to England for ten days leave, before returning to Germany.

At the end of the war Michael was a Major in Eisleben on the river Saale south of Bernburg in Saxony-Anhalt and part of the military presence spread around Germany until the Military Government took over. One of his tasks was to liaise with Burgomasters, it was then he met Herr and Frau Kerkhoff and their four daughters who lived on a large farm in the village of Hotensleban . The Burgomaster could speak no English so his pretty 22 year old daughter Roselies acted as his interpreter. Herr Kerkhoff took on the responsibility of disseminating the information to the other Burgomasters in area, considerably easing the load for Michael. When the British took over from the Americans they were told that the Russians would not be coming to the sector but would be responsible for an area further south so the civilian population had no reason to panic.

Roselies Kerkhoff

Michael came to know the family well, Frau Kerkhoff was very frightened that as wealthy farmers with young four daughters they would not be safe if the Russians took over. Michael had been able to reassure the family that there was no danger, but a few days later orders came that the British Army would move out the next day and the area would become part of the Russian Sector. All officers were under strict instructions that there be complete secrecy, the British didn't want to panic the population into a mass exodus into western controlled sectors.

As an officer Michael was bound by military rules and there could be serious consequences if he disobeyed the order but he had given his word to the family that they were safe. That morning, after wrestling with his conscience, Michael visited the farm and warned them the Russians were coming. Frau Kerkhoff burst into tears, the family would have to leave their home and abandon their farm that night, taking with them as many of their most valuable possessions as they could carry. Fortunately they had farm wagons and several cars so could transport a certain amount of furniture and household goods. Roselies left the room and returned with a red rose which she gave to Michael, she never forgot the young officer who warned them, however she is mistaken in that he helped them through the border. Michael was not at the frontier that evening, but in the requisitioned house of pro-Nazi German doctor in Eilsleben. He was entertaining a Russian platoon commander and his orderly with food and a great deal of wine on the night before the British left and the Russians took control.

The Kerkhoffs were very friendly with an elderly retired Army officer Major Ludecke- spelled phonetically in her second letter as Mayor, and asked Michael if he would warn him as well. After weighing his options Major Ludecke chose to remain in his home and hope for the best. This proved to be a fatal decision, as soon as the Russians arrived they sent him to a concentration camp. Given his age and lack of further information as to his whereabouts it is unlikely he survived this incarceration. Roselies refers to the Major and his son in the following letter. She says 'he died this year and only his wife lives' – seemingly talking of the son.

On 2nd August 2000 Roselies wrote:

Dear Michael,

Which surprise the call today of your friend. I already had a bad conscience not having answered your nice letter immediately but I was completely engaged for 6 weeks when the family of my daughter visited me. I just rang you up and start the letter as promised. When I red your letter some tears were dropping and the past returned. Thank you once more! Your memory seems to be as well intact as mine, but what happened 55 years ago was so important for all my life that it's understandable. In order to give you a little impression of me I put some photos in the letter. You can choose which one you want to keep and others I want back because I have no doubles. I explain them at the end of the letter.

And now your letter. I did not know that your help was against the order, the more we have to thank you. Only less people have the courage of my father and you, you can be proud! Yes, my father died 1962, he had cancer, was smoking too much. My mother died 10 years ago. My oldest sister was a doctor of medicine. I, as known, 5 years interpreter and then 9 years head of personal department of Schering Concern in Dusseldorf where my husband was the director and manager. I come to know him there, he was a wonderful boss and the best husband I could imagine. We married 1959 and he died 1969 heart infarkt. I never intended to marry again, there would be nobody similar to him. My daughter was born in 1960 and we love us very much and I am sorry that she lives in France, but that is the stream of life.

I have many friends play golf almost every morning, the place is not far and the landscape is wonderful. But what a pity I have Parkinson's since February this year and not so fit as I was. Still I am able to live alone and to look after my house and garden, what shall I want more in my age. And now I have one friend more who is called Michael.

By the way you mentioned the Mayor, his name was Ludecke. He had only one son to whom I had contact, but he died this year and only his wife lives. I informed her about you.

Your life was also very interesting and you came to know the world, could your wife accompany you? I suppose not. She looks so sympathetic.

You asked me, whether we got back our farm, a little part of the field. The buildings were destroyed during the Russian time and the place looks awful. We sold the field now, it was of no use for us and our children. My husband was a doctor of agriculture but working in the chemical industry. In order to realize his hobby he bought 1935 an island 104 ha near the east sea (8) which was also confiscated by the Russians. After reunion the firm Siemens took over the island and I tried for 3 years to get it back without success it is 4 ha too great, but in 2004 I still get some money for it. The island would have been a wonderful golf place, but it is over 900km far away from my home and who could look after it?

Now I stop. Excuse the mistakes and the bad typing. On the backside I still explain the fotos and that's it for this time.

Many greetings to your wife and the friend who called me,

Yours as always,

Roselies

Roselies with her son

Roselies

Michael remained in contact with Roselies until she died in 2013. After the death of his wife Elizabeth, he made the journey to Bavaria, reunited with Roselies and met her family.

Notes

1. *Roselies letters are as written - I have made no attempt to correct them.*
2. *Projector Infantry Anti-Tank Grenade Launcher in use from 1942 'a hollow charge ' projectile launched from a spring loaded tube shaped launcher typically crewed by two personnel. Developed hurriedly after Dunkirk and the loss of British anti-tank weaponry in Northern France. The PIAT proved to be effective against all contemporary enemy armoured vehicles. Became one of the most famous anti- tank weapons of WWII along with the American 'Bazooka' and the German 'Panzerschreck.'*
3. *Wolseley helmets were worn by the British Army between 1899 -1948*
4. *HMS Warspite a Queen Elizabeth class battleship, the 7th of 8 ships of that name launched in 1913. She served during WWI & on numerous operations in WWII earning the most battle honours of any ship in the Royal Navy and the most battle honours for any individual ship.*
5. *Taq-e-Bostan (Kurdish 'Arch of Stone' Persian 'Arch of Bostan') an archaeological site on the Silk Road caravan route with some of the finest examples of Persian sculpture, arches and reliefs carved into the rock dating from the Sassinid Empire of Persia - the dynasty that ruled western Asia between 226 to 650AD.*
6. *Qum has a semi-desert climate with its main water supply coming from the*

surrounding mountains through salty rivers. From the beginning of its Islamic history, the city of Qum became the centre of the Shi`a in the area, and by the end of the first Islamic century, more than 6000 Shi`a had settled there.

Qum is:
* *a world-renowned centre of Islamic learning.*
* *an agricultural city, producing wheat, cotton, pomegranate, fig, pistachio and melon.*
* *an industrial city, manufacturing carpets, pottery, plastic products and building materials.*
* *a commercial city, due to its location at the crossroads that connects northern Iran to its south, and the vast number of pilgrims.*
* *a regional centre for the distribution of petroleum and petroleum products. The city has a natural gas pipeline from Bandar Anzali and Tehran and a crude-oil pipeline from Tehran runs through Qum to the Abadan refinery on the Persian Gulf. Additional prosperity came when oil fields were discovered at Sarajeh near the city in 1956 a large refinery was built between Qum and Tehran*

7. *Reina del Pacifico a Passenger Ship of the Pacific Steam Navigational Company launched on 23rd September 1930. In service from 9th April 1931- 27th April 1958 when she was scrapped. She had direction finding equipment, a gyrocompass, 4-stroke engines and 4 screws, and a speed of 18 knots and was the fastest and largest motor liner of her time. In 1937 former Labour British Prime Minister Ramsey MacDonald died on board at the age of seventy-one while on a cruise. During WWII she was requisitioned as a troopship taking part in the landings in North Africa, Sicily and Normandy.*

8. *East Sea -the Baltic*

In the 1950's after a period of training Michael was seconded to Parachute Regiment where he took command of a Company in the 3rd Battalion, re-joining his Battalion in Berlin in 1954.

Shortly after his arrival the Battalion continued their overseas tour with a year in Kenya during the Mau-Mau insurgency. Kenya was followed by tours in Aden and in Cyprus while EOKA were active. After a period the Ministry of Defence and the Joint Services Staff College he returned to the Battalion in Hilden, Germany. His next posting was as Brigade Major in Berlin; Michael was on duty when the Russian's closed the border at the beginning of the isolation of East Berlin from West Germany and the erection of the Berlin Wall. This tour was cut short by his promotion to Lieutenant Colonel in Command of the KOYLI Depot in Pontefract to train new troops.

During his varied military career several of Michael's postings were staff appointments, he completing his Army service as HQ Director of Infantry in Warminster retiring in December 1975. The system that retired officers could continue to serve on the staff as a RO (retired officer) at reduced pay ensured that Michael continued on the staff as an RO until 31st December 1982 aged sixty two.

CHAPTER 8

With the RAF in India 1945-1947
Norman Waspe

Young Norman Waspe was a couple of months past his twelfth birthday and living in Hampstead, North London when War was declared in 1939, so it was not surprising that by 1944 his two major passions were aeroplanes and ships. His ambition was to join the Fleet Air Arm, so despite being too young to enlist, he hadn't quite reached seventeen, he decided to visit the Recruitment Centre close to his home. The recruiting FAA officer rejected him outright when he realised Norman was a qualified electrician, but suggested that he went next door to where the Royal Air Force, who were seeking electricians, were recruiting. Norman remembers that when he entered he saw a very pretty WAAF with the most beautiful legs he had ever seen, a sight that encouraged him to enlist in the RAF as a Volunteer Reserve. Young men were conscripted at seventeen and a half; however at this stage of the war there was a shortage in recruiting, and, as Norman was in a trade that was in demand with the RAF, he was called up at seventeen, reporting to Cardington in Bedfordshire. His service commenced on 3rd February1944, he was described as being five foot eight inches tall, fair haired, blue eyed and fresh complexioned. Norman was posted to Skegness for eight weeks basic training where among other things gained a nickname, 'Lofty' and learned which end of a rifle to hold!

Norman Waspe 1944

After basic training on 6th April 1944 Norman was posted to RAF Hereford No.11 School of Technical Training, also known as RAF Credenhill as a tradesman. The site had been requisitioned in 1939 and the site was officially opened on 15th June 1940. The camp comprised of both wooden and brick huts and nine Hinaidi hangers, five of the hangers housed aircraft for training purposes, two were workshops, one was an instrument school and the remaining hanger was used as a gymnasium and for church purposes. When Norman arrived there was a 112 bed hospital and a recruitment training wing that could accommodate up to a thousand recruits at any one time. He was at the station for eighteen weeks on courses which took place over three periods of six weeks. One of the courses was to train radio operators; the new recruits would sit at benches with headphones on and listen to 78 records of Morse code. There would be twenty questions; one example was to see if the men could recognise three dots followed by another three dots or three dashes

133

followed by three dashes as being identical. Norman had not joined the Air Force to sit listening to radio signals so he ensured he failed by deliberately giving negative responses. He qualified AC2 as an electrician and just before Christmas 1944 he was posted to RAF Winthorpe in Lincolnshire, Bomber Command No 5 Group.

Norman spent the last months of the war servicing and repairing the stations heavy bombers. After VE Day Bomber Command began disbanding the Station, brand new Lancaster's were flown away and control of RAF Winthorpe passed to Transport Command. The Squadron stood down, for Norman and his mates it was time to get ready to go to Japan; the Japanese surrender in August 1945 heralded a change of plan, he was posted overseas to a Transport Command in India, servicing Dakota's at RAF Palam, outside of Delhi on 2nd October.

Norman thought that India was a fantastic place and enjoyed his time there in the period prior to Independence and Partition. In the midst of the political turmoil that was taking place in the country, the RAF station was a tranquil place; Norman described life as being segregated from the towns, like being in purdah, not interacting with the civilian population!

Life in India was extremely comfortable for the men. The food on RAF stations was always very good, as well as being a taste of home. Noman didn't have to make his bed or clean his boots all the while he was there, he employed a bearer to look after him for just 2 rupees (3/-) a fortnight . The bearer also looked after nineteen other aircraftmen so was earning a very good wage; he didn't do menial work, a lower caste Indian would clean the rooms, so the bearer would be a cut above the other Indians on the station.

Norman had his twenty-first birthday while at RAF Palam; his parent's sent him money to buy a watch for sixty rupees, around £4.10. One evening he went off to town with his mates and realised that he'd left the watch on the table by his bed. None of the men believed that he would ever see his watch again; things had a habit of disappearing if they were unattended. However when the bearer woke him with his tea the next morning he was greeted with "You are a very silly man sahib, you left your watch on the table, if I had not found it you would have lost it!" The bearer then opened a tin box and returned the watch.

While Norman was at RAF Palam there was the opportunity to go up on test flights in the Dakota's, sometimes two or three times a day! The electricians and engineers would fly as second crew with the pilot, it was easier to work on the air cooled engines and generators in flight; on the ground they would have to be constantly running and in danger of overheating. On one occasion the pilot levelled out over Delhi for engine checks, he feathered (stopped) the port engine then restarted it; he then went through the same procedure with the starboard engine, this engine restarted sluggishly so the pilot feathered the engine again- this time it wouldn't restart. The pilot sent out a 'Mayday' call, received permission to land and made his final approach. Norman remembers "It was quite a sobering sight to come in to land and see two ambulances, fire engines and loads of blokes at the end of the runway!" The plane landed safely, but when the pilot opened the throttle, with only one engine working the aircraft began to turn in circles on the tarmac.

One Sunday morning a young pilot entered the crew room, he wanted to take up his plane to check it was serviceable and asked Norman if he would fly with him and then sign off the Dakota as airworthy. When the men reached the plane Norman saw a group of fifteen to twenty uniformed young women in khaki sari's waiting for a joy ride. All the women piled onto the aircraft, when the doors closed they sat facing into the middle of the plane and put on their safety belts. The skipper radioed 'all secure', taxied onto the runway, took off and levelled out before advising the women they could now take off their seat belts and move around anywhere except the crew area. Norman entered the cockpit to find the pilot trying to keep the plane level as he circled, the excited passengers rushed from one side to the other to look out over Delhi. Norman was sitting in the co-pilots seat when he became aware that he was alone, the skipper was socialising while the plane was flew on autopilot. Everyone belted up for the landing, the pilot taxied to dispersal and the women disembarked; when Norman and the pilot stepped onto the runway their passengers saluted then clapped.

India was full of mongrel dogs scavenging for food, occasionally one of the dogs was adopted by the aircraftsmen, so it was that Norman acquired 'Snooks' from a man who was about to be demobbed. Many of the strays had mange which was very contagious; keeping Snooks healthy was made easier by the fact that on the opposite side of the road to the RAF station was an Indian Army Regiment with horses who had a veterinary surgeon. The Indian soldiers were very friendly and all spoke excellent English.

When India became Independent, all RAF personnel left the airfield, handing everything over to the newly formed Indian Air Force and setting sail for Singapore on 1st April1946. Norman left Snooks with a couple of men in the RAF Signals, he later discovered that when they were posted separately they took the difficult decision to euthanize the dog rather than risk it being abandoned.

When they arrived at the Depot in Singapore with its massive long hanger they discovered this was full of spares for Japanese aircraft. Norman's role now was as a motor transport electrician working on all manner of vehicles.

On their first night in Singapore the monsoon rain was the heaviest in fifty years. The young men had gone to the camp and the NAAFI and were making their way to the lorries when Norman found his path blocked by an enormous storm drain full of water. He attempted to step over it, and managed to fall into four feet of water.

The system for demobilisation was based on criteria such as age and length of service, however the RAF was short of electricians, so Norman was retained for an extra six months Towards the end of 1947, coming up to his fifth Christmas as RAF ground-crew Norman was about to be demobilised. Because he had served an extra six months he was eligible to fly home rather than take the more usual troop ship. Aircraft in the 1940's were considerably slower than they are today and they only flew during the day so the journey was long and tedious. The Lancaster left Singapore at 10am, landing in Colombo, Ceylon, to overnight and refuel. The second day they landed in Karachi, the capital of the newly formed Pakistan; they stayed for two nights, leaving late in the afternoon of the third day because the aircraft was deemed unserviceable and needed repairs. Norman is uncertain where they stopped that night, except it was somewhere at the eastern end of the Mediterranean. It was late in the evening and very cold after the heat of the Far East, the crew were wearing light weight khaki uniforms so they changed into the warmer RAF blues. The fifth day of travel brought them to Luga, three miles from Valletta on the island of Malta, there had been a degree of uncertainty as all RAF flights would stop two days before Christmas, if they weren't in England by then they would spend the festive season elsewhere. They left Malta late, at 2am but arrived at RAF Lyneham 4 o'clock in the afternoon just hours before the no-fly deadline came into force.

Leading Aircraftsman Norman Waspe 3202052 RAFVR (Royal Air Force Volunteer Reserve) served from 30th March1944 until the 31st December 1947 plus 82 days leave. His overseas posting in India and Singapore was from 2nd October 1945 until 10th December 1947. Civilian life in1948 was difficult, even for skilled tradesmen such as electricians; there were huge numbers of demobilised service men, many with skills, flooding the labour market. Norman changed careers and became an ambulance driver, first for the Red Cross and later for the National Health Service. He retired after forty years in 1988.

Notes

Hinaidi Hangers: named after the RAF Station in Iraq. Handley Page built an aircraft of the same name – the Hinaidi hangers were tall and narrow built to store the aircraft with its wings folded back. They were cheap and quick to build so frequently to be found on RAF airfields overseas.

Hinaidi hanger

No 5 Group Bomber Command: was the most famous Group in Bomber Command, taking part in some of the most specialised and daring attacks of WWII, noted for their high accuracy bombing and the introduction new weapons operationally such as Barnes Wallis's bouncing bomb, the Tall Boy and Grand Slam (earthquake) bombs .

The South East Asian Theatre: was in the Pacific, it included Burma, Ceylon, India, Thailand, Indochina, Malaysia and Singapore.

Dakota Aircraft: The Douglas DC-3 was a fixed- wing propeller-driven commercial airliner, one of the most significant transport aircraft ever made. The military version the C53, had a crew of four and accommodated up to twenty eight troops; used as air ambulances, personnel transports and freighters, it was designated the Dakota in Britain and the C-47 Skytrain in America. The British twin- engine military transport was manufactured by Douglas Aircraft Co. in Santa Monica, California, had two Pratt and Whitney Twin Wasp engines, with a range of between 1,500 and 2,215 miles. The Dakota entered service with the RAF in March 1943; during WWII over 1,900 were supplied to the RAF under to lend/lease arrangement with America.

Indian Army: By the end of WW 2 the Indian Army had become the largest volunteer army in history, 2.5 million men in 1945. More than 36,000 Indian servicemen were killed, 34,354 were wounded and 67,340 became prisoners of war.

In May1942 the Woman's Auxiliary Corps was formed, recruits had to be at least 18 years old, by December that year the age was reduced to 17. Volunteers duties were clerical or domestic, they could enlist for Local or General Service, the latter could be sent anywhere in India. Despite the fact that Indian women during this period did not socialise or work with men, and were hampered by tradition and caste, 11,500 women, the majority Anglo-Asian, served in the WAC's.

CHAPTER 9

NATIONAL SERVICE 1950
Raymond Hayne

When the summons came, which in my case was in the autumn of 1950, there was an element of resignation in my reaction. I was interviewed in August for the November intake. We were given intelligence tests to see which unit we would be sent to, for example "When the sun is up what colour is the sky- pink, red or blue?"

Raymond
Hayne

There was also something of adventure about it, as when eventually I went to join the Signals Unit to which I had been allocated, it was Catterick Camp in Yorkshire, which will be a location well known to many. The journey took me through new and hitherto unvisited places – like Grantham and Thirsk! I doubt if I had ever been north of London at that time! When we arrived to the chilliness of the Yorkshire Dales, it was (as far as we Southerners were concerned), just about as far north as we could go; but then we met lads from Aberdeen, who likewise thought London was some twenty miles south of Doncaster! The bringing together of young men from a wide variety of backgrounds was traumatic, but a very, very good thing. Grammar School boys having to rub shoulders with sons of Port Glasgow dockers was excellent all round and a number of misconceptions corrected.

Fresh intakes of about 200 conscripts of the same age arrived every two weeks and were put through the traumatic experience of square bashing. For the first few weeks I was pretty homesick but I soon got over that. Another good thing was that we were taught a trade, in my case this turned out to be as a touch typist, - a teleprinter operator, which in future years proved to be a help when it came to electronic keyboards. For Royal Signals Corps one needed to be good at English, be able to communicate and to spell, on active service there was a lot of decoding especially relating to troop movements. We also had to type in code- we often had 50 blocks of 5 letters and you cannot take your eyes off the page or you very quickly lose your place so you had to be able to touch type. We trained at Catterick for a year, six months of which was learning to touch type, so you did a year's concentrated training for a year's work.

The third "plus", was that when we came to be transferred to our units, most of these were abroad, in 1952 I travelled from Harwich on a troopship to the Hook of Holland then by train to join the British Army of the Rhine, at a Spa Town of the name of Bad Oeynhausen close to Minden; it is a bit like Bath and of course the *Bad* bit is the same word. At this time it was the Headquarters of B.A.O. R. before this was moved to Munchen Gladbach in the South of the British Sector. It was a wonderful place to be just then, as it had every possible facility one could imagine. The Kaiser's Summer Palace had been converted to serve as the NAAFI Club; we had our own theatre, swimming pool, sports club, and freedom to use a number of other attractions, such as the hot baths. The countryside was quite lovely too.

As we were engaged in high security work we were discouraged from fraternising and forbidden to enter the local pubs so we had virtually no contact with the civilian population. We did have a very good social life, on our days off we would swim in the morning, play tennis in the afternoon and go dancing in the evening, we didn't have a problem finding partners in the RASC because we worked with members of the Women's Royal Army Corps.

We were quartered in a civilian detached four storied house, there were no specially built barracks at that time so troops were in civilian accommodation with a separate cookhouse. Army food was very good, much better than at home where rationing was in force. There were plenty of shops and while cameras were much cheaper than in England, coffee was very expensive and there was a thriving black market ....

I did attempt to learn German soon after I arrived and enrolled in a language course; however everyone I met wanted to practice their English, spoken, usually with an American accent, so I eventually decided there was no point in continuing.

I was impressed with the German concentration and work ethic; they seemed to be recovering from the war more quickly than in Britain and were working hard building cities and roads. Although we had little contact with the population at large we did meet some of the Germans working for the Army, we had a team of decorators arrive at 7am one morning, they had a half hour break at 11.30am took another a half hour for lunch and finished for the day at 7pm.

Contact with local residents was not encouraged overmuch, although there was, inevitably some rapport; this was particularly difficult with young people, understandably resentful about our presence, humiliated and angered by our occupation and victory, which led to the end of one who had been a role model, e.g. for the "Youth Movement", and of all the hopes and aspiration he had given them for the "New Germany" of their future.

Reaction from the older generation to our presence there was, interestingly, quite different. Secretly they were saddened by what they saw as a terrible distortion in the ideal of their national identity; the German People were and are a noble and proud race and I don't think it is too much to say that they were ashamed at what had been done in their name. They realised that the ideals of the Nazi regime could only end in tears, and looked upon us who served in the army there as deliverers rather than occupiers. Friendships were made with such as these and in some cases endured long after we returned to civvy street.

Lifelong friendships were made with each other as well of course; I did lose touch with a particular pal, Gerald Towell who was billeted with me, and although we spent all our free time together during our time in Germany, and I spent my "demob" leave with him in Plymouth, we lost touch almost immediately after that. However, after sixty-two years (and through the wonders of modern computer technology), we met up again last year, and as he and his wife live in Cheltenham, we meet up again from time to time.

During the war years prisoners of war in Devon were allowed out of camp for weekends if families would offer overnight accommodation. Gerald's parents were loving and outgoing people, they welcomed Fritz into their home during hostilities. Fritz's family lived in a farming community within 20 miles of where we were stationed, so Gerald would visit them on occasion. I was invited one weekend and was made very welcome. I remember it was very rural, they still ploughed with oxen, couldn't afford tractors. I asked to go to the toilet and was directed through a scullery, opening the door to come face to face with a cow! Gerald remains in contact with Fritz to this day and frequently holidayed in Germany after returning to England.

Shortly before we were due to complete our duty to King/Queen and Country (the former changed during my time abroad) we were invited to sign on. I must confess I was not really tempted; but the experience had been a good one overall, and I learnt much about life and myself during the two years of service; if *only* we could have some form of national service now!

I found England had changed a lot when I returned; the 1950's were a golden age, a young Queen on the throne, a new Elizabethan Age, much laxer, with rationing ending and more money about.

Conscription

Conscription in the United Kingdom existed for two periods in modern times, from 1916 -1919 and from 1939 – 1960.During both World Wars it was known as War Service or Military Service, from 1948 it was known as National Service.

Conscription during WWI began in 1916 when the British Government passed the Military Service Act. The Act specified that single men aged between 18 and 45 were liable to be called up unless they were widowed with children or ministers of a religion. There was a system of Military Service Tribunals to adjudicate upon the claims for exemption on the grounds of performing civilian work of national importance, domestic hardship, health and conscientious objection. Married men were exempt from the original Act but this was changed in June 1916. The age limit was eventually raised to 51; recognition of work of national importance also diminished and in the last year of the war there was some support for conscription of the clergy.

Conscription lapsed in 1920, but as a result of the rise of Nazi Germany and the deteriorating international situation the Cabinet of Neville Chamberlain introduced a limited form of conscription 27th April 1939 with a Military Training Act passed a month later. Only young single men between the ages of 20 --22 were to be called up, they were to be known as 'Militiamen' to distinguish them from the regular army. These men were not to be issued with a suit in addition to a uniform and to be having six months basic training before being discharged to an active reserve.

At the outbreak of war on 3rd September 1939 the National Service (Armed Forces) Act superseded the Military Training Act and the first intake was absorbed into the army. The National Service Act imposed a liability to conscript men of conscription to all men between the ages of 18 -41, they could be rejected for medical reasons or if they were engaged in vital industries or occupation (for instance lighthouse keepers).

By 1942 all men between 18 -51 as well as all females between 20-30 resident in Britain were liable to be called up. Prior to 1942 men under 20 were not liable to be sent overseas Men of 51 who had retired, resigned or been dismissed from the forces before the war were called back and those who reached their 51st birthday while in serving were liable to serve until the end of hostilities.

All women were released at the end of the WWII however Britain did not completely demobilise in 1945 as conscription continued after the war- the last of the male wartime conscripts had been released by 1949.

Peacetime conscription was formulated in the National Service Act of 1948- from 1st September 1949 healthy males 17- 21 were expected to join the Armed Forces for a period of 18 months and remain in the reserves for 4 years. In 1950 as a result of the Korean War National service was extended to 2 years.

As well as in Korea where members of the Gloucestershire Regt took part in the last stand during the Battle of the Imjin River, National Service personnel were used in combat operations including the Malayan Emergency, the Cyprus Emergency, in Kenya due to the Mau Mau Uprising and in the 1956 Suez Crisis.

National Service came to an end from 1957- all those born on or after 1st October 1939 would not be required. The last men entered service in November 1960, call ups formally ended on 31st December 1960 and the last National Servicemen left the armed Forces in May 1963.

CHAPTER 10

A Short Term Regular in Malaya 1954-1957
Terry Davis

In 1954 when I was seventeen and working in a brewery I knew I would soon be called up for National Service, you were paid £1.8s. a week and you went where you were sent. If you signed up as a short term regular you were paid £2.8s. per week and you could choose to join any regiment or corps- so I signed up for three years and chose to join the Royal Engineers. On joining the Army I served one year in the UK, training and doing two courses, one at Brompton Barracks and the other at Kitchener Barracks- the latter being a heavy plant operator's course.

Terry Davis front row 2nd left

The Army had two big construction jobs coming up in 1955; one was to build a fourteen mile jungle road in Malaya, the other to start work on Christmas Island ready for the atom bomb tests. I was lucky and went to Malaya in late 1955.

Our flight, full of military personnel and families, left Stansted on a Handley Page Hermes airliner often used during this period in a troop carrying role. We had to stop off in various places in order to refuel, Rome, Cyprus (where we broke down so spent half a day in Nicosia) , Bahrain, Delhi, Karachi, Calcutta (we had two overnight stops in India) .

As we were crossing a large expanse of water, possibly the Bay of Bengal there was a strong smell of oil and the cabin filled with smoke. One of the four propellers had stopped and the pilot made the decision to shut off the offending engine. He poured more power into the other three engines in order to gain height, possibly in case he was forced to glide in to make an emergency landing, this resulted in strong vibrations throughout the aircraft. We landed at Rangoon in Burma for repairs which obviously interrupted and delayed our journey. Apparently the air for the cabin came through the engine then through a purifying plant hence the smoke. We were offered food in Rangoon but as it consisted of a little blue bowl filled with cold rice and three raw fishes complete with heads and tails no one was hungry! Out of the windows we could see men on the tail busily painting out the Russian symbols on an aircraft given to the Burmese Government by President Nikita Khrushchev.

My first impression of Malaya was of the humidity as soon as I got off the plane at Singapore after a four and a half day journey. I felt like there was no air, I was also aware of not unpleasant smells from the open air shops that that sold spices and sandalwood. After WWII the bomb damaged city was rebuilt as before by the Malays, Chinese and Indians with huge monsoon drains – nothing like the modern city we see today. It was a Saturday afternoon when we arrived and we went straight to Nee Soon Transit Camp before heading for our unit at the main camp just outside of Kuala Lumpur.

We found the Malays quite friendly but the Chinese and the Indians kept more to themselves, the only Chinese that spoke were the ones who had gift or tailoring shops. One thing we found a bit strange at first was that you could see Malay men, even those in the Malay Regiment, walking along holding hands.

On 12th January 1956 I was sent with about twenty other young sappers to erect a base camp at Ayer Hitam, one end of the Ayer Hitam to Kemayan Road. Here I learned a painful lesson, Ayer Hitam was a tented camp, our job was to erect all the brand new large tents, we wrapped the guy ropes around our arms and pulled the tents up. The trouble was, as we found out to our cost later, was that as the tents were all new the guy ropes had been treated with creosote, creosote on skin in the hot sun was not a good mix! We all got quite bad burns- lesson learnt!

We went up country by rail; it was a bit of a worry to see there was an armoured car on the tracks to go in front of the train for the whole journey. By the time we arrived in Malaya things had settled down a bit after the Malayan Emergency but there was still a threat from CT's (Chinese Terrorists). We had trained and armed them during WWII then when the conflict was over the Malayan Communist Party, determinedly anti- colonialist, led by Chin Peng, began a guerrilla insurgency. There were some hot spots known as 'Black Areas' where we had to be careful and where we were not able to travel at night. It was rumoured, that because we were providing infrastructure Chin Peng had ordered we be left alone because we were benefitting the country, but whether that was true I don't know.

Our main camp in Malaya was at Sungie Besi, approximately six miles south of Kuala Lumpur. Our accommodation was in a series of 'Bashas' each holding about thirty men. These had an overhanging roof, a step up, there were no walls, just an approximately four foot screen around the structure at the bottom made of atapp, a type of palm leaf- ideal for creepy crawlies. The rest of the building was open on all four sides.

Most of the guys were National Service and had less to spend than us regulars, most of our food was taken in camp - I can't remember there being many places to eat in K.L. , at that time almost the only place we went to was the K.K. Bar. In most of the places food seemed to be cooked at the side of the road, which didn't seem a very good idea!

Another food delight was if we had to use the 24 hour ration pack, these were nothing like the guys get now, most of the main meals in the pack came from tins, sausage and beans or bacon and beans, streaky bacon in a tin in the tropics- not good- the fat in the tin melted! But needs must or we'd go hungry. Other staples in the packs were boiled sweets, Mars Bars, toilet paper, salt and paladrin tablets.

In the camp were 56 Ghurkha Field Squadron, 11 IND (Independent) and my unit 410 IND Plant Troop. I don't know why but I was given the task of loading the plant onto flat railway cars and trying to make sure they stayed on. Not easy when the plant was on steel tracks, the flat cars had a steel deck and the Indian shunt drivers were none too gentle when shunting trains.

As the railway was a couple of miles away from the camp I had to stay and sleep on the flat car every night- not very good as it rained nearly every night. When the time came to start the road I, along with two other sappers were sent to 4 troop Royal Australian Engineers, with our dozers. 410 built East, 11 (IND) built west and we in the centre at Ayer Kring built east and west to join up.

I found the Aussies quite a good bunch; they were not as rigid with things as the British Army. For example they had a box of 303 ammunition which was very old and so was expendable, we were allowed to use this, with permission to go into the jungle and try to shoot wild pigs. Two were shot at different times giving us fresh meat for a change. I and another guy went out one day and were just about to go into a tree line when two shots rang out and two rounds went just above our heads into the trees. We made a hasty retreat back to camp as we didn't know if it was a couple of Aussies larking about or something more sinister.

If you were in Base Camp you had to go on a morning parade for inspection, while on parade you were given (and you had to take) a Paladrin tablet and a salt pill. When the parade moved off the ground looked like it had a covering of tiny buttercups, these were the Paladrin tablets that were spat out! They were little yellow pills always known as the 'Yellow Peril.'

I transferred from the plant section to MT (Motor Transport) the job entailed collecting vehicle and plant from around Kuala Lumpur and delivering to Johore Bahru at the bottom tip of Malaya. We had a pioneer Scammel and trailer, one ton Ration Truck and a Dingo armoured car for escort. The round trip took about a week, we were not allowed to travel overnight due to the possible risk of ambush, we had to pull off the road and stay overnight in any military camp.

One time I was driving the Scammel and trailer mid- afternoon through a village.

To get through the village I had to drive through a checkpoint chicane made up of four 40 gallon drums filled with sand. At that time of day all the Rubber Tappers were going to unload the rubber they had collected during the day. The Tapper carried the rubber in two buckets on a yoke on their shoulders... On the nearside Scammel wing there was a white painted pole, I just touched the yoke with this pole, spun the tapper round and the rubber went everywhere! At the time we all thought it very funny but I have felt guilty about this ever since.

As Royal Engineers we had a construction job to do- finding and killing, if needed was left to the Infantry- and a very good job they did too. We had a fairly quiet time, all we had to do was work check our machines and around the area in the morning and, if needed, protect ourselves.

In 1957 I returned to England on a troop ship, a voyage that took six weeks, considerably longer than the four and a half day flight that brought me to Malaya. Because of the Suez crisis we were unable to use the Suez Canal so sailed around South Africa. Someone on board had 'Asian Flu' and was in isolation; the result was that the ship was quarantined when it made the ports of Durban and Cape Town, where we stood off shore in the Bay. It was especially disappointing in Durban where 'The Lady in White' was to be found, she organised dances for the troops during and after WWII – but we were unable to set foot on shore.

Note

Chin Peng was born in Ong Boon Hua, Setiawan, Perak, British Malaya 21st October 1924 and died aged 88 on 16th September 2013 in exile in Bangkok, Thailand. He was the long- time leader of the Malayan Communist Party and fought British and Commonwealth forces in an attempt to establish an independent communist state. He continued to campaign after the MCP defeat and Malayan Independence, seeking to establish a communist government while in exile. He eventually signed a peace accord with the Malaysian government in 1989- one of the conditions was that he would not be permitted to return to Malaysia.

CHAPTER 11

Berlin during the Cold War 1961- 1963
A Second Lieutenant's Story

At the end of the Second World War Germany was divided up among the Allies; the western part being shared by the Western Allies, United States, Great Britain and France whilst the eastern part was held by the Soviet Union. The division in political terms was very marked the east being communist and the west capitalist. As the cold war developed the border between east and west became a focal point for tension and the border was closed with wire. Berlin, however, lay over one hundred kilometres inside East Germany and in 1945, having been Hitler's capital, it was declared a 'free city.' This meant that the Allied Powers had the right of free movement in any part of the city. This must have been very tiresome for the Soviets! Berlin itself was divided up in a similar way to the rest of Germany. West Berlin was held by the United States, Great Britain and France whilst East Berlin was held by Russia; nevertheless free movement in any part of the city was permitted by treaty for the Allies.

Thus Berlin was an extraordinary city; a hot bed of democratic capitalism situated in the middle of a communist state. Many of the German people who lived in East Germany were unhappy about the Soviet occupation and countless attempts were made to escape to the west. Since the east/west German border was closed and the border between East and West Berlin was open the City became an attractive escape route for those wishing to leave. The border was guarded by Grenztruppen der DDR (GREPO) but there was no physical barrier between the two parts. The number leaving escalated and in August 1961 the East German authorities decided to act.

In a move that appeared to take the western allies by surprise the border was closed and work began on building a wall dividing east from west. Berlin became the focus of world attention the Soviets and their communist German Government (DDR) declared that the wall (Fascist Protection Rampart) was a rampart against fascism. The stage was set for a period of political tension probably unmatched in its intensity.

Berlin Wall 2007

As a very newly commissioned Second Lieutenant fresh from Sandhurst it was all very exciting. Units were brought up new heightened readiness levels and our training increased very greatly; our fairly relaxed life style changed dramatically and our workload. In addition to our primary role as Platoon Commanders we subalterns had a considerable number of extra duties directly linked to the political situation.

The Wall became a considerable focus for our lives. There were three infantry battalions in the British Berlin Brigade and these were rotated through the patrolling pattern along the Wall. The British Sector was in the central part of the border; it was to a considerable degree the most photogenic of the areas, because it included the Brandenburg Gate, the Reichstag and the Tiergarten in addition to that there was a Soviet Memorial for the Russian soldiers who had perished in the Battle for Berlin. This extraordinary Russian Memorial with two Russian tanks on plinths, was typically Russian in architecture, it was guarded by Soviet soldiers.

Treptower Park

Tiergarten memorial

The Wall was patrolled by the Western Allies on foot and in armoured vehicles. During winter Berlin is extremely cold and patrolling was a pretty miserable occupation. We were equipped with German made military vehicles; these were generally reasonable but were inferior to their British equivalent. One exception was the armoured vehicles that we used for patrolling the frontier. These vehicles were actually British Humber One Ton trucks that had armour added. These became known as the 'One Ton Pig.' They were pretty primitive, had no heating and the radios were fixed outside in bins which was pretty 'Heath-Robinson.' From time to time as we patrolled we observed escape attempts, these in the main were unsuccessful as the GREPO guards engaged the escaper with live fire. The rules of engagement were such that we were not permitted to open fire unless life in West Berlin was directly endangered which was very frustrating. Our patrol route ran from the French sector in the north down to the American sector in the south.

An imposing building close to the Brandenburg Gate is the Reichstag the German parliamentary building. Today it has been magnificently restored but during my time in Berlin it was a burnt out shell, all that remained were the walls and a small area of the roof. Being so high and so close to the Wall it provided a splendid place to observe all that was going on in East Berlin and, as a consequence, there was a permanently maintained Observation Post (OP) on the roof. It was the responsibility of one of us Subalterns to supervise the OP and to change the soldiers manning it at regular intervals, getting to the OP entailed climbing a series of ladder fixed to the walls of the buildings. Climbing these ladders was not a task for the faint hearted.

A duty that was very different was 'The East Sector Tour.' When one was detailed to carry out this duty one went first to Brigade Headquarters at the Olympic Stadium to be briefed by the Intelligence Staff. We were given entry and exit times and the route to be followed once inside the Soviet Sector, one was required to collect low level intelligence and to be seen exercising the right to free movement. Entry was made via the American Sector in Friedrichstrasse at Check Point Charlie. As soon as our little army Volkswagen car crossed the border marker the vehicle picked up the 'Heavies.' This was a car full of tough looking operatives who would follow wherever we went; they took photographs of all our actions and hung around slightly menacingly if we dismounted. To add interest to these tours we would attempt to lose the Heavies and watch their discomfort if we managed gives them the slip.

Site of Checkpoint Charlie 2007

One more testing and unpleasant duty was the Eiskeller Security Platoon. The

Eiskeller is an area in the north east part of West Berlin, by some accident of history the area is an enclave of the west entirely surrounded by East Germany and joined to West Berlin by a single rough track. A handful of farmers lived in the area. At one time the DDR had taken over the area and prevented the inhabitants from leaving. As a result the Eiskeller was secured by a small British force. The strength of the force was about thirty five and each subaltern was required to take his platoon plus some signallers and a cook to live on the site for about ten days at a time. The area was surrounded by high wire with observation towers manned by GREPO. Whenever one of the farmers or their family wished to leave the areas they had to be escorted by military personnel. The perimeter had to be patrolled every hour and one in four of these had to be on foot. Driving around the patrol route became very difficult as the ground became very boggy and even more difficult in heavy winter snow. Vehicle patrols consisted of two units moving in mutual support which means that one truck remains in readiness to cover with fire if needed whilst the second moves forward, the procedure is repeated throughout the patrol.

One rather young officer, whilst working at the Eiskeller decided that rather than get all the soldiers out of bed to carry out a vehicle patrol correctly he would do the job himself. With his driver he set off in a single vehicle. After a period his radio progress reports ceased but the Operations Room signallers initially thought that it was an equipment malfunction. When it became clear that the officer was very long delayed a report was made back to the battalion headquarters. A search was ordered and the officer's empty vehicle was seen close to the frontier; it was empty. Very quickly a rifle company was stood to and flown into the Eiskeller by American troop carrying helicopters to secure the area.

The patrol vehicle driver in a very shocked condition appeared. He said that he had been threatened by GREPO who had crossed the boundary and arrested both the occupants of the truck. He did not know where the officer was but reported that he had been taken away. This situation caused considerable excitement and wild speculation. I do not remember how long the officer was held in the east. Eventually he was formally handed back at the Gleinecker Bridge which was the location for the spy swaps [*Gary Powers the American U2 pilot was traded for a Soviet agent here in* 1962.] the officer was hurried out of Berlin, indeed I never saw him again, his room was cleared and he left the army and vanished.

Long before the time I came to Berlin, shortly after the Berlin Airlift of 1948-49 Major General Charles Coleman was the British Commandant in Berlin. The land around the city is very flat and one of the places where it is possible to broadcast is in the British Sector in Charlottenburg, The Russians by agreement had a radio station there where they could broadcast, they came and went in the normal way because they had absolute freedom to do that. One day the Eiskeller was cut off by Soviet troops. General Coleman ordered a cordon to be put around the Russian radio station in much the same way as the Eiskeller had been cordoned. The Russians, not unreasonably, pointed out that they would need food and water to survive, the General could only agree. When asked when the cordon would be lifted the reply was that just as soon as the Eiskeller cordon was lifted. The Eiskeller was freed as was the radio station. The General was made a freeman of Charlottenburg and became known as 'Barb Wire Coleman.' He eventually became my father-in law.

After the Nuremberg trials in 1947 a number of leading Nazis were imprisoned in Spandau town prison. My room in the Officers' Mess looked out over the prison. When I arrived in Berlin there remained four prisoners in Spandau, Rudolf Hess, Baldur von Schirach, Albert Speer and Grand Admiral Karl Donitz. The prison was an important political meeting point where all the wartime allies took it in turns to run. For a month at a time each nation provided staff this included the Prison Governor, the prison warders, cooks, medical facilities, interpreters, the military guard and, of course, the language. Commanding the Spandau Prison Guard was another duty which fell to us subalterns. The prison was a forbidding looking structure the outer perimeter wall was very high and observation towers were sited at strategic points around its length. Each tower was manned by a single armed soldier. The commander and his deputy were required to change the tower sentries every hour and to do this the troops were marched around the inside of the perimeter wall changing old sentry for new. Along the route the party passed through a garden that was maintained by the prisoners. On sunny days one would meet the prisoners; we were not allowed to speak to them and we could recognise them by a number worn on their coats.

I used to do the handover of the prison duties for my Regiment when we handed over to another nationality. Normally the security duty was carried out in Combat Kit but the international handover was done in Ceremonial Dress. On the first occasion that I handed over to the French I was rehearsing in the barracks when the Commanding Officer came to inspect us and watch and ensure that we were up to scratch. He said to the soldiers "Now listen to me: when the French officer steps forward and kisses your officer on both cheeks you are not to snigger." The little wolf whistles that came from within the ranks was very audible. Needless to say there was no kissing but I felt very apprehensive throughout handover ceremony. I remember the words of the handover: "Sir, On behalf of Her Majesty the Queen I hand to you the responsibility for the Military Security of this prison."

There were three routes into Berlin for personnel of the British Garrison: the air corridor, the single autobahn and the British Military Train. The Military Train ran each weekday; it had a military complement consisting of an armed guard, a Train Warrant Officer, two interpreters and the Train Duty Officer (TDO.). The TDO duty fell to officers in the rank range Second Lieutenant to Captain. The duty commenced when, as TDO, one reported to Charlottenburg Railway Station at about nine o'clock. The train military staff was then inspected and the train was boarded. The train guard personnel then secured all the doors of the train with wooden hasps. The Train Warrant Officer, a member of the RASC would check the passengers and collect the passports and travel authorisations for the TDO to check. The locomotive was provided by East German Railways as were the train operating personnel. The departure time was I think 0930 so off went the train. Lunch was taken in some style in the Restaurant Car. Lunch consisted of soup, tinned roast chicken, tinned carrots and peas and sautéed potatoes, pudding was tinned fruit and cream. Since passengers travelled only very occasionally the monotonous menu was not important.

At the point where the train left East Germany to enter West Germany the train was stopped at Helmstedt. Here there was a 'show station' with shops with bright lights to demonstrate what a fine place East Germany was to live. I never saw anyone in the shop nor any change in the goods displayed. The TDO with the interpreters dismounted and marched to the Soviet security office. Here the documentation was handed to the Russian official. This man was invariably rudely officious and the TDO would sometimes make him the subject of mild humour. Having delayed the train for as long as possible it was released to continue its journey to Hannover.

In Hannover the TDO was free to roam about but one felt slightly limited by the fact that uniform was worn and a briefcase was padlocked to the wrist. In the late afternoon the procedure was repeated for the return to Berlin. Dinner was served and the menu was identical to that at lunch.

In the normal course of events if a young officer erred in some way he was awarded a punishment normally consisting of extra duties. The nature of the orderly officers' duties in Berlin meant that it was not appropriate to award extra orderly officer duties and they were replaced with extra TDO duties. Travelling on the train on consecutive days was pretty boring, it quite put me off train travel.

In October 1962 the Russian leaders hotted up the Cold War by sending missiles to Cuba where Castro was their ally. The missiles presented a very real threat to the United States and the President, John F Kennedy, took very bold and immediate action stating publicly that if the vessel bearing the missiles continued on its way it would be sunk by the US Navy. There was a terrifying stand-off and the world held its breath as a nuclear war seemed a certainty if neither side withdrew. This event became known as the 'Cuban Missile Crisis.'

In Berlin we were warned that if the vessel was sunk the Soviets would retaliate and this retaliation might well take the form of Russia taking out Berlin itself. We were taken to conduct reconnaissance's of the bridges over the Havel River where we would be expected to halt a Soviet advance to force a political decision. We young officers were excited at the prospect of some major action whilst our senior regimental colleagues who had fought during the war and in Korea were less enthusiastic. There was a single television in the officers' mess and we gathered around it as the story unfolded. Eventually Kennedy won the day and the vessel carrying the missiles turned away.

My two year tour of duty in Berlin, or as the Americans called it "The Big Bear Town- the Outpost of Democracy," was exciting and at times exacting. As well as the purely military aspect we lived a very full social life and played a great deal of sport.

I eventually served in a very many overseas stations but I will always look back with affection to the exciting times that, as a very junior officer, I spent in a part of the world that was always in the media spotlight during the Cold War and where I learned a great deal about life.

Notes
Spandau Prison
Was constructed initially as a military detention centre in 1876. From 1919 it was also used for civilian inmates holding up to 600 prisoners at a time. In1933 the prison held opponents of Hitler who were tortured and abused by the Gestapo while in 'protective custody.' At the end of that year when the first Nazi concentration camps were built all prisoners held in state prisons in so called 'protective custody' were transferred to the camps. At the end of WWII it was operated by the Four Allied Powers to house Nazi war criminals sentenced after the Nuremberg trials. On 18th July 1947 seven men were

imprisoned there:
Karl Donitz sentenced to 10 years released early September 1956
Konstantin von Neurath sentenced 15 years released early November 1954
Albert Speer sentenced 20 years released early September 1966
Baldur von Schirach sentenced 20 years released September 1966
Erich Raeder sentenced Life released early September 1955
Walther Funk sentenced Life released early May 1957
Rudolph Hess sentenced Life died in prison 17th August 1987 aged 93.

Only four fully served their sentences, Neurath, Raeder and Funk were released early on grounds of ill health. Hess was the only prisoner in Spandau between 1966 and his death in 1987. The prison was demolished that year to prevent it becoming a Nazi shrine.

CHAPTER 12

MEMORIES OF VIETNAM 1971
Richard Whaley

In December, 1970, I was stationed in Barnstorf, Germany with the 42nd ADA (Air Defence Artillery) Nike-Hercules Missile unit supporting the German Air Force. I was the commander of A Battery at the time and we controlled the nuclear warheads that were on the Nike-Hercules missiles. A 1st Lieutenant (1LT) friend of mine from OBC (Officer Basic Course - an introductory course to become an officer usually lasting three months), who was the Commander of B Battery called me and said that he had talked to the ADA Branch Officer in the Pentagon and he wasn't going to Vietnam as we had been discussing our future assignment. He suggested I give them a call, too, so I did.

Rich and Ramona Whaley

As luck would have it, the ADA Branch Officer, a Major, told me he was just looking at my file and I was scheduled to go to Fort Benning, Georgia in January, 1971 for Infantry training and then deployment to Vietnam. My orders said I was assigned to the Saigon Support Command. As a 1LT that sounded good to me.

So, I went home and told my wife, Ramona, who took it well and said we could rent a house in Provo, Utah and she'd work on her Master's degree while I was in the Republic of Vietnam (RVN). So, a few weeks later, we were off to Ft. Benning.

Infantry training was the pits but I did enjoy calling in Artillery rounds. The PT was tough as we didn't do too much in Germany, but I made it anyway. I did get lost on the compass course because I thought I could take a short cut which turned out to be a mistake (I knew better, but did it anyway). Fortunately, a guy from Utah ran into me and knew where we were and we got back to the starting point...a little late, however. I took a lot of ribbing for my mistake. But I never made it again!

On the way to Utah with Ramona I managed to get stopped by the cops in Texas for speeding and I had to go to the courthouse immediately. Fortunately the judge was in court and he chastised me for speeding. I told him I was heading to Vietnam and apologized. He waived the fine and I left. It took us a few days to find a house in Provo. It had no a/c but it did have a large backyard and a great apricot tree. So, once we were there, I had some leave and we made arrangements for the household goods to arrive, which they did before I left.

In early March, we went to California to say good-by to my family who were in San Jose. My Dad took me to the airport and told me that "I wish I was going in your place." Then he told me to say good-by to Ramona and he walked away. I kissed her for a long time and then left and headed into the gateway.

After my reacquaintance with the compass and Infantry tactics at Ft. Benning, I shipped out to Vietnam the first week of March 1971, leaving a young wife in a rented home in Provo so she could attend Brigham Young University (BYU). Unfortunately, in those days, people could smoke anywhere on a plane so our 20+ hour flight to Vietnam was the pits for me. But, finally we arrived at Tan San Nhut Airport. As we were flying in fairly low into Saigon, I looked out the window and noticed the bomb craters, rice paddies, etc. Then when the plane landed and the doors opened, I was hit first with the tremendous heat and humidity and then the smell! It was a sickening smell of rotting material, sweat and Muc Bom sauce, which was a spicy (and stinky) sauce the Vietnamese put on their food. It really stunk and I never ate any food with it on it.

Upon landing we boarded buses and headed to the BOQ (Bachelor Officers Quarters) at Camp Alpha where we'd wait for further transportation to our units. My orders said I was to be assigned to the S4 office (which deals with logistics and supplies for the units and their missions) in Saigon which seemed a lot better than an Infantry unit!

I was taken to a large warehouse where we were out-fitted in jungle fatigues and all sorts of equipment, all of which fit into two heavy duffle bags. Then off to our BOQs until our units picked us up. The first night in the BOQ, (actually just barracks with double bunks) I heard a very large explosion a short distance away. It turned out that two officers were fragged (1) and one was killed within our compound. There were an unfortunate number of these fragging attacks in the last couple years of the Vietnam War. This was a sobering welcome! I have always known that sometimes officers do things that anger the enlisted soldiers, but for them to start killing their officers is never good. I knew that this was a moral issue I had not expected. I figured we had enough to worry about from the VC (Viet Cong) and shouldn't have to worry about our own troops. But obviously that was not the case.

Cu Che tunnel entrance   *Cu Che mantrap*

The next morning, I went over to the Commander's office to check on transport and I was told by the NCOIC (Non-Commissioned Officer-in-Charge) that my orders were cancelled and I was going north to Da Nang with further deployment from there. I was also told, "Sir, you are going north to Da Nang and then probably

Cambodia." That didn't sound good at all. Saigon might not look good but Da Nang didn't sound any better and Cambodia really sounded bad! That didn't make me very happy at all. I demanded to see the Commander and that didn't do me any good, either. I was to leave in a couple of days. So, I just figured there had to be a reason. My concern was that there was a major operation into Cambodia and I figured that was where they wanted to put me.

One night when I went over to the Officer's Club for dinner, I got into a discussion with a guy who was heading home. He asked me if I wanted a woman because the Vietnamese were good at sex. I told him that I was married and not interested. He told me I would "screw some of them before I left". I said I wouldn't (and I didn't) and asked "How could you face your wife if you did something like that?" He didn't say anything.

Finally, five days later, I got on this C-130, a Flying Box Car heading for Da Nang—fully combat loaded with a bunch of other guys, all of us weighed down with combat gear (no one had a weapon yet, however). The plane flew over the tree-tops, as we began our descent through the clouds and rain (Monsoons were just beginning); the MSG (Master Sergeant) sitting next to me commented that he was as glad we were landing as was I. He said, "You were starting to turn every shade of green possible." I was about to lose my lunch, breakfast and supper for the past month! Well, it WAS one bumpy flight, that's for sure. But, we landed, grabbed our gear, got on the buses and were transported to our mosquito infested BOQs. And, with no large fan to move the air around the heat and humidity was stifling.

The next day, I learned that it was not yet determined which unit I'd be assigned to as there were no Nike-Hercules missiles in Vietnam! What a shock! Two days later, I and one other guy from the Fort Benning Infantry class were still unassigned. I did learn that one of us was going to be assigned to the 5th Transportation Command and the other was going to the 101st ABN at Phu Bai. Well, I didn't have any idea what Phu Bai was like, but I figured that since I was on a downward path from Saigon and I knew what the 101st would be involved in, I better get praying even harder! I did. I went to the 5th Trans and the other fellow went to Phu Bai and was, I learned later, killed in Cambodia. Such is often the fate of Lieutenants.

My arrival at the 5th Trans was uneventful and I was given a room in a hootch which, surprisingly, had air conditioning! I met the Commander, a Transportation Corps officer and he told me I'd be the S-4 because they didn't really know what to do with an ADA Lieutenant. He decided that I could be the S4 because that position was universal as far as duties are concerned. I told him, that was fine and I'd read the manuals and learn my job. I also learned that the command ran the Da Nang Port operations for all logistics in Northern Vietnam. So, I became the 5th Transportation S4.

So, here I am, a 1st Lieutenant ADA officer, who went through Infantry training going to a Transportation command that dealt with trucks and the Da Nang port. Fortunately, I had an NCO who knew what he was doing; I sure didn't. My MSG NCOIC, was a big, highly competent black NCO. I mention this because one must remember that the early 1970's saw a lot of racial discord in the military—and we were not exempt in my unit in Vietnam—as I shall explain later. He knew his job and, best of all: he knew mine, too! It gave me time to learn.

My first Sunday in Da Nang was fast approaching so I found the unit chaplain and asked him where the members of the Church of Jesus Christ of Latter-day Saints (LDS) met. He said there weren't any in the area. I told him I was one and wanted to go to Church. He couldn't help me or wouldn't. So, I started asking around and then, of all things, I found out that my jeep driver was LDS but inactive. He told me where they met (at 80th Group Compound) but wasn't sure of the time. I said he could take me there at 1000 hrs. He said he would but he didn't want to go in and I said that was okay, he could just wait for me in the jeep.

That Sunday we pulled up at the chapel and as I started up the walk-way I could hear them singing, "Come, Come Ye Saints." I knew I was in the right place! As I walked through the chapel door, the Branch President stood up and pointed at me and said, "You are LDS aren't you?" I said, "Yes I am." He then said, "We have been praying for you to come here. You are going to be in the Branch Presidency. Come up and take your seat." All I could say was, "Thanks! I had a very nice job in Saigon and you got the Lord to send me here instead!" We all laughed and I was sustained and installed in the Da Nang Branch Presidency as 1st Counsellor.

Life was fairly easy and routine in Da Nang—other than the occasional rocket attacks, not much was going on. As the S4, I had access to vehicles, which helped the Branch members as I could get a truck or something to transport them if we wanted to go to the movies at the airbase or to the beach. The Branch President was over supplies for the Corps, another member was over the Officer's Club system, another was a Warrant Officer who handled all the personnel records and another was the Senior Sergeant over the Corps Depot Motor Pool. So between all of us, we were able to determine when any LDS guy came into our area, we had transportation, steaks for our parties, parts for our vehicles, and recreation when we wanted it. We were known as the "Mormon Mafia" as my Colonel called us. He told me, "Nothing moves in Vietnam without the knowledge of the 'Mormon Mafia!'" It was funny—with an element of truth in it, too.

I arrived at 5th Trans around the 20th of March. The next week, on March 29th, my second wedding anniversary, and before I was assigned a weapon, we got hit. The sirens went off, the machine guns opened up and flares were going up into the air. Mortar rounds were coming in some distance from my location. I wasn't sure what to do and I didn't want to climb into the bunkers because snakes were known to be inside and I don't like snakes. So, I just hunkered down behind some sand bags and waited until the "All Clear" sounded.

This was also the day the Marines pulled out of Monkey Mountain to redeploy back home. They were our protection, conducting nightly patrols around the area and "Charlie" (the Viet Cong) laid low but now that the Marines were gone, "Charlie" sent his "welcome" to us. No one was injured (seldom did they hit anyone—although they did hit the Officer's Club one night which upset everyone!) but I do remember saying to myself: "what am I doing here?!"

As the S4, I was in-charge of the local Vietnamese work force, many of whom were women. They were involved in housekeeping, cleaning the offices, etc. Because of my position, I hired and fired, hence I was viewed with some degree of "fear." Losing a job with the US Forces was very serious because you couldn't get a job anywhere else and we paid very well compared to the Vietnamese economy.

During my first week, I was warned that the Mama-sans would steal things from your room so you had to be careful. I figured I'd put a stop to that before it began. I put a can of C-rations with a spoon and a can opener on the desk I had scrounged up. Sure enough, when I came back to my room at the end of the day, it had been opened and the contents eaten and the empty can left on the desk.

The next morning, I got the translator to gather up all the Mama-sans and when they were assembled, I told him to translate exactly what I was going to say. He said, "Okay." I then held up the empty can and said that one of the Mama-sans had stolen this from my room and if anything was ever taken again, I would fire them all immediately and hire all new people! That would have been a disaster for them because they needed the money. He hesitated and I told him to translate it. He did and there was a lot of head-turning and murmuring. They all looked at my hooch maid at once and she looked down; I never said another word and I never had anything ever taken again.

My quarters consisted of a small room in a Quonset hut on Camp Baxter which had been a hospital at one time. And it had air conditioning! One of my "major" duties as the S4 was to keep the air conditioning unit in the BOQs operating. Now this may not seem like much, but it was so hot and humid and we had no windows in the hooch's, if it went out, it was truly miserable! As luck would have it, it died one night. Within minutes guys were pounding on my door demanding I get it fixed and, of course, I said I would.

The next day I tried and tried to find a new compressor with no luck. Then in the early afternoon, I discovered that a Korean contractor had one, so off I went to see him. No luck, he said he didn't have it. When I got back to the office, my MSG told me what to do: bribery! He said the Korean loved Jack Daniels Whiskey and it would take two bottles to have him "find" and install the compressor.

Off I went to the Class Six store to buy two bottles of whiskey. Now, I had never ever used my ration card so when the clerk said he'd have to punch it, I handed it to him and he asked how come I never used it and now wanted to (it was illegal to buy items for non-authorized individuals)? Well, I explained the situation and he smiled and said "OK". Then he said, "You are a Mormon, aren't you?" (How he knew that I do not know.) I sheepishly smiled and looked at the two bottles. He said, "Here, let me put them in this brown bag for you!" I thanked him and left.

Walking back into the contractor's office I asked if he had a compressor. "Nope." One bottle came out of the sack. "Nope." I put the sack on the counter; he looked in, smiled and said, "I 'member there might be one in the back. I go look and see." Two hours later, cool air was wafting through the BOQ and I was a "hero!" I hated having to bribe the guy but there was nothing more I could do.

The Gospel and Church standards are well known in the military so it is impossible to hide, even if you wanted to. There was a "tradition" at that time that when you got promoted, you had to buy a round for everyone in the Club. I knew that I was scheduled to get promoted to Captain and I had a problem because I didn't want to buy drinks for any one. So, I went to the club manager and made a deal: when I came in and ordered drinks for everyone, he'd put a case of soft drinks on the counter and that'd be it. Plus, since not all that many officers ate at the club at night, I figured it wouldn't cost me more than two dollars.

The next day, the Colonel called me into his office and when I walked in, he said I was out-of-uniform and then the S1 (Administration Officer) came in and called everyone to "Attention!" and began reading the promotion orders. The Colonel pinned the Captain's bars on my shirt and congratulated me! I thanked him very much and he said he'd see me at the club in the evening. I agreed.

That night when I walked into the club the place was absolutely packed—only standing room! It had never been so crowded; I knew it was going to cost a lot more than $2.00!! As soon as I was seen, the noise subsided and everyone was waiting to see what I, a Mormon, would do. I looked at the bartender and said, "Drinks for everyone!" There was literally an audible gasp from the crowd, but when he started putting cases of soft drinks on the bar, everyone stood and applauded! I wonder what they would have thought had I ordered beer?! Sure glad I didn't.

One day, I was asked to accompany the unit chaplain to see the local village elder. It seemed that the village Buddhist Temple needed electric lights and they didn't know what to do. So, the chaplain decided that the S4 could figure out a solution. When we got to the hut, the elder placed glasses of tea on the little table for us to drink. I knew this was an act of hospitality but I now had another situation I hadn't planned on. So, I thanked the elder and asked if I could have glass of water instead as my religion forbade me from drinking tea. He wasn't upset but asked what religion prohibited the drinking of tea. So, I told him and explained why and he told me he appreciated a person who would follow his faith and was pleased to have me in his home. The chaplain, I could tell, was not very happy with me (he was also the chaplain who told me there were no LDS services in the area.). I agreed to arrange for electricity to be brought into the Temple and get an electrician to string lights, make the hook-ups, etc. He was pleased with the agreement and the next day it was completed.

In early May, the Colonel went on leave to Thailand where he met his wife who flew in from the States. During his absence, his Executive Officer (XO), an Infantry LTC (Lieutenant Colonel) assumed command. He was a hard-driving individual who gave orders only. The second day of the Colonel's leave, the XO called me down to the port and began telling me some of the things he wanted me to do. It suddenly became apparent that he was directing me to do some things that were illegal and a violation of policy. I suggested that I could accomplish what he wanted by doing it another way, but he ordered me to do it his way. In my brash youth, I told him I couldn't, in good conscience, do it that way and violate the law and policy. He then relieved me on the spot.

Getting relieved in a combat zone is basically a kiss-of-death as far as a junior officer's career is concerned. So I was really depressed as I left the port and went back to my hooch. The next day, he called me into his office and began to tell me how he was restructuring my shop and duties. I told him that I could not accept the position under such restructuring. He kicked me out of "his" office.

The next five days were very long as I could just see my career floating away. Finally, the Colonel returned and shortly after his arrival I was asked to report to him immediately. I figured this was the end as I walked down to his office. As I walked in, he got up from behind his desk, stuck out his hand to shake mine and asked, "Rich, what happened?" He had never called me by my first name so I figured I was really in for it. After I explained what had happened, he informed me not to worry about it, my career was in tack and he was assigning me as the next Company Commander of Headquarters and Headquarters Company (HHC) as the current commander was due to depart for the States. I told him I'd do it but I would like a new First Sergeant as I knew the current one was part of the problems the company was experiencing as was the Company Commander. He agreed to do that and I left quite relieved.

The following morning around 0630, I went down to headquarters and noticed the XO sitting on his duffle bag in front of the HQ building. When I walked in, I asked the S1 what was going on with the XO? I was told that after my conversation with the Colonel, he called in the XO and fired him telling him to get out of his command immediately. I was not happy to see someone fired, but, in this case, I didn't lose any sleep over it, either.

Now, this probably doesn't sound significant but one must understand that getting command time is something sought after very much and for me, a non-Transportation Captain to be a commander in any sort of a Transportation organization was most unusual—especially as there were others available. In a few short days I assumed command of HHC, 5th Transportation Command. The Change-of-Command was accomplished and I was "in-charge."

Within 24 hours my new First Sergeant and I found out what a real mess we had on our hands. Drugs were rampant, racism was serious, criminals were literally running an extortion and prostitution ring with impunity, and extorting money from white soldiers. There was much work to do.

I was assigned a new Executive Officer who was probably a good staff guy, but was really lacking in leadership ability; he just didn't have it. And this became dramatically obvious when the second night in command as I was walking to my hooch with my XO when the VC hit us around midnight. As soon as the rockets and mortars started coming in, our machine guns opened up and the sirens went off. We hit the ground and then got up and headed for the TOC (Tactical Operation Center).

Normally, my position was in the Company TOC with the First Sergeant and the XO would check the positions. But when I looked at my XO I knew he would instil nothing but fear in the troops if he didn't get killed, so I told him to stay in the TOC and watch things. When I got there, I saw my new First Sergeant and quietly told him he was in charge, to sound the alarm, continue to issue the weapons and not, NOT to take any orders from the XO. He understood. I told him I wanted to check the fighting positions and I'd be back.

The troops came tearing out of their bunks, grabbing their weapons and getting into their fighting positions. I crawled from position to position giving orders, making sure everyone was where they should be and that they were ok. I immediately noticed that several foxholes only had one soldier when they should have had two. I came upon a position where a newly arrived soldier was crouched.

He looked like the guy from Mad Magazine: big ears, freckles, etc. He was scared out of his wits, shaking so badly he could hardly hold his weapon. I rolled into the position and chatted with him for a few moments. I asked him where his buddy? He said he didn't know but thought he was in a bunker. I kidded him a little and then told him I was really glad he was here protecting me. He said, "Really?" I put my hand on his shoulder and told him to continue to do his job because my wife was counting on him to protect me. Interestingly, that calmed him down. He sort of smiled and said he'd be okay and she wouldn't have to worry. So, with a pat on the shoulder, I took off to the next spot.

The rockets didn't last too long (they usually didn't) and they didn't hit anything of importance, which was also normal, but it still is scary. I got back to the TOC and, shortly thereafter, the all-clear signal was sounded. Now began the job of accounting for all the weapons. That took about an hour before it was concluded. We had no wounded or killed but a lot of scared guys. There was also one ticked off Company Commander: me! Fully 1/3 of the positions I had checked were not manned.

The next morning, I held a Company formation and informed everyone that I was not happy that so many had not gone to their fighting positions (I discovered that many were strung out on drugs—a major problem at that time and one which took considerable effort to get a handle on). I told them that this was not only unacceptable to me, but also dangerous, and would not be tolerated. At our Commander's Call, I ordered all the Platoon Leaders, Section Leaders, and Sergeants to ensure everyone was out and in their positions in the future—whether it was a practice alert or a real one and that I was holding them personally accountable. I was pleased that we had no further problems during the remainder of my command time during several attacks and practices.

Shortly after assuming command, my exuberant Security Officer decided we needed to all familiarize with our assigned weapons, so with my approval, the next morning he set up a range on the beach and the company all went out to fire. As the CO I was first, of course, and an interesting thing happened.

I fired my first shot and it went through the bull's eye! My next shot went through it again and the Security Officer said I had missed but then he took out his binoculars and said I had hit the hole again. I was surprised to say the least. Then I fired a third time and again I hit the same hole! Three shots in the same place with my .45 caliber pistol!!! I had never before, nor since, done that. I recall the troops being highly impressed that the "old man" can really shoot! This turned out, I believe, to be significant as I later found out.

The company had several problems, amongst which were drug usage, racial issues and shacking up with the Mama-sans. I decided that I needed to address all three of these issues and get control of discipline. I knew this was going to be a big challenge and Top agreed but knew it had to happen and was supportive of me.

I began finding out who the pushers were and what units they were in and how they were getting the drugs. And, as I figured, most of them were from the minorities in the unit. This was a real sensitive situation because any time any one said anything about minorities you were facing rants of being a racist. But, names never really bothered me so on I went.

As we began to clean up the drug and discipline problems, the First Sergeant and I got our first anonymous threats. Sadly, this wasn't unknown and, in fact, every Company Commander had been "jumped" at one time by a "soldier". I had no intention of allowing that to happen. As I was driving to a location one day, I commented to my driver that I sure wished the guys would clean house on the druggies. Well, he took that as license to do so. That night about 10 PM I got a frantic call from the CQ (Charge of Quarters- equivalent to Military "Police") over the radio in my hootch that there was a riot in the barracks and I needed to get there fast!

Not knowing what was going on, I yelled at the new S4 to come with me immediately. I knew I could trust him. I put on my clothes and strapped on my pistol. He did the same and followed me on the run to the unit. Now, I had a standing rule that you NEVER put on your weapon unless you were prepared to use it and you NEVER drew your weapon unless you were prepared to use it and possibly die. Everyone knew that.

The troops had surrounded a couple of my "criminals" and were going to beat them up. My arriving on the scene stopped the fracas when the troops saw me, I heard someone say, "The Captain can shoot, don't push him!" Suddenly I remembered my hitting three bulls-eyes." I think, even today, that one event may have saved my life. I knew it was the Lord who put those rounds through the target; not me! No one ever threatened me again and I was the ONLY Company Commander in the unit who was never jumped or intimidated by his thugs—and we all had them! I may not have handled this in the right way but the out-come worked! And I did sleep with a loaded, cocked .45 by my side for about two weeks after this event, however.

But now, the hoods wanted their weapons so they could take action. I told them they could not be armed and that I would protect them the remainder of the night. One of the hoods, (a Puerto Rican from South Chicago) started to mouth off so I ordered him to get into his room and poked him in the stomach. He snarled at me, "We're going to get you." I told him, "Be my guest, but don't miss, because if you do, I'll put a bullet between your eyes!" He popped up, "You'll get court-martialled." To which I responded, "You'll never know as you'll be dead." He went into his room and I resolved the problems the next morning. I figure that these punks knew I was deadly serious and they knew I could shoot so they didn't follow through with their threats. I ordered the CQ to get two guards posted to cover these guys' barracks. I also instructed the guards that no one was allowed in, or out, of the barracks until morning.

One morning, shortly after assuming command, I walked into my mess hall for breakfast and noticed a long line with several of the "brothers" doing the "Dap" (that was a complicated handshake that many African-American soldiers used in greeting). I had noticed that sometimes this was so involved it was disruptive. This was the case now, because no one could move ahead of the line or through it unless they had "greeted" every black in line, and vice versa. No non-Blacks, of course, could do the "Dap" hence they had to wait until all the Blacks had gotten their food, which wasn't happening because you couldn't go around them.

I called the Mess Sergeant over and asked how long this was going on and he said something like 15 minutes and the troops were getting angry. I told him to announce that the mess hall was closed and the line shut down. He smiled and said he understood, but a lot of troops were not going to get breakfast. I told him I understood but that's the way it was. He made the announcement and with much grumbling, the troops looked over at me and began to file out.

At lunchtime, I walked in about 15 minutes after the opening and noticed the same thing going on. I called the Mess Sergeant over and asked him if the same thing was going on and he confirmed it was. "Close the mess hall and shut down the line," I told him. He did so and now there was even more grumbling—even from the "brothers" who were starting to get the picture.

When I walked in 15 minutes later at dinner, I noticed that there was no "dapping" going on and the line was moving smoothly. Funny, but when I was noticed, there was applause from the troops. The Mess Sergeant came up to me and said, "It worked; I doubt we'll have any more trouble." We didn't. Amazing what a hungry stomach will do for discipline! Dinner sure tasted good that night, as I hadn't eaten either.

The racial problems within the 5th Trans Command continued to increase and finally resulted in a large demonstration of black soldiers in front of the Command's Headquarters yelling about racism and how we whites weren't fair, etc. I noted a couple of guys from my unit (the ring-leaders) and I figured I best keep my eye on them. The Colonel was furious when I told him that there was a perception amongst many of the minorities that they weren't being treated fairly in promotions, etc. and I suggested as a way to diffuse the tension, that he go out and disburse the demonstrators and appoint someone to listen to their complaints. That would give us time to work within our companies. The Colonel refused to take personal action but did agree to set up the ombudsman approach. I said "I'll go talk to them and call the MPs if needed. We can't allow a riot to happen in the unit; that will destroy any credible we may have." I went out to convey our concerns and decisions to the demonstrators.

I went out and walked up to one of the leaders of the demonstration, who was in my unit. He was from South Chicago and got into the service because the Judge gave him the choice of jail or Army! (I hated that stupid type of ruling!) I looked him in the eye (that seemed to intimidate them for some reason) and asked what was going on. He told me that some of "his" people were being discriminated against. The whites were getting all the promotions and it wasn't fair. I told him I'd look into the problem and fix it but first they all had to stop the demonstration and go back to work or their hootch. There was a long pause as he considered it and then he turned and told everyone to leave and the problem would be taken care of. I breathed a long sigh of relief and he and I headed to my office to talk.

So, we went over to my office and sat down and discussed the problem. What had happened was that a Caucasian SSG (Staff Sergeant) had called a Black Private a racial name. As we discussed what happened and what led up to the confrontation, it became quite clear that both were in error. I told the leader that, and, surprisingly, he agreed with me. I told him I'd talk to both of them.

I was beginning to wonder when this racial stuff would ever end. I was again faced with a dilemma. So, I called the NCO in first and talked with him. He indicated that the PFC was a "slacker" and a "pain in the ass" and had a big mouth and the NCO was fed up with it. I then talked with the PFC and he said the NCO was always making racial comments and that made him mad. So, now I am stuck. I called in Top and asked him what he thought. He indicated that he thought both are right and both are wrong. He suggested that I give both a verbal reprimand and see if that would resolve the resentment. And, that's what I did. I chewed them both out for what they each did and said if it happened again, I'd take more severe action against them. That seemed to clear the air. At least, I didn't have a problem with them again.

I think I had established a sense of "fairness" with the minorities and they knew I wouldn't take anything from them and wasn't going to be intimidated, either. I also wouldn't allow anyone to abuse them because of race.

The problem was "solved" but not the underlying racial tensions that existed Army-wide of course. But what it DID do was let both "sides" know that I'd listen but not accept disrespect from EITHER side to either side, so-to-speak. This type of issue would come up again and did.

The Colonel, (thinking about racial incidents that had happened a few months before I arrived), ordered that the officers set up a walking patrol amongst themselves in their company areas for the next couple nights. So, I got my Platoon Leaders together and discussed how to comply with the order. It was decided that we would NOT carry a weapon (although the COL had told us to do so) as that would indicate we were afraid of our soldiers and I did not believe that US officers should ever be afraid of those whom they lead. I also took the first shift, as I knew if there was going to be trouble that was when it was most likely to happen.

That night as I was walking through the area, I heard footsteps behind me. I turned but couldn't see anyone as it was very dark, so I continued on towards a lighted corner and stepped around the corner waiting to see who was following me and why. At this point, I was beginning to wonder if not having our weapons was such a smart thing to do. Suddenly, coming around the corner was a black soldier who had been a rehabilitation transfer into my company. He had been in trouble before and the transfer was his last chance. We had talked when he came in and I told him that this was a new unit and his past was over; what he did in the future was what was important. I gave him a moderately responsible position and he appreciated that. Now, he was in front of me carrying the club I used to beat off wild dogs which he had taken it out of my office.

I asked him what he was doing and why did he have my club? He told me that I was walking through the "brothers'" area and he was going to make sure nothing happened to me. I thanked him but assured him that I could handle myself. I told him the "brothers" might not like him guarding me. He just smiled and said he was going to make sure I was not hurt and that he had not forgotten that I had treated him fairly and it was the least he could do for me. He followed me for the next two nights and nothing happened. He also came under considerable verbal "abuse" by his "brothers"—but that didn't deter him.

Sometime in June, I learned of a Black History Class that was going to be taught on the base by a Black Major (remember, I was only a Captain?) and I thought I might just go in and see what he was going to teach. The first class was relatively benign but I sensed that he was moving heavily into the Civil Rights issues of the day so I decided to go the following week. I noticed that everyone else was Black and several were from my unit (the demonstration ring leader being one of them.)

The following week, this Major went on a rant about how whites were slave-owners and kept the Blacks down as an underclass (considering his rank, he looked rather stupid for making such a comment and later, even more so as the next Commander was a Black Colonel). Then he went on about how there needed to be a pay-back as whites deserved whatever could go their way.

Well, that did it for me! I raised my hand and when he called upon me I think he had forgotten I was in the classroom. I stood up and looked at the class and said, "I just want you all to know that the first time anyone walks up to my house with the intent of doing harm to me or my family, I will put a bullet between their eyes! Just like I would expect you to do the same were I to do that to you."

The troublemaker stood up and stuck out his hand for me to shake it and said (and I'll never forget this): "Sir, I can respect that!" The tension in the room died immediately and, suddenly, the whole tenor of the class changed and we learned a lot.

The days continued getting more hot and humid. I hated it because you'd put on a clean pair of fatigues and within minutes they'd be damp from the sweat. And even though my office (and hootch) had a/c, the jeep obviously didn't and I was always out seeing what was going on in the unit. I suppose the NCOs and troops got tired seeing me around, but that's the way I was.

In those days, Company Commanders could promote up to E5 (the lowest NCO rank a Sergeant or a Specialist) and recommend up to SSG. There was also a BIG push for "equality" and "diversity" to the extent that minorities really had an "edge" on promotions and some were being promoted who were unqualified. This "disparity" was what the demonstrators were upset about. Well, as luck would have it, I had two guys up for E5, a black and a white. I picked the white kid (although I didn't know who was who by the records and evaluations). So, I get called into the Colonel's office because of my decision which put my promotion balance out-of-whack. He wanted to know why I didn't pick the black kid.

Fortunately, I was ready. I told him that the white kid could read a map and the other couldn't and the responsibility called for someone who could read a map. I then told him that I had arranged for the black kid to learn how to read a map and if he did well, all things considered, he'd get promoted the next month. That seemed to please the Colonel. And the next month, the black soldier got promoted.

Most of the work in the unit was routine transportation stuff: move supplies from here to there, account for it, handle discipline issues quickly and effectively and wait for the end of the tour. But, we had a problem with hooch maids selling themselves to the troops for cash.

I didn't like it and tried to stop it but knew it was an up-hill fight. Some progress was being made in controlling this problem and then the Corps CG issued a directive that "female guests could visit troops in their rooms up to 11:00 PM." I went through the roof and headed for the Colonel.

He wasn't very happy at all as he knew the problems that would cause: drugs, VD, etc. to say nothing of the morality issue. After he got me "calmed" down and dissuaded from going higher, we put together a "sign-in" plan that was about the best we could do to control the problem. I never really stopped it but did make an attempt. One of the saddest things was in an adjacent company when one of the young girls (usually mid-late teens) was raped by an entire platoon and carried outside the gate where she was picked up by the Vietnamese police and hauled off. I was so mad at that company commander for allowing that, I didn't speak to him for days.

Then one of my troops came to me with a problem: "his" hooch maid had gotten pregnant and he wanted to marry her. Since I had to give permission for this to occur, I talked with him for a while and learned that he was from a small town in Maine, had a girlfriend there that he really wanted to marry but felt an obligation to this Vietnamese girl. The "girl" was actually 10 years, or more, older than he and was looking for a way to the States. After doing some checking around and learning that this woman was sleeping with any number of guys, I called him in and told him that I would not give permission for him to marry and that he would give her one month's salary which I would ensure that he did, and that he was being returned to the States within the week (it always helps to have people you know in positions to do you a favor) as his tour was being cut short. In the interim, he was to stay away from her and keep his pants on. (I also got her transferred out of my Company area.) He was very relieved. I don't know if that was the right thing to do or not, but it seemed the best I could do considering the circumstances.

Drugs were rampant amongst the young soldiers during my tour and something that caused all sorts of trouble: fights, robberies, etc. I had one kid who was using several caps each day. Pure heroin cost a dollar a cap (a couple grams) and it was readily available. This soldier was a pitiful case: he had a wife and three young children (he showed me their pictures) and was terribly hooked. I wanted to get him off the stuff, so I called up an MP friend who ran the local stockade.

I told him that I wanted to lock up one of my guys for two weeks. When I said I was not charging the guy with anything, he wouldn't do it. But, after explaining my purpose, he reluctantly agreed.

So, I get the man, doped up and all, put him in my jeep and we drive over to the stockade and lock him up. I told him I'd come and get him the next day when he dried out. Two days later I called to see how he was doing. Well, he was okay, but the first night was pretty rough with his withdrawals etc. At the end of the week, my friend informed me that this soldier stayed all day long near the gate because "the Captain said he was going to come back and get me." I did--at the end of the two weeks.

When I came to get him, he was cold sober, and smiled—first time I ever saw him smile and he was a great guy, lucid, engaging and obviously quite smart. He thanked me for helping him. I told him that I was sending him back to the States to the detox unit in Oakland, CA so he could get proper treatment. He was really happy. His flight was to leave in a day or two—enough time for him to fall right back into his old habits. I was really upset with him so I got a couple guards who transported him to the transfer point and signed him in for his flight. I forgot about him—or so I thought.

A couple weeks went by and I get a telephone call from Saigon wanting to know what happened to the soldier? His wife had contacted her Senator because he did not show up at the Oakland hospital. I didn't have a clue. A quick call to the transfer point and I learned that he had escaped; they didn't know where he was. We put out a bulletin to the MPs to find him.

A couple more weeks pass and suddenly, he appears in the Compound, ragged, wearing only his fatigue pants, needing a shave and in deplorable condition. He had sold everything he had to get drugs and now had no place left except to come see me. Now, he was a deserter having been gone 30 days, so the problems are worse. Again, using one of my friends, I got the paperwork arranged and had him returned to the States and hand-carried by two armed guards to the Oakland Hospital. They notified us that he was turned over to the hospital and signed in. I never heard what happened to him from that point on; I just hope he was able to recover—but I have my doubts.

There was a young man that I was teaching the Missionary Discussions to who was under charges to be kicked out of the Army on drugs. He was a good guy, got off the drugs and I baptized him in the South China Sea. That was a unique experience: a blue ocean, white sands, barbed wire and machine guns behind us on the beach and the two of us dressed in white participating in a Gospel Ordinance. It was quite a juxtaposition of all that is good against all that is evil.

He was discharged from the Army even though I intervened but couldn't stop the process as it was too far along but he got an Administrative Discharge. A couple years later, he wrote me from England and was serving in the same mission I had served in: British South. That was a success story.

Attending Church was the highlight of the week for us guys. We always arranged for some sort of meal: steak, chicken, etc. after the service--anything to create a sense of brotherhood and maintaining commitment. Sometimes we were able to drive over to the Da Nang Air Base and see a movie (the Air Force always lives good!) I know that some would criticize us for doing that on the Sabbath, but it was the only time we could relax and we figured it was a worthwhile event.

Towards the end of my tour, I was called to be the District Mission President. That kept me busy. We had a lot of missionary work going on both within the military as well as with the Vietnamese. We had two Vietnamese Sisters attending with us for a while; I don't know what happened to them. My last month in-country, we had 30 baptisms so I guess we were doing something worthwhile.

One thing we learned was that we had about a week to find our LDS Brethren once they got in-country, or we'd lose them to drugs, sex, etc. Fortunately, we had a member who was in the personnel section in Da Nang and he was able to usually get us the name and unit of assignment pretty fast and that was our top priority.

We had a young officer in our Branch who was semi-active and struggling with his testimony as well as his marriage. I found out that there was a Marriage Retreat being held in Japan by the chaplains and I talked him into meeting his wife there. He reluctantly agreed.

The week after the retreat, he came to Church and informed us that it was the best thing that ever happened; he and his wife talked things over, resolved some differences and fell in love all over again. A few days after his return, he was killed while trying to disarm an unexploded rocket that hit the compound. I heard the explosion and had a bad feeling but didn't learn until a few hours later what had happened. It was a downer for us all. Just made us all realize that you never know when your time is up and to be prepared. We held a very touching Memorial Service for him; it was tough.

Mid-tour I was able to take leave and come home. My First Sergeant warned me not to do it; but I, like he, went anyway. The return was really tough and is the only time I ever came close to going AWOL. This experience had a downer for me in one respect.

We flew into San Francisco International Airport on a chartered flight out of Da Nang. We were all in uniform, of course, and about an hour out, the senior officer on-board got on the intercom system and told us all to leave the plane immediately, talk to no one and go directly to our connecting flights or ground transportation. I couldn't figure out what could be the problem; I soon found out.

As many know, there was a very vocal minority of people in the nation who were anti-Vietnam. Their dislike of the war resulted in many acts of anti-Americanism, anti-military, anti-government actions. While not as large as the media reported, they were very vocal and made good press. Many, of course, were college aged and, personally afraid of going and being killed. What I didn't know was that they met many of the in-coming flights with their brand of "Welcome Home!"

As soon as the doors to the plane were opened, we heard chanting and yelling coming from the other side of the gangway. Being in the front (officers debarked first), I entered the terminal to see a cordon of screaming people carrying signs such as "Baby Killer," "Make love, not war," "No more War" and all sorts of other stuff. Moving through the gauntlet, people screamed invectives at us, spat upon us, and threatened us to hit them—which is just what they wanted. I saw TV cameras and other media nearby, so I knew if we did anything, it'd be all over the news and "proof" that we were bad people. Seldom in my life have I been so upset and dismayed at my fellow citizens. No amount of "apologies" can make up for that experience.

My two weeks home was great!! Ramona proved she was one caring and wonderful wife! On the 4th of July, we were asleep in the bed and suddenly, a cannon was fired! I yelled, "Hit it!" and was on the floor half-way under the bed when I woke up. Ramona was sitting up in bed looking at me like, "What IS the matter?!" When I explained what I was doing, she laughed and reminded me that Provo was not Vietnam. I laughed, too, sort of. It turned out that there was a flag raising ceremony at the Provo Cemetery a block away and that is why a cannon was fired.

Well, finally, the time came to go back. As I indicated, getting on that plane was the pits. Ramona, being tough, did not cry; nor did I. I called her from San Francisco and I felt like going AWOL, but I didn't. I flew back to Vietnam.

The next several months were fairly "dull" -- few attacks. But we did move the unit to the Navy Base. The one good thing about this was that the Navy Mess Hall was GREAT!! They really have great access to food!

One day I was walking through the barracks and I saw some undergarments hanging on the back of one of the bunks. This surprised me as I thought I knew of all LDS in the area and certainly in my company.

I asked the First Sergeant if a Private had just come into the unit and he said that he came in yesterday. I asked what he was being assigned to and when I learned it was to the night-time patrol, I asked to see the Private.

A short time later the Private knocked on the door and I told him to come in. He came in and saluted and I returned it. I then looked at him and asked if he was LDS. He paused and then said he was. I reached across the desk and shook his hand as I told him I was as well. He looked very relieved. I then asked if he could type and when he said a little, I told him if he'd learn how, I'd make him a clerk in the office.

The next morning I came in and Top told me the Private had stayed in the whole night typing and now could do it quite well and would make a good clerk. I was pleased and we immediately assigned him to that slot. Interestingly, I got a letter a few days later from my wife and she indicated that a new family had moved into our ward and the wife told her that her husband was in Vietnam! The husband was the Private! A coincidence? I do NOT think so!! He was very good and helpful to the Company and even when I left, he kept checking things out. The day after I left, my Farewell trophy was in the Post Office and it got hit by an in-coming mortar during an attack so I never got it but he told me no one was hurt and that was much more important to me!

The months went by with nothing really difficult but the heat and humidity was the pits! I really hated that above all else. Then came Christmas and I decided to go on R&R (Rest and Recreation) for a week in Hawaii. I received permission to leave and arranged for my wife to meet me there on the 22nd of December. And she did.

When I got off the plane we all climbed onto the bus and being the highest ranking officer, I sat in the front seat. When we up to airport doors, we could see lots of people were waiting for their soldiers. The doors opened and off I went! Interestingly, Ramona was standing in line with her friend whom we would stay with for a few days and her friend yelled, "I told you he'd be the first one off!" Well, they were all laughing and so was I!

On Christmas Day, I was VERY sick and Ramona took me to the Emergency Room on the Military Base we were staying at. We sat and waited for the doctor and as we did there was a Marine Colonel sitting next to us when a Marine Private walked into the clinic and he was wearing his hat. The Colonel looked at him and told him to take off the hat because you don't wear a hat inside. The Private grabbed his hat and quickly left the room. It was funny.

Soon I was called in and after a quick exam the Physician Assistant told me I had either the Hong Kong flu or malaria but the doctor would have to figure it out the next day. I was not a happy camper as a guy in my company had died the week before from malaria and I hadn't been taking those anti-malaria pills either. I was worried but, fortunately, the next day the doc said it was just flu. So for the next several days I laid in bed and ate nothing. I never even got out of the beach cabin onto the beach. So, our R&R may have been "cheap" but it certainly was NOT what we had planned.

Then came the day to head back. Although still sick, Ramona took me to the airport and left me and went on to her friends. I got on the plane and wound up sitting next to an Admiral's Aide which turned out to be a blessing.

Several hours later we arrived in Guam and landed to refuel. There was a mechanical problem and we were delayed several hours so we took a short tour of the island and then got back onto the plane. We started up and then turned around and went back and were told the part had not been fixed and the plane would be staying overnight and we all had to get off.

So, the Aide and I got off and he told me to stay with him as he'd take me to the hotel with the Admiral. In doing so, we wound up getting the last room. I was grateful but others were not, that's for sure. I went into the room and slept for a couple hours and then met the Aide in the dining room for dinner. It was the first food I had had in five days; it was good.

The next day we arrived in Da Nang and it was raining. My unit sent a truck to get me and it was the only one available because others were on a mission. The rain was pouring down and there was no roof on the cab. When we got to the Headquarters and the First Sergeant saw me, he got me to my room and told me to go to bed as I looked pretty ill. I did as he said and literally slept for over 20 straight hours before I woke up.

When I woke up, I got showered and headed up to the office and when I walked in the clerks said "the Boss is here!" Top told me there were 15 guys waiting for an Article 15 as they caused a lot of trouble. Then I learned my XO had been relieved the day after I left and things went to pot. Well, I took care of the issues and the company was back in step.

While at that location, I became friends with a South Korean Officer who liked to play chess and wanted to improve his English so we associated a lot. I learned the Koreans had a much different take on discipline and were very tough on the Vietnamese, even to the point of killing them if they wanted to. Really bad.

Finally, January arrived and I got "The" telephone call and, it went like this: "Captain Whaley, you can have a one month drop in your tour if you can be at the Transfer point in two hours. Can you make it?" I told them I was packing already; I made it. The S-1 got the call, I said a quick "good bye" to the new Colonel, the new XO, my First Sergeant and turned over the company to my new clueless XO and left.

My last "fond" memory of Vietnam was having a battery of 175 mm Artillery open up with a pre-planned fire at 2:00 AM the morning I left. Scared the heck out of all of us! But, we were leaving so, who really cared? We didn't. The next day we got on the plane and cheered our lungs out as the wheels went up and we left that sad, sad land. Oh, did I tell you the airline attendants got better looking the closer to the States we got?

Observations

During the time I was in Vietnam, we had a vicious typhoon that hit and caused all sorts of problems with flooding, loss of electricity, etc. The heat and humidity was terrible: well over 100 for days in a row but one adjusts (I even asked for long-johns to be sent to me when "winter" hit as it got down into the 80s and that seemed so cold!) The majority of the Vietnamese I met liked Americans and appreciated us—contrary to what the media told the nation in those days. Mosquitoes were not too bad as we sprayed regularly—which is no fun if you are in the area when the spraying took place. Snakes (Cobras) were around but I didn't see them nor did I see any of the tigers that were shot up on Monkey Mountain. Dogs were a big problem as I mentioned earlier, but we got control of them ultimately.

Food was good—at least in the rear. Powdered eggs and milk got old but considering it was a lot better than C-rations the guys in the boonies ate, who could complain. The Navy REALLY ate great and we'd go down to the Navy Base occasionally and, eventually, our unit was actually transferred onto it—which was a lot nicer than Camp Baxter.

Morality within the ranks was not good, but many Officers didn't help. When I out-processed at Ft. Lewis, I had to go through a doctor who checked our records. He asked if I had ever had VD to which I responded, "No." Then he described the symptoms and I again told him, "No". He then said I didn't need to be ashamed and could tell him the truth. Well, that ticked me off and I told him so. I asked him how many guys who out-processed had sex while in Vietnam and he said over 95%--I told him he was looking at one of the under 5%, grabbed my paper work and left. I don't know if his statistics are accurate or not; I'd like to think they weren't.

The people in the USA were clueless as to what was going on; all they had were the media accounts which were, in my opinion, very slanted against the war. I have never believed that we actually lost the war; but the media, the left and the gutless politicians gave it away. The people who really paid the price were the Vietnamese. As my Vietnamese secretary, Quie, told me: "Captain, what is going to happen to us when the Americans leave?" I didn't want to think of the consequences; it wasn't pleasant. We let them down and should not have.

The countryside was a gorgeous green, the beaches a brilliant white and the ocean, a deep blue. It would be a great place to visit—in the fall when the temperature drops however!

I got a Bronze Star for stopping a riot and a few other medals. Nothing big, no great glory, no bloody war stories; I just did my duty as ordered to do.

Someday, after much time has passed and the current biased group of academics, politicians, military, and media-types are gone, someone will tell the true story of Vietnam; now is still too close to be objective…if that is ever possible.

Notes

5th Transportation Terminal Command was first deployed to Vietnam on 29th September 1966 tasked with the mission of operating the port of Qui Nhon. In June 1970 they moved to operate the deep water port at Da Nang. By November 1971 the geographical area of responsibility for sea and land transportation covered over 3,000 square miles.

Monkey Mountain a name given by the Americans to So'n Tra Mountain on the Son Tra Peninsula overlooking the bay of Da Nang and the East Sea. Da Nang's port Tien Sa (translates to Fairy Landing) Terminal is located at the base of the mushroom shaped mountains western face.

1) Fragging (from fragmentation grenade) in the US military refers to the act of murdering members of the military, particularly commanders of a fighting unit. Additionally, the term can be applied to manipulating the chain of command to have an individual or a unit deliberately killed by placing the personnel in harm's way. Originating among US troops during the Vietnam War, the term was commonly used to mean the assassination of an unpopular officer by his own fighting unit. The precise number of such killings during the course of the war are not known but at least 230 cases of American Officers killed by their own troops have been documented and there are approximately 1,400 unexplained officer deaths. Between 1970 and 1971 there were 363 cases of "assault with explosive devices" against officers in Vietnam.

Fragging has been recorded as far back in history as the Battle of Blenheim in 1704.

2) Article 15 of the Uniform Code of Military Justice Nonjudicial (NJP) refers to certain limited punishments awarded for minor disciplinary offences by a commanding officer.

Richard Whaley was born on June 14th 1943 in Moline, Illinois. He became a member of the Church of Jesus Christ of Latter-day Saints (commonly known as the Mormon Church) in October 1961 and spent from March 1963 to May 1965 on a Mission in England.

*Rich Whaley and author
Salisbury, Wiltshire 1965*

In January 1969 he completed Reserve Officer Training Corps (ROTC) at San Jose State College in California and was commissioned a 2nd Lieutenant in Air Defense Artillery (ADA). In April he attended an Officer Basic Course (OBC) at Fort Bliss, Texas before reporting to his first assignment at the 42nd ADA in Barnstorf, Germany in July. In September that year he became the Commander of 'A' Battery, 42nd ADA.

He reported to Fort Benning in Georgia to take an Infantry course en route to Vietnam in January 1971. Rich was promoted to Captain in May 1971 and became Commander of Headquarters and Headquarters Company (HHC), 5th Transportation Command. He returned to the United States in January 1972 and became Executive Officer (XO) of the Medical Company in the US Reserve unit at Fort Douglas, Utah.

June 1974 he was one of only 12 LDS Chaplains on active service – he received a Branch Transfer to the US Army Chaplains Corps upon being selected by the LDS

Church. *The following month he was at Fort Hamilton, New York attending the Chaplain Officer Basic Course. In September he reported to Fort Polk, LA and assigned as a chaplain with Basic Combat Training Brigade (BDE). In December 1974 he was assigned as the only chaplain at 3rd Basic Combat Training Battalion (BN), on Fort Polk, LA.*

In June, 1977, he was assigned to the 3rd BDE in Friedberg, GE as a Chaplain. In June 1980 he reported to Fort Monmouth, NJ for a yearlong Chaplain Officer Advanced course and promoted to Major. September 1981 he was assigned to the ADA School, Fort Bliss, Texas, as School Chaplain; the first LDS Chaplain ever assigned to a military school teaching among other subjects, Ethics. He also was sent to the Defense Language Institute in Monterrey, California to take a Spanish language course.

June 1984 he was assigned to the Chaplain School at Fort Monmouth, NJ as an instructor in Religion, Tactics and Pluralism. May 1987 he was assigned to the National Training Center at Fort Irwin, CA in the Mohave Desert (southwest of Death Valley in California) as the first Army Chaplain ever to be a Trainer/ Observer/ Controller and started a program that is now in all training centers.

May 1988 he was promoted to Lieutenant Colonel. June 1989, reassigned to the Chaplain School as the Department Chair of the Chaplain Officer Basic Course at Fort Monmouth, NJ.

May 1990 assigned to Combat Operations Division to rewrite Army Chaplain Tactical doctrine. June 1993 retired after turning down promotion to Colonel and the Army Corps Chaplain slot in South Korea.

July 1993 began work with Resources Consultant Inc. (RCI) in New Jersey. Moved to Utah in 1995. May 1998 promoted to Northeast Regional Manager for RCI and retired in 1999.

May 1999 until retirement in September 2013 -- hired by the LDS Church as an Assistant Endorser and worked with Military Relations Division training and selecting chaplains and dealing with the military, travelling around the world dealing with issues involving the LDS Church.

CHAPTER 13

Northern Ireland 1976 - 1978
David Shaw

It arrived early in the morning of the 10th May 1976, a beautiful, sunny and warm day in a year that was to go down in history as the hottest on record - even in Ireland which was not called the Emerald Isle because of droughts. I set off for Liverpool docks in good time to board the overnight ferry to Belfast. I searched around for Captain Larry Brown in vain; he wasn't there to meet me so I pulled into a quiet spot close to the rendezvous and waited as I had no idea where to go in a city which was one of the most dangerous in the world at that time. It was just that problem that had delayed Larry; he had been caught in a bomb scare and after a tense half hour for me I was scooped up and followed him to Lisburn in County Antrim, some eight miles or so from Belfast. I was about to become the Staff Captain Q Quartering in Headquarters 39 Brigade.

The simplest way to describe the job I had to do and the conditions that surrounded it , is to reproduce a piece I wrote in 1968 for the journal of the Prince of Wales Division, the administrative grouping of West Country, Welsh and West Midlands regiments to which my Regiment the Devon and Dorsets, belonged.

David Shaw 1976

STAFF CAPTAIN Q QUARTERING IN NORTHERN IRELAND 1976-1978
or
What's it like to be an eminent drain surgeon....
Musing two or three years ago about my career prospects it became clear to me
that the next important step in what I hoped would be a speedy climb up the
ladder to grasp my Field Marshal's baton, was to get myself a 'good' Grade 3 staff
appointment . You know, something like GSO3 Operations in a busy theatre, GSO3
in Intelligence in Northern Ireland or the Middle East or a Staff Captain's job in
AG2(our Personnel Branch in MOD.) One hears jokes throughout one's service
about appointments such as G3 Drains Outer Hebrides and how this is akin to an
MP's application to join the Chiltern Hundreds, and so it was with some horror that
I slipped open the brown envelope containing my posting order which told me I was
to be the Staff Captain Q Quartering at 39 Brigade and was to report for duty in two
weeks' time.

I thought I had done reasonably well at Regimental Duty so I asked my CO what
I'd done. He said he thought it was a pretty reasonable job and that I should shut up
and get on with it.

So be it, I said, thankful anyway to get any Grade3 job in these days when they are
so hard to come by. A quick phone call to AG2, who told me that quartering in 39
Brigade was a vital job and I had been specially selected for it, still left me dubious.

What was I to do, I didn't fancy a long tour in Ireland but I couldn't afford to
resign either. I 'borrowed' a copy of Building Regulations, packed my boxes and
booked myself a ferry passage on that well known tub, The Ulster Queen. Apart from
the odd scrounging foray into the Quartermaster's store as a subaltern, inspections
with the CO as Adjutant and slightly more involvement during a short while as a
Company Commander I had very little to do with the Q side of life. If I wanted
ammunition I asked the CSM; if I wanted a camp bed or some compo (composite
rations) it was the CQMS and if the family needed a strip of masking tape there was
always a chum in the MT. I never quite knew where it all came from. Furthermore,
as far as I was concerned, the DOE (Department of the Environment) were the
people who laid paths in the barracks where no-one wanted a path; they never came
to fix the loos in one's house; they had a compound at the far end of the camp with
big padlocks on it and they seemed to work for about three hours a week. They
were called the Ministry of Public Blunders and Wonders and everyone knew why.
Finally the Estates and Surveying Services were the people who sold surplus married

quarters in Catterick and Blandford and who were nothing to do with me. These were the thoughts that passed through my head as we chugged slowly through the night bound for the Emerald Isle. I didn't get much sleep possibly because I was thoroughly miserable but the more likely reason was that my cabin mate was a 15 stone drunk on his way home and his snores were only marginally quieter than the pneumatic drill he had left on the M6 motorway.

I arrived in Belfast in the early morning and it was raining-exactly how I'd left it the last time. It was a miserable, depressing sight and what was more, the chap who I was relieving and who had promised to meet me wasn't there as he had been held up in a bomb scare in the city. All was soon well, however, and on my first day I learned what my responsibilities were to be. In basic terms this responsibility was for all emergency and permanent accommodation occupied by soldiers in the Brigade area, land negotiation, acquisition and relinquishment of property, Works Services and liaison with DOE and the department until recently known as the Defence Land Agent. I was to look after 60 locations scattered throughout Belfast ranging from battalion bases to small observation posts.

My predecessor had spent most of his time building or modernising bases. It quickly became clear to me that as the security situation improved and the RUC and UDR accepted more responsibility and the conservation of manpower became all important, one of my main tasks was going to be concerned with concentrating the same number of troops in fewer bases. This meant that not only would bases close but more accommodation would have to be built in the ones we were going to keep. Added to this was the Government's decision to inflict further cuts in Defence expenditure which meant there was much to do and much less money with which to do it.

My days were very busy. I spent almost every day down in Belfast with one or other of the Units, coming back to my office at teatime to go through a piled 'in' tray and sort out the work collected during the day. The 'on site' meeting became the thing and with money being so scarce these became necessary for even the small jobs. In this way cheaper solutions were arrived at or agreement was reached that it probably wasn't necessary at all. I began to realise that I was meeting new people daily and that this was the ideal staff job – I spent very little time pushing paper and polishing my backside. It gave me great pleasure to plan a £50,000 project literally on the back of a fag packet, plan it in detail, organise the building coordinating a number of different contractors, and see it finished, working and occupied three months later.

During my time there I had the pleasure of seeing most of the Prince of Wales's Division battalions in the Province. I saw 1 STAFFORDS in Hastings Street, 1 RWF in Monagh, 1D and D in North Queen Street, 1 WFR passing through to help out 3 Brigade, 1 R HAMPS in Ballykelly and their successors 1 GLOSTERS there too. The RRW's reputation in Holywood still lingers as does the 1 DERR's in Ballykinler. 1 STAFFORD's slogan 'Good ere innit' was still plastered over Albert Street Mill when the bulldozers knocked it down! The Division was also well represented on the various staffs which raises the tone a bit.

As well as its sad and frustrating moments the theatre produces some of the most amusing situations for Paddy jokes. As an example of the first, a director of an Irish firm was asked by an officer what sort of turnout he had had on a particular day during the Ulster Workers' Strike. The answer was 100% and he expected an even better turnout the next day! My favourite Paddies are the ones who thought Sherlock Holmes was a block of flats and the one who threw himself off a six storey building because his foreman had told him he'd flown in Wellington's during the war. Finally, and this one is true, we had a senior officer who had to decide which of the Brigade officers should umpire a UDR exercise. There were two who were available; the Staff Captain 'A' whose name was Boocock and the Ordinance Officer whose name was Alkins. So he sent a memo to Captain Allcock and thus left it to the Chief Clerk to decide whose tray it would reach.

As I reach the end of my tour I have processed some six hundred 'works services' and spent on behalf of Her Majesty half a million pounds. I have handed back twelve major security bases to their owners and have seen over fifty units through Belfast. I have got wet almost every day for two years and I know Belfast better than I know Exeter. I have talked to thousands of Irishmen who are fed up with the business as we are. I have met some who want to see us go but many more who don't. I have seen both the RUC and the UDR hold their heads up and work extremely well on their own. I have seen a wicked waste of life and wanton destruction and I have seen brave soldiers and brave people who just want to live in peace. The mysteries of 'Q' are no longer mysteries and I have enjoyed almost every minute of my time here. It has given me immense professional satisfaction and I would pass on one small message to regimental officers who have always considered themselves to be either 'G' or 'A' men. That message is don't exclude the 'Q' side because it is full of QM-type mumbo jumbo. Finally if you are ever offered this job- take it.

Having settled into the job and having made the transition from warrior to worrier, I really enjoyed the challenge, the 'crack' and the people. We also had a lot of fun to balance the tricky situation and frustrations we encountered so often. I relished the freedom to get on with my job and the trust placed in me to do it. Our little blue Mini, the Branch transport, was out almost every day and must have been clocked by the IRA but we led a charmed life. Late one evening I was returning from a late meeting in Belfast on a nasty, wet and misty night when the engine conked out. I was just outside a notorious pub in south-west Belfast frequented by the IRA and their sympathisers and very much out of bounds to us so there was no possibility of seeking help there, but as I contemplated my circumstances, and my probable fate, a noisy group of drunken Irishmen came out and spotted me. They weaved up to the car which by now was pretty steamed up inside and I slipped my right hand with the cocked pistol in it down the side of the seat nearest the window. It wasn't long after Robert Nairac, the Irish Guards officer, had been abducted on the border and, we thought, murdered by the IRA so I thought my time was up. "What's the problem?" was shouted at me to which I shakily replied through the tiniest gap at the top of the window, "Broyken doyin and need a poosh" in my best or worst Irish accent. Five or six of them heaved and pushed and the little engine coughed and spluttered into life. I was off 'kangarooing' down the road with a wave of thanks through my window and arrived in Lisburn shaken but not stirred. God was most certainly on my side that night and I thanked him sincerely for the rain which probably helped my deliverance as I didn't have to get out of the car and I promised once again to be good.

My friend and colleague Rod McLeod, was a Royal Engineer who dealt with everything on the maintenance side that I did not. Our offices were next door to each other's and we worked together much of the time. I never saw him again after we left Northern Ireland which makes me think he left the army - but he did brilliant cartoons to illustrate some of what we were doing there. He was a talented artist and his mocking sense of humour helped brighten up the dreariest days as his work circulated around the building.

The Army had taken the lead in Northern Ireland ever since it arrived in 1969 to relieve a beleaguered and dispirited Royal Ulster Constabulary that had taken a hammering in Londonderry in particular, but seven years later the RUC had grown in stature, reputation and, above all, professionalism so Police Primacy was restored. The policy had made an uncertain start but joint operations continued and generally worked well although tensions and misunderstandings occurred more than occasionally when the Army, on a four or six month tour and anxious to make its mark, tended to forget that the RUC were playing the long game. Policemen, like members of the Ulster Defence Regiment, had to live there and whatever situation they dealt with during duty hours the same face appeared in the supermarket when off duty albeit in a different set of clothes.

The Loyalist strike caused severe disruption and considerable challenges to crowd control during demonstrations both for and against it. We had grown to expect demonstrations on the anniversaries of the Easter Uprising and during the 'Marching Season' in July but the potential was always there for mass involvement from the smallest incident that would ignite unrest. Our crowd control methods developed, together with all our tactics, over the years and usually we were deployed to keep the two factions apart. Any deployment that occurred outside the unit's TAOR (Tactical Area of Responsibility) across a boundary or that involved more than one unit was planned and directed at Brigade HQ and the same system worked for operations across brigade boundaries.

The day's work began with the Brigade Commander's briefing. All the HQ staff assembled in the Operations Room at 8am and the overnight Duty Officer summarised the activities of the preceding eight hours. Had there been a serious incident the Commander would have been informed as a matter of course and he would have been woken to authorise searches of property as a safeguard against soldiers on the ground running amok but the routine still had to be briefed to him and once that was done each staff officer was asked what he was doing that day in order to co-ordinate activities and to prevent treading on each other's toes. When I commanded the battalion in South Armagh some ten years later, I began the day in a similar manner.

The mid-seventies was an active period in the life of the Province and of Belfast especially. Most days produced incidents of varying severity and although the Intelligence branches were well on the ball there were often matters that escaped even them. The six o'clock news was another time to gather and the Commander, whisky in hand, would sit in front of the television to catch up on the parts of Belfast that Intelligence did not reach. The RUC, despite its numbers and the bravery of many of its members, was still relatively impotent without a steady flow of intelligence. This was the life blood of any police operation and especially so in a counter-terrorist situation. It was getting better all the time but, as any would admit, still not good enough to pre-empt the activities of either the terrorist or the 'ordinary, decent criminal.' The line between the two was a fuzzy one as well; as the police chief in Cyprus wisely said during the EOKA campaign there, "Give a chap a mask and a pistol and the first person he bumps off is the one to whom he owes money; only then does he get on with the more ethnic business." It is also a well-known fact that people's perceptions can differ greatly; for example, one man's terrorist is another man's Freedom Fighter.

'Operation Bravado' was the RUC and the Army plan to cope with the firemen's strike in 1977. Any strike where the police and army are called in to 'aid the civil power' is difficult to manage as new skills have to be learned quickly but in Northern Ireland matters were complicated hugely by the security situation. A fire in a Protestant area, for instance, would often have to be approached by an Army-manned fire engine from a Catholic estate. Obstacles, and sometimes riots and shootings, would face the troops and precautions had to be taken. Such precautions usually involved an operational clearance that took time to put in place and meanwhile the building burned down. If I was not on duty in the Operations Room I would be on the ground doing what I could to get the various civilian agencies safely to the right place to help and in a fit state to fix the problem. For example, if a fire hydrant had been booby-trapped it had to be cleared and any damage incurred repaired. During this process another building burnt down.

Much of a brigade staff officer's work was done at his desk in the Lisburn HQ and while mine involved a certain amount of paperwork most of my job had to take place on the site meeting people, finding out what was required, planning a solution and co-ordinating the programme of work. I loved the freedom it gave me and with very few exceptions I enjoyed working with the majority of hard-working Irish people who simply wanted to get on with life. In a similar way the RUC and the UDR, local workers on Army property, and even just government premises ran the risk of being targeted by terrorists from both factions and we had to take care of their security.

Flax Street Mill was an old, rather derelict, place that had been occupied by the Army in Belfast early in The Troubles and the decision had been taken just before I arrived in 1976 to refurbish it. One of the largest and most complicated projects I had to manage, it was completed just a few months later and this was another of the joys of working in an operational theatre – red tape could be swept away and I had considerable flexibility to do just that. We stripped out the old partitions made from cardboard packing cases and replaced them with stronger plasterboard working a shift system of almost twenty four hour duration to get it done as quickly as possible, taking care to deliver materials during the night rather than use drills and hammers as soldiers were living in the next section. The 'finished' product was well received and worth the effort but a couple of months later a section of roof was reported leaking and rain water ruining some of our good work. There was nothing for it but to get up there and find the source of the problem so my closest colleague from the District Works Office and I set off next morning to search. High above the city we were crawling along the apex of the leaking section when we both heard the 'buzzing of the bees' around us. Someone was firing at us and it was time to get out of the way, moving considerably faster than hitherto, when I felt a burning sensation on my left thigh. I explained my lucky escape to Diana as having 'walked into some barbed wire' and we had to arrange for the Royal Engineers to erect a screen on the roof to enable repairs to take place in relative safety.

Brigadier Dick Gerrard-Wright was relieved by Brigadier John MacMillan who was quite different but equally effective. It is a facet of the 'club' as we call the Army that we are still in regular touch with both families and our children have grown up knowing each other well not least because they had Lambrook School in common. David Godsal and I soldiered alongside each other at a number of stages in our careers, completely by chance and this is something civilian careers lack. We first met in Exeter in about 1970 when we were both just married and at the end of our careers we worked together as fellow Directors of the ABF (Army Benevolent Fund), he at regional level and me at the national one. In between we were, amongst other things, students and Directing Staff at the Staff College together. David was another Lambrook Old Boy and his own sons followed him there.

Jeremy Gaskell and his family were neighbours in Hamel Road, a married quarters 'patch' inside the wire fence that bounded Thiepval Barracks, and we became good friends; such that we holidayed together when we could escape from the Province and I was very pleased to see Jeremy's name on the ABF's employees' list when I arrived there some twenty years later. We found, as civilians, we were like-minded souls in a somewhat strange environment and he and David Godsal were strong allies when I had to 'fight' the vagaries of Head Office. The 'club' of which I speak often, the Army, is unlike almost any other; some friends are made who become simple acquaintances but others are friends for life and I see Godsal and Gaskell as often as I can these days some forty years later.

Back in NI other hazards involved being infested with fleas while looking at a derelict pub with a view to turning it into a temporary SF (Security Forces) base and only realising I had 'visitors' when I arrived back in Lisburn. I went home to change and did so in the pouring rain in the garden of that house we occupied in Hamel Road. Stark naked, I rang the bell with the intention of asking Diana for a towel before I burnt all my clothes; the door was opened by one of her female friends who I didn't know very well, and who had come to coffee. I covered my lower regions in embarrassment which showed my youth and inexperience; wisdom tells you to cover your face.

Diana and the family enjoyed a reasonably normal life although we lived 'behind the wire.' Care had to be taken not to stray into difficult areas of Belfast, many of which were out of bounds anyway, but shopping in Lisburn and Belfast was straightforward once we got used to being searched at entry gates, in road blocks and entering shops. Extra time had to be built into any excursion plans to cope with such eventualities and the main thing was to appear normal, to be patient and not to do anything out of the ordinary. Northern Ireland is a friendly place and the countryside is beautiful so the family would return from a happy afternoon spent walking or visiting and not wanting to hear of the nastiness I had been experiencing as I went about my job. Explosions and shootings were commonplace and family life was disrupted when we soldiers were called away at weekends or at all times of the night to cope with some incident or other.

H Jones, my old boss and friend, was the Brigade Major of 3 Brigade which had responsibility for operations on the border and he and Sara lived in Portadown. At this time, with much historical precedent going back to Partition, the border areas of County Armagh, Fermanagh, Down and Tyrone were not only challenging and dangerous for the military but similarly so for the police as they had to cope with the smuggling that was profitable to the perpetrators and thus rife. It was a way of life and, for Republicans, was almost a 'legitimate' activity from their political perspective. Sara remembers how many dinner parties started with her husband present but how often he had to go into the Headquarters at some stage in the evening leaving her to carry on without him. On one occasion we were there H had to go before supper had even started. Without any fuss Sara dished out the tasks that needed to be done. Someone carved the meat and I served the drinks. Sara, as always, was the perfect hostess; undoubtedly irritated but totally unfazed by the situation. H arrived home as we were leaving. We all became used to having an empty cupboard inside our front doors for visitors to place their weapons and radios before having dinner. After H was killed leading his battalion in the Falklands in 1982 I am afraid the same ritual over hosting applied; when Sara had a party one of us took on the carving and another the drinks duties but this time H wasn't coming back.

The garrisons all over Northern Ireland were busy places but facilities were better than in the outlying bases and they were occupied by 'kindred spirits'; everyone was in the same boat, there were friends on hand for our children and excursions to the Devil's Causeway on the Antrim coast and similar places were much enjoyed . Jo was about to have her 6th birthday and, fed up with jelly on the ceiling and ice cream on my shoes (admittedly, not that often as I had missed most of my children's birthdays over the years), I suggested we celebrate it with a visit somewhere such as the cinema, the circus or the zoo. She chose the zoo. Good, I thought; Belfast Zoo is a good one and we were going midweek so it wouldn't be crowded. She could choose six friends, we would borrow another car and take what would be eleven of us including Jeremy and his friend to the zoo, see all the animals, finish with a fizzy drink and ice- cream and return home.

The day arrived and off we went; fraught grown-ups and lots of excited, babbling and laughing children. On arrival, it quickly became obvious to me that the man taking the ticket money was a good Catholic as he was busy removing some anti-Vatican graffiti (God bless our Pope, to which someone had ye to the end of Pope) from the side wall of his booth. 'Two adults and nine children please', I said. He looked at me, then at Diana and then at the line of children who did, I suppose, look as if their ages ranged from 10 to 3 and said 'Well done Sir; we'll call that two adults and three children.' That was the number I paid for and learned another thing about the Irish - they look after their own.

I shared an office with Mike Boocock who was a fellow infantry man and Staff Captain looking after personnel and welfare matters. Apart from getting to know each other's work well from overheard telephone conversations, misdirected post and a deal of exchange of ideas and questions we became good friends. He and his family lived in a quarter outside the wire and one that was mixed up in the local civilian housing estate. One day I offered to give him a lift home as his car was in the garage and on arrival noticed that his neighbour had placed a pink bathroom suite in his driveway. It was a colour that Diana called 'germaline pink'; very nasty. As Mike opened his door his neighbour appeared and greeted us. Being polite I said hello and complimented him on getting rid of such a disgusting coloured suite. 'That's the new one that's just being delivered', was the withering reply.

Sadly soldiers and policemen, together with many innocent civilians who became caught up in the violence, were killed or injured in The Troubles and the middle seventies was a particularly violent time. This poem was left in an envelope for his parents by Steven Cummins, a soldier killed on active service in Northern Ireland, to be opened in the event of his death. He didn't write it and no-one knows who did but it became one of the nation's favourite pieces and I am one who thinks it is a magic homily.

Do not stand by my grave and weep;
I am not there. I do not sleep.
I am a thousand winds that blow.
I am the diamond glints on snow.
I am the sunlight on ripened grain.
I am the gentle autumn rain.
When you awaken in the morning's hush
I am the swift uplifting rush
Of quiet birds in circled flight.
I am the soft stars that shine at night.
Do not stand by my grave and cry;
I am not there. I did not die.

'Normality' meant that the children went to school locally although there was an armed escort on the bus and that when Jo had an accident at school and was admitted to hospital with concussion it was the Lagan Valley rather than the Musgrave Park which had an SF wing. Both she and Jeremy did well at school. Northern Ireland schools were well run; they concentrated on the three 'Rs' which meant that our children were lucky to be well grounded and Jeremy started school at four rather than five. We normally took our holidays on the mainland because it was essential to get away from it all but I was told on one occasion to take a week off and at such short notice decided we would stay in the Province. We hired a cabin cruiser on Lock Erne, hid the car in a locked garage and had a lovely time being 'normal' among local people and foreigners enjoying a holiday in a beautiful and romantic part of the country.

At the height of The Troubles life was cheap with the news telling us daily of some new atrocity, disaster or accident. When life is so depressing you need some lightening of the gloom and that comes, invariably, via the soldier and his sense of humour, fun and the ridiculous. Sgt Oggy Jones was a Devon and Dorset NCO who had been a member of my training team at the Depot and with whom I had served in the Battalion often, and he used to come up with some gems. Quite where he got them I never knew but in later years, when he was the proud wearer of both the Queen's Gallantry Medal and the George Medal earned in extraordinarily dangerous circumstances and having obtained a BA at university and, later a Master's degree, understanding dawned. He had always been a thoughtful and considerate soldier; quietly spoken and with a kindly twinkle in his eye, he made no song and dance about his ambition to better himself and simply absorbed information wherever it interested him. The quotes came out when he found an opening during a conversation about some ghastly business in the Province he produced a superb one from Thomas de Quincy which I then researched:

'If once a man indulges himself to murder, very soon he comes to think very little of robbing; and from robbing he comes next to drinking and whistling on the Sabbath, and from that to incivility and procrastination. Once you begin on this downward path you never know where you are going to stop. Many a man has dated his ruin from some murder or other that he thought little of at the time.'

Someone thought I had done a good job as within weeks of leaving the Province I received a cable (a signal, in Army speak) from the PA to the GOC of South East District in whose command I was. It congratulated me on my award but gave no hint as to what it was. I rang her to be told it was an MBE which chuffed me no end. General Tim Creasey, who was GOC Northern Ireland at the time, wrote afterwards: *'For two years you have held the appointment of Staff Captain Q at HQ 39 Infantry Brigade. During this time, by professional skill and long hours of work you provided a most efficient service to some fifty four major units that have served in this active brigade. Your contribution to the efficiency and morale of these units has been outstanding and I am very pleased that your fine efforts have secured official recognition.'*

What the job in Northern Ireland taught me was the stimulus gained from doing an important job well and probably for the first time in my life I realised the real meaning of responsibility. I began to despise the inefficient, the sub-standard and the second rate because in the circumstances in which I found myself these things simply would not do. The job undoubtedly helped to secure my place at the Staff College as I had been tested in a staff post in an operational theatre and had not been found wanting. The MBE was the icing on the cake and I was deeply honoured. Diana and I, accompanied by Jo aged 7, went to Buckingham Palace in November 1978 for the Investiture.

David and Diana Shaw with their daughter Joanna at Buckingham Palace November 1978

I was ordered to do two things between leaving Northern Ireland and arriving at Staff College. The first was to organise and run the Battalions KAPE (Keeping the Army in the Public Eye) tour of the West Country and the second was to attend the Combat Team Commanders Course at Warminster. I led a small selected KAPE team to visit all our Freedom cities and towns, schools and recruiting offices setting up displays on the way. One such display was at Allhallows, my old school, and I combined the visit with a reconnaissance to see if it would suit Jeremy who, in 1978, was five years old. The old place was just the same but the Headmaster was dreadful - and put me off within five minutes; Jeremy went to Sherborne instead.

In Warminster in 1978, when H Jones was an instructor on the Company Commander's course, he kindly invited me to dinner on the first evening together with some other Devon and Dorsets, who lived locally and he and Sara gave us a delicious and very alcoholic meal. H never did anything by halves and none of us went home before two in the morning. Home to me was a room in the Mess and I was not in bed for long. The first lesson of the day did not go well; H was not my syndicate instructor and had not had time to warn the arrogant and pompous cavalry officer who was, so my bleary eyed and untidy appearance did not go down well. I was summoned to the Chief Instructor at lunch time to be told to buck up my ideas and I went on to enjoy the five week course and to do well on it.

Another more positive occasion that involved H was when I was put in command of a tank squadron and was roaring across Salisbury Plain enjoying the speed and flamboyance of armoured warfare training when the infantry in the combat team became bogged down and a counter attack to relieve them had to be planned. I made the plan and gave the orders but the infantry still couldn't achieve the aim so I handed over command of the tank squadron to the Second in Command, leapt down and took over the counter attack on the ground. With H as Directing Staff and the bit between my teeth we roared up to the objective screaming blue murder which frightened the 'enemy' into submission. The day was won and I went back to my tank well pleased and with H's plaudits ringing in my ears. Little did I know at the time but that exercise was held up on future courses as an example of how to unlock a seemingly hopeless situation. The word 'Ratchet' was used a lot in conversation by H, but usually his expression was used in the context of 'the plan all seemed to be going well then it all turned to rat shit.'

H was always at the front of any attack on this course, encouraging commanders to lead by example. On another day we were racing at breakneck speed into a final assault when H went down into an old shell hole that was immediately in his path. He came up the other side and almost garrotted himself as he failed to see a length of barbed wire that was intended to keep people on foot out of it. The trouble was he was running fast and didn't see it. He was taken off to hospital and appeared again the next day, bandaged up but with no harm done.

Four years later, in 1982, I was the Brigade Major of 49 Brigade; we were on exercise in Germany and whatever we were doing we kept an ear on the reports from the Falklands. On the dreadful day when it was announced that H had been killed leading a counter attack in order to unlock a blockage during the battle for Goose Green I was shocked and very sad - but I wasn't surprised. This was a tactic he had always employed in training and, later, when the post mortems were taking place as to why he acted in that way I was able to offer my own explanation; that it was H's way, and it could just as easily have come off. Indeed the impasse was unlocked but at great cost. 2 PARA had lost its Commanding Officer and we had lost a friend; the country had gained a hero, his VC was a special one, as they all are, and I have always felt privileged to have had him as a mentor.

The years 1976-1978 were brief but packed and passed quickly. They were formative ones for me; at thirty years old I was learning about the stages of my profession that followed platoon command and at the same time I had to juggle the demands of a young family. Diana was a supportive wife and a brilliant mother; Jo was 5 at the start of my tour in Northern Ireland and Jeremy 3 and Diana had a worrying time of it. She and the other wives had to cope with a husband who was working long and unsocial hours on a good day and dangerous ones on a bad one - and our wives never knew what sort of day it was going to be. As a matter of fact neither did we!

At the end of 1978 we settled into a new home in Camberley where I was to attend the Army Staff College course which was to last 15 months. The Staff College was difficult to get into but, if one was successful there, it was another launching pad on the career ladder.

David Shaw was commissioned into the Devon and Dorset Regiment in 1966, commanded an armoured platoon in Germany for 3 years and was training subaltern at the Wessex Depot in Exeter for the next 3. Four more years at Regimental duty saw him serving in the UK, Belize, Northern Ireland and Cyprus as an anti-tank officer, Adjutant and Company Commander. He was Staff Captain in 39 Brigade in Northern Ireland from 1976 -1978 where he was awarded the MBE.

Brigadier David Shaw CBE 1995

He attended Staff College at Camberley in 1979 followed by 2 years as a Company Commander with the Devon and Dorsets in British Army of the Rhine (BAOR), in UK and NI. Next, he was the first Chief of Staff of the newly raised 49 Brigade followed by a year as Second in Command of the Cheshire Regiment in Hong Kong. He was promoted and posted as the Directing Staff at Staff College Camberley, 2 yearts later he went to command the 1st Battalion of his Regiment seeing service in the UK, the Falklands, Belize, Denmark, Kenya and Northern Ireland. He was mentioned in Despatches after this latter tour.

David was promoted to Colonel in 1989 to be the Chief of Staff of Eastern District in Colchester, during which time he oversaw the move of the HQ to York in 1992. He was appointed CBE in that year. Next he was Divisional Colonel of the Prince of Wale's division in Lichfield from where, in 1995 he was promoted to Brigadier to Command 42 (North West) Brigade in Preston.

He retired from the Army in August 1998 at the age of 52, and after 34 years' service, to become Divisional Director (West) of the Army Benevolent Fund and was selected to be the Director of Regional Fundraising and Liaison in June 2002 responsible for 18 regions across the UK, Cyprus and Germany; he was also the charity's principal link with the Army and retired in 2010 after 12 years in the charity sector. He was Deputy Colonel of the Devonshire and Dorset Regiment and a Trustee for 16 years until the Regiment became part of The Rifles in Feb 07, Chairman of the Regimental Association for 10 years (now an Honorary Vice President) and he was Honorary Colonel of Wiltshire Army Cadet Force for 7 years handing over in 2006.

David Shaw married Diana in 1969 and they have 3 grown up children and 5 grandchildren. Joanna is married and lives in Oxfordshire, Jeremy is a financial consultant in London and Georgina, also married, lives in Portland. His main hobbies are field sports and country pursuits and he is an enthusiastic supporter of cricket, rugby, golf and tennis. He used to include 'fell walking' among his hobbies until a young Army cadet asked him whether he was alright now! He and his wife live in Codford St Mary in the Wylye valley in Wiltshire where they are fully engaged in village and church matters. He sums up his life so far as having been a 'fortunate, and happy, captain of the second XI.'

CHAPTER 14

Expedition to Afghanistan 1977
Alan Kells

On 15th July 1977 three Landover's drove through the gates of Barker Barracks, the home of the Queen's Royal Irish Hussars in Paderborn, West Germany. A fanfare of trumpets and the cheers of the assembled Regiment wished good luck to the two officers and eight soldiers bound for Afghanistan to follow the route that the ancestors of the Regiment, the 4th Light Dragoons, had taken in the first Afghanistan War of 1839.

The idea, conceived almost a year before, was to combine adventurous training with reliving Regimental history. The aim of the expedition was twofold. Firstly to provide the challenge of driving 13,000 miles in seven weeks and secondly to retrace the trail and the adventures of the 4th Light Dragoons. Once approval had been gained from the Regiment and from the Headquarters of the British Army of the Rhine, the considerable organisation to make an expedition of this kind a success began.

The members of the expedition were chosen and various tasks allotted to them. The vehicles to be used by the expedition, three reasonably new long-wheel base Army Landover's and trailers were civilianised by repainting them the Regimental colours of green, blue and yellow. They were thoroughly serviced and modified for the heat. Each Rover had canvas beds with mosquito nets installed and sufficient petrol cans carried in side panniers and trailers to enable 1,200 miles to be covered without refilling. A comprehensive medical chest was assembled, and the expedition sergeant went to a British military hospital for three weeks where they injected as much medical knowledge as they could into him. Another expedition member was sent on a water purification course so he could make the local water drinkable when the 29-gallon capacity of each Rover ran low. In an attempt to avoid the dysentery that often accompanies travel in the Middle East, the expedition carried tinned and dehydrated food for consumption east of Istanbul. In Europe fresh food was bought and cooked.

Running concurrently with all this activity went the historical research. The British Museum kindly photocopied three hundred pages of a book that was to be the basis of our journey. Written by William Taylor, a Troop Sergeant Major of the 4th Light Dragoons only two years after the Regiment returned from Afghanistan, the 'Scenes and Adventures in Afghanistan' gives a colourful and detailed account of the campaign, as well as a fascinating insight into the life of a soldier at that time. Taylor's book was read to the expedition at all relevant places along the 'trail' and his graphic, often verbose descriptions gave us a strange feeling of reliving history.

Sixty-eight industrial enterprises were contacted by the Commanding Officer Lt Col Webster, asking for financial or material support for the expedition. The response was poor, but those who did react favourably proved most generous. Courtauld's supplied each member with jeans, a waterproof suit and a parka, all made to measure and of excellent quality. They also made a financial contribution, as did Wilkinson Swords, General Food and many other individuals. Ingersol sent watches; Pye tape cassettes as each Landrover had a stereo cassette player. Thames Television, although unable to help sent 'Rock Follies' T-shirts. Finally, Southern Coolers Ltd constructed a proto-type cooler with the aid of Danfoss, Danish Company, which we installed in one of the Landover's. This proved invaluable in desert heat.

By 10th July 1977 all the political clearances, including Pakistan that had been causing anxiety because of political unrest, came through, and on the 15th, well prepared and excited we set off.

July 1977 Barker Barracks, Paderborn, Germany.

The route to Afghanistan was one of great contrasts. There was a gradual change from the picture postcard beauty of Germany and Austria to the more austere countryside of Yugoslavia and Greece. The transition from West to East was striking, after the fifth day of driving we crossed the Bospherous, and encountered children begging beside the roads. Even children three and four years old would beg for cigarettes and shout 'buckshees, buckshees,' even though the Landrover put up a big sign saying 'No buskshees today.' Often groups of beggars besides the roads were aggressive, they would beg and shout to the first Landrover, but getting no response they would leer angrily at the second and throw stones at the third. I, in the green Landrover, always led in these areas.

A strict system was worked out in order to keep the three- vehicle convoy together. It was necessary to close up before and after towns, and for the leading vehicle to be responsible for making sure the other two were within sight behind. We were astonished at the poor standard of driving of the locals and their apparent disregard for life. The mixture of narrow, bad roads and vastly over-laden vehicles travelling at high speed evidently leads to many crashes. We took great care as we passed awful accidents and wrecked vehicles with wreaths beside them.

We drove continually through the day apart from meals, and the 'exercise' halt every two hours. We passed through major towns and cities without stopping, as our aim was to begin the 4th Light Dragoon trail as soon as possible and have a more leisurely journey back. On several occasions we drove through the night in order to cover less interesting countryside. We had planned on averaging 30 miles an hour and covering 350 miles a day, in fact we maintained this schedule on the journey out.

Iran was surprisingly clean and 'western' with much evidence of oil money. The change crossing the border into Afghanistan was dramatic- the process of actually crossing the border was agonising. We spent the day in total confusion trying to find the officials and the documents they needed. Luckily Staff Sergeant Roxborough had repaired a bus belonging to an extraordinary young American woman who was leading a tour, she knew the ways of the East and had been across this border many times. She took us under her wing and we were only held up one day. One unfortunate group of tourists in a minibus had been there three days and were still totally confused.

The Landover's were bearing up well; it was interesting to note how the different coloured vehicles developed their own characteristics, and how the crews began to identify with their own Rovers. The blue Rover was known as the 'Ming' wagon as it and its crew of Lt Hurst, Cpl Cowper [REME] and Cpl Briggs were always dusty and scruffy. The yellow was known as the 'Dent' wagon after a slight bump in Iran when a truck reversed into it, which upset the crew- Staff [of life] Roxborough, Cpl McCartney, Cpl 'Hat' [as he never took his cowboy hat off] Hadfield and Trp Boyle very much. The expedition leaders Landrover with Sgt 'Medic' Kells and Trp Schofield was known as the 'Tea Leaf' wagon because anything that went missing, the rest of the expedition said, ended up in the green Rover!

The roads in Afghanistan have tolls, which are controlled by the tribesmen of the neighbourhood. These allow them to continue their ancient custom of robbing all travellers and amused us greatly.

Toll tickets &
toll roads

We drove through the astonishingly hot lifeless deserts to Kandahar, Kabul and finally through the more humid bush vegetation to Karachi along the 'trail'. We arrived in Kabul after 14 days of hard, interesting and thankfully trouble free driving.

The historical background to the First Afghanistan War of 1838 is a fascinating tale of courage, hardship and incompetence. In the early 19th Century Afghanistan was a loose confederation of chieftains who owed some allegiance to a weak, nominal King, Shah Shujah. He was expelled from the Kingship in 1809 and was then supported in exile by the British at Ludhiana. Dost Mahommed Khan; a powerful local chief emerged as leader. He was Amir at Kabul, but was hardly recognised by his brothers in Kandahar and not at all at Heart by the local prince who still owed allegiance to Shah Shujah.

Heart in 1837 was besieged by a Persian army with some Russian support and many Russian officers. A Russian envoy, who was subsequently disowned by the Russian Government, was installed at Kabul with Dost Mahommed. Naturally in India these activities were taken to imply a Russian threat and Lord Auckland, then Governor General, conceived a plan to get Ranjit Singh, the ruler of the Sikhs, to depose Dost Mahommed with who he was already in dispute over Peshawer and restore the feeble and unpopular Shah Shujah.

Lord Auckland's idea was that the British forces would help Ranjit Singh, but the 'Lion of Lahore' as he was known, made his terms for co-operation too high and in the end even refused British troops permission to go through Sikh Territory. Instead it was decided to send an Expeditionary Force made up from a specially raised force with British officers and many Indian sepoys, as well as elements of the Bombay and Bengal armies.

The Expeditionary Force that totalled 21,000 included two Squadrons of the 4th Light Dragoons [later the 4th Hussars] that combined with the 8th King's Royal Hussars to form the Queen's Royal Irish Hussars. The Commanding officer of the Regiment at this time was Lt Col Scott, who was given command of a cavalry brigade; so command of the detachment of the 4th –16 officers and 300 men fell to the Second-In-Command Major Francis Daly.

The Regiment, stationed at Kirkee in India, received orders for the detachment to march to Bombay in November 1838. They embarked on the 'Cambridge' and proceeded towards the mouth of the River Indus. The voyage was uneventful except for one occasion when the ship ran aground on a sandbank of the Gulf of Kutch. The captain made all the troops jump up and down on the deck together until the ship broke free and continued northwards.

On 30th November the two Squadrons landed at Hajamro Creek on the mouth of the Indus, 70 miles north of Karachi. When all the horses and stores were ashore the force was reviewed by the Commander-In Chief, General Sir John Keane.

This was the first campaign of the British Army in Queen Victoria's reign, and although both the Bombay and Bengal columns were only to support Shah Shajuah's army- the grand title of the 'Army of the Indus' was invented. The whole campaign was supposed to be a 'Grand Promenade' to which officers from all over India flocked for adventure and prize money. The light-hearted way in which the officers regarded the forthcoming campaign was aptly demonstrated in the huge amounts of baggage- one 16th lancer brought with him 17 camels laden with his personal equipment.

The regular part of the Indian army, both native and infantry, were dressed in the same fashion of the Regiments of the British Line. This was originally so that the renowned red lines should strike terror into their Indian foes. The 4th Light Dragoons wore a heavy scarlet uniform with green facings- totally unsuitable for the heat and guerrilla tactics of the Afghans.

The Bombay column consisted of the 4th Light Dragoons, 1st Bombay Light Cavalry, Poona Local Horse, three infantry battalions, artillery and sappers, totalling five thousand six hundred men. The column marched northwards through the lush landscape and humidity towards Hyderabad along the west bank of the River Indus.

In his book Taylor gives detailed accounts of the towns, Tatta and Juruk and the countryside; we found little changed! The inhabitants were dressed as they had been in 1839, with long baggy robes and wrap around headgear. The towns we found had no drainage, as we drove through them in convoy the confusion and filth assaulted our senses. The roads in this part of Southern Pakistan were, I should imagine, much the same as in Taylor's day....we bounced and braked to avoid deep holes and strangely unconcerned locals. The detailed route we found difficult to follow as the whole area had been radically changed by the control channels of the Indus.

The marching Bombay column suffered from the heat during the day and the cold at night. Dysentery broke out and remained endemic with the Army of the Indus throughout the campaign.

At Tatta, Taylor recounts the tale of a magician who was a very imposing figure, his only 'assistants were a man who beat a tom-tom or drum and a beautifully formed girl, about 5 or 6 years of age, whose supple graceful movements excited general admiration.' The conjuror took a basket, having demonstrated it empty he made the girl climb in. Then he, in an apparent rage 'plunged a sword to the hilt in the basket, twice or thrice and every time he took it out it was reeking with gore. The half smothered groans convinced spectators that a murder had been committed and three soldiers rushed into the circle for the purpose of seizing the criminal. The conjuror held them off with his sword, then the little girl bounded into the circle unscathed!'

The column approached Hyderabad , which was described as being of 'considerable extent but of little strength.' The Amirs of the town were supposed to be sympathetic to the British, but closed the gates. The whole Bombay column rubbed its hands in delight at the thought of prize money but when preparations were made for the attack, 'to the great disappointment of both officers and men' an envoy came from the town and bought British friendship. The troops camped outside the town beside the Indus, which is an amazing 1,800 ft wide at this point. During this time an iron supply steamer approached the town, all the population flocked out at the sight and threw themselves prostrate 'in perfect ecstasies of wonder.'

The Bombay column marched on through Laki and Sehwan to Larkhana, three hundred miles from Karachi. Constant harassment by Baluchi tribesmen as the column moved northwards caused daily casualties. These Baluchis followed at a safe distance on the flanks, stealing camels, murdering stragglers and attacking foraging parties. At Larkhana the column left the lush vegetation and clouds of mosquitoes of the River Indus and set off across the desert towards the Bolan Pass in the Suliaman Range. Because the supply system was almost non-existent, as any depots had been raided by the tribesmen, the column was almost brought to its knees by lack of food and water. Sir John Fortescue wrote 'it was very evident, that the expedition, dangerous in its mere conception, was to be made yet more hazardous by sheer mismanagement.'

The Mogul system of supply and transport had failed. The army was beyond the reach of the merchants and the 'carrier' tribes that had supported all the British campaigns in India, and the unfortunate Bombay column was put on half rations after Larkhana. '½ lb of flour, ½ of red rice and about 4 oz. of meat, often of no use because there was no fuel to cook it.' The lack of forage and water reduced the already insufficient band of oxen and camels still further- so the Infantry had to carry much ammunition as well as their personal equipment.

Landrover convoy

In 1977 our expedition covered the distance between the Indus at Larkhana and the Bolan Pass – even driving through this barren land with no shortage of food or water we were very uncomfortable. Observing the large distance the 4th Light Dragoons had to cover in the desert, combined with the continual harassment from tribesmen we felt great pity and could understand the horrors of the march.

Taylor recounts an interesting incident that occurred when, after an exhausting march in the desert heat, the column halted for a few hours rest. When reveille was sounded the unfortunate infantry was too exhausted to form up. The officers, obviously very worried, remembered it was St Patrick's Day and the band were ordered to strike up Irish tunes. ' The effect was electrical, the poor devils whose limbs had a short time previously refused to perform their accustomed office, felt that this was an appeal to their proverbial bravery and powers of endurance, and gratified vanity did what threats and remonstrations had failed to effect. A faint smile lit up their features and rising slowly from the ground they tottered on their way.'

The column marched through Jhal and Gandava where they found supplies, reaching the mouth of the Bolan Pass on 9th April. The column entered the Pass 'a huge chasm running between precipitous rocks to the length of 70 miles, rising in that distance 5,637 feet from the plains below.' The other half of the Army of the Indus, the Bengal column, had passed through the Bolan two weeks before; the Bengal ? column found the Pass strewn with the rotting corpses of men and animals. The troops marched back and forward across the Bolan River as many as eighteen times a day, sharps flints laming camels and horses. Whenever the road narrowed it became a scrum of shouting, exhausted men and screaming animals.

The Bolan Pass of 1977 is not such a nightmare! We found it not unduly impressive, the ascents were well graded, but we could imagine traversing the river, little more than a trickle now, and following its narrow snakelike course.

A "COKE" STOP NEAR KANDAHAR 28·7·77

In 1839 the whole chasm lay in the domains of Mehrab, Khan of Kelat, who had been paid a large sum of money to keep the Pass open and to provision the British force. Even so the Beluchi harassed the column. Taylor wrote 'a handful of men could have eventually stopped our progress had there been but another Leonidas amongst the wild inhabitants [sic] of this magnificent defile.' After eight days dreadful going the column arrived at Quetta where they found sufficient food for men and animals. The verbose Taylor describes his relief at leaving the Pass and said 'sparkling streams, orchards and vineyards while the carol of the lark broke with many home associations charmingly on the English ear.'

Quetta was 'a miserable mud town with a small castle and one gun on a rickety carriage.' Now it is a large modern town that still enjoys an excellent climate. But the orchards and vineyards are gone, an earthquake we were told , was responsible for changing the water supply and now the surrounding countryside is a virtual desert.

During May 1839 Mehrab Khan was accused by the British of withholding supplies, but he rightly pointed out that the land just could not supply food for 50,000 men and 30,000 animals. Mehrab did his best, he sent off men to guard the ripening crops and guarded the route over the Bolan for communications to India, which the British had failed to do. Again supplies began to run low and the men were on ¼ rations. So after the much-needed rest the column marched towards Kandahar at night because the day heat was too great reaching 125F in the shade.

Overloaded lorry Heret – Kandahar July 1977   *Camels near Ghazni July 1977*

The Baluchi attacks on grass cutting parties became so serious, William Taylor describes, that on 'one occasion 'A' squadron of Her Majesty's 4th Light Dragoons was immediately ordered out in pursuit under the command of Major Daly. We proceeded towards the hills at full gallop, and at length came in sight of the enemy who were in a close body of from three to four hundred men, they suddenly disappeared from view, although the country was till perfectly level, and presented no apparent means of concealment. On reaching the spot we found they had ensconced themselves in a large stone pit or quarry, into which it was impossible for the cavalry to penetrate, and the sharp and well directed fire from all the salient points of the rocks afforded the least shelter, indicating to us their different lurking places. Patiently watching our opportunities we sent a volley into every recess or cavity where a rag was to be seen fluttering, and Major Daly observing a party of about ten or twelve clustered in some bushes which lay almost within a bound of his horse gallantly dashed the animal down the descent, followed by Lieutenant Janvrin, the quartermaster of the Regiment, and with a couple of hog spears, which they happened to have with them they dispatched several of the party. The others made their escape by plunging deeper into the recesses of the quarry.'

'The night now setting in, the Beluchis took advantage of the obscurity to steal out of their lair and creep through our lines one by one. They did not get off, however, without further loss. Hearing a rustling noise within a few feet of me, whilst on watch, I listened attentively, and felt convinced that some of them were endeavouring to effect their escape by crawling along the ground on their hands and knees. I plunged my spurs in my horse and clearing the distance at a bound , just as I observed two men rising from the ground, I cut them both down, notwithstanding a most determined resistance, in the course of which they fired twice at me. We returned to the camp well satisfied. Major Daly and two troopers had been wounded in the affair.'

Water was very scarce as the column approached the Khojak Pass- the last mountains before the Plains of Kandahar- Taylor mentions that after a 15 mile march nearly 100 men had died from sheer physical exhaustion.

Today the Pass is if anything more impressive than the Bolan, as the road is not tarmac, and we could easily understand the circumstances described by Taylor 'a camel laden with camp equipment, missed its footing and was precipitated into the abyss with its conductor, and both were immediately, of course, dashed to pieces.'

From Khojak the ground levels to the hottest and most lifeless plain leading to Kandahar; for us this was the most exhausting part of our route-the heat was so oppressive that opening the window of a Landrover was like opening an oven door.

There was no grass, only stones stretching as far as the eye could see.

Both columns unite before Kandahar and it was the general hope that Dost Mahommed could be brought to battle, but he retired to Ghuznee. Shah Shujah triumphant and unpopular entered Kandahar with great pomp and ceremony.

The Army made camp outside the town. After a few days the troops recovered from the exhausting march, but they soon bored of Kandahar, finding it a 'large and filthy city, containing about 80,000 inhabitants [sic].' Soon sickness broke out , the diet of mutton and ripe fruit combined with living under canvas resulted in much fever, dysentery and jaundice. Taylor recounts that one incident occurred when 'two of the marauders fell into our hands. In order to put an end to, and diminish these vexatious losses it was determined to make a terrible example of the prisoners, in the hope it would have some effect upon their companions. They were accordingly tried by a court martial, composed of native officers, and sentenced to be blown from the mouth of a gun. Having been led into the marketplace at Kandahar, they were ordered to draw lots as to who would first undergo this dreadful doom.

The younger of the prisoners, a stripling of about nineteen years of age, whose firm and gallant bearing excited universal sympathy and admiration, responded to this command by at once embracing the mouth of the gun from which he was instantly blown to atoms. His companion, a grey- headed man, upwards of sixty years, sat looking on, unmoved at this terrible scene, and coolly smoking his hookah. One being ordered to take his place at the gun he did not exhibit the least appearance of fear, and just as the match was about to be applied, the officer in command attested it and directed the prisoner to be taken away, the Shah influenced, it is said, by the entreaties of Sir Alexander Burnes, having granted his pardon. This unexpected release produced as little emotion on the part of this stout old man, as the near approach or the fate of his youthful companion had elicited.'

Our expedition found Kandahar unchanged, extremely hot and dirty. A local policeman described the inhabitants as dangerous! Several of our number went down with violent stomach upsets during our visit.

The Army stayed at Kandahar for two months, waiting for the crops to ripen and supplies to arrive. By 27th June General Keane was ready to go on, and, resisting the urging of his political officers, decided to take most of his force with him.

Keane was also informed that the fortress of Ghuznee, 130 miles N'E' of Kandahar was of no great strength, so he left his heavy siege guns at Kandahar after having laboriously dragged them over the passes. This bad intelligence had been the

result of the fact that, as the Army of the Indus was only 'political' support for the
Shah's army, it had no intelligence system itself. So all the information came from
the political officers 'of whom a very low opinion was soon formed.'

On the 21st July the army came across the fortress at Ghuzee, Keane at once
realised his mistake. It was a 'place of great strength, both by nature and by art....
its fortifications rising up, as it were, on the side of a hill, which seemed to form
the background of it.' Storming the fortress without siege guns would have been
too costly, and the army had insufficient supplies to lay siege. The Shah suggested
bypassing it but Captain Thompson of the Bengal Engineers volunteered to blow one
of the gates with gunpowder.

Afghan forts had, and still have, walls made of mud six to eight feet thick at the
base and perhaps three feet at the top, all pierced with numerous loopholes for wall
pieces. It was known that the defences had been strengthened, six months provisions
had been laid in and the garrison at Ghuznee increased to 3,000 men commanded by
Dost's son Hyder Khan. Another son, Afzul Khan, hovered outside with a force of
2,000 cavalry ready to operate against the invaders' flanks.

It was the Kabul gate at the north of the fortress that had not been barricaded ,
and under cover of darkness Lt Durand of the Engineers and a party of sappers laid
300 pounds of gunpowder and a 29 ft fuse. The explosion took the gate and most
of the surrounding wall, and at 5am next morning the fortress was taken after a most
gallant defence by the Afghans.

The 'impregnable' fortress of Ghuznee had been captured at a total cost of 17
killed and 165 wounded. The Afghans lost 1,200 killed, 300 wounded and 1,500
prisoners taken. A report was despatched to England describing the capture in 12
long paragraphs [more words than Wellington used to describe Waterloo.] Peel later
said 'it was a most brilliant achievement of our armies in Asia.'

Large quantities of supplies, many animals and war materials were won at
Ghaznee. One soldier found 600 gold pieces in a jar, he attempted to hide his find
from the 'prize agent', who eventually found out and removed it. Another amusing
tale is told of a private noticing a cheap looking shield discarded in a pile of booty for
auction, being a jeweller in private life, advised his captain to buy it- who later found
it was pure gold.

Taylor describes Ghuznee in fair detail and much of it remains unchanged
today. 'Nearly equidistant from the town and the fort, and surrounded by luxuriant
orchards and vineyards, stands the famous tomb of Mahommad of Ghuznee. It

consists of an oblong building 36ft by 18, and about 30ft in height, and is crowned by a mud Cupola. The gates are said to be of sandalwood, and were taken from the temple of Somnath by the conqueror, whose remains lie entombed there. The gravestone in the interior is made of the finest white marble, but its once rich sculpture is now nearly defaced, and it presents few traces of the Arabic characters with which it was formerly inscribed. Over the last resting place of the hero, and in a sadly decayed state, are suspended the banner of green silk, and the enormous mace he had so often borne in battle.'

'In the plain to the south of the hills stand two pillars, or obelisks, of brickwork, about 100 ft in height, and 12 in diameter at the base, which are said to have marked the limits of the bazaar of ancient Ghuznee, and which present form serve only as conspicuous landmarks for the traveller.

The two obelisks and the tomb are as they were in1839- although the gates of Somnath were removed 3 years later by the British, a cause of much ill feeling. Today the fortress is still a fortress so we weren't allowed in. When we took photographs, Afghan soldiers appeared and wanted to remove our cameras- only after much talking did we manage to get away! The expedition was surprised to find so many European looking locals, some with strikingly naturally red hair. It seems conceivable that they are the descendants of the British- perhaps even the 4th Light Dragoons!

When the news of the fall of Ghuznee reached Dost he sent his brother Nawab Jabber Khan to ask the British what terms they had to offer him. When the brother returned with the answer of political asylum in India Dost Mahommad marched out to Argandeh on the Ghuznee road and formed up his army of 13,000 men and 30 guns. The Afghans' morale was low after the news of Ghuznee. Dost rode among them, Koran in hand shouting 'support me this time and then go to Shah Shajuh if it fails,' but none responded, they all drifted away to the hills. So without an army or crown Dost fled to Bamian in the Hindu Kush, his son Akbar Khan covered his retreat with a few horsemen. He was chased by Captain Outram but the British force was frustrated as the man guiding them was sympathetic to the Dost.

Today the road to Kabul is very beautiful, and the hills on both sides of the long valley running from Ghuznee are spectacular. There is little greenery but no shortage of rivers to the land south of Ghuznee. Again, as in Quetta, the lush vegetation that Taylor had found had disappeared.

BELLA HISSAR FORT KABUL 2·8·77

JON SCHOFIELD HAVING A SIDE SHINE
KABUL 2·8·77

On 6th August 1839 General Keane came across the pitiful sight of Dost Mahommed's guns abandoned at Argandeh. The next day Shah Shujah rode into Kabul at the head of a great procession, with Burnes, the political officer, by his side. Bayonets gleamed and cannon roared in salute and the sight of the ancient city with its ring of hills was splendid and inspiring - as it is today.

Although the Kabulis received the Shah [who travelled with the Bombay column] glumly he was once again on the throne. Shah Shujah who had been very fond of his old palace, the dominating Balar Hissar was said to have run around it eagerly, saddened by the manner in which it had been neglected.

Everyone was pleased except the Afghans. General Sir John Keane became Lord Keane of Ghuznee and a new medal called the Dourani Order was given by Shah Shujah. Lord Auckland's policy had been implemented, and Shah Shujah restored, albeit with British help and not by his subjects. The Army of the Indus had been a great success and became the Army of occupation. It enjoyed good living and plentiful food. 'The British soldiers' relates Taylor 'could go as they pleased in no danger.'

A race meeting was organised just outside Kabul, and Shah Shujah offered a beautiful gold hilted sword as the prize. 'The officers rode their own horses, and turned out in gay striped jackets and jockey caps so that, but for the dark faces and turbaned heads it would not have been difficult to imagine ourselves suddenly transported to Ascot or Epsom. In the final race, Major Daly, who had become in the eyes of all those watching the champion for the Bombay column, and an officer in the 16th Lancers of the Bengal column, were neck and neck, and when Major Daly won there were delighted cheers from the Bombay column and the congratulations of his brother officers.'

The 4th Light Dragoons spent one month of good living in Kabul, then received orders to march back to Bombay. Many were sad to be leaving Afghanistan. It seemed certain there would be more trouble, only later did the Regiment understand how lucky they had been to leave when they did. A year after they went Akbar Khan rallied the Afghan chiefs and the British, who had mishandled the whole situation, were defeated. Shah Shujah was deposed and the remainder of the British Army of 4.500 soldiers and another 5,000 camp followers were forced to retreat in the winter snow towards India. Akbar Khan had given a promise of safe conduct but he could not restrain the tribesmen. The frostbitten windswept force perished in the defiles of Gandamak- a few of the officers and ladies were taken hostage but the bulk died in their tracks. Many gallantly struggled on towards the fort at Jallalabad, but in the end, only a weary Doctor Brydon, on a dying horse, managed to reach the fort.

A 4,500 strong, well equipped British force had been destroyed by tribesmen due to the incompetence of the political and military chiefs. A year later Generals Pollock and Nott subdued the Afghans- the deaths at Gandamak were avenged.

In September of 1839 the 4th Light Dragoons set off from Kabul with the Queen's, the Leicester's, the Bombay Light Infantry and some gunners on the return march to Karachi. Supply dumps had been established and the Baluchi tribesmen gave no trouble – they were glad to see the British go. At Ghuznee Taylor was surprised to find the Kabul gate rebuilt and the whole fortress looking as if nothing had happened. Most of the wounded left at Ghuznee were dead, so the column continued along a direct route to Quetta over the wild desolate hills. This march lasted five weeks, it was often so cold that the force found many streams frozen. After the cold mountains the column once again found itself in the desert making for the town of Sibi. As they progressed southwards many men and horses were lost from exhaustion and disease- one of them being Captain Ogle of the 4th Light Dragoons. Taylor said of him 'he looked upon the private soldier as something more than a mere automaton placed at his disposal, few men have left behind a memory so associated with everything that is valuable and estimable in social and military life.'

So retracing the route of the advance they arrives at Sukkur on the Indus. After a pleasant six weeks rest they marched without incident to Karachi where they boarded a vessel for Bombay, from where they marched back to Kirkee.

Major Francis Daly returned on 30th March 1840, 18 months after the two squadrons had set out. Three officers and fifty-eight soldiers had died. Lt Col Scott received the CB and he and Major Daly were awarded the Dourano Order. Each soldier got medals 'Afghanistan' and 'Ghuznee 1839' and two Battle Honours were given to the Regiment.

The 1977 expedition did not have time to follow the cross-country route as it would have had to on foot. The return journey made by the Regiment long ago was mostly without incident. They had done little actual fighting in the First Afghan War but they had acquitted themselves very well and on this note we felt that retracing their steps today was exciting and worthwhile. The aim of the expedition was duly completed and we set off on the return journey.

Staff Sergeant Alan Kells -Operations Intelligence/ Information Officer United Nations International camp Cyprus 1979 – all others are officers from various countries.

We decided to alter our route back to go through the deserts of Western Pakistan to Zehedan, Kerman, Isfahan and finally back on the old route to Tehran. This route begins at Quetta and we had to apply for political clearance for this change of plan. The dirt road to Quetta was hazardous as we encountered heavy rain in the desert, which turned dirt roads into quagmires. The phenomenon of desert rain and flash floods can be a frightening experience; the desert suddenly becomes a sheet of fast moving water!

It was evening when we left the small town of Nasirabad when our Landrover came up behind an unmoving queue of converted Bedford trucks. These trucks had the doors removed and a complete wooden superstructure built around the cab so that they can seat at least six across the front seat and carry three times the normal load. The vehicles were then painted with gaudy designs and finished by fixing multitudes of Christmas decorations all over them. We walked in ankle deep mud and after waking some other truck drivers, one of whom was 'high' on drugs, we moved on.

After bogging down and fording wild torrents we thought we were clear of the confusion, when we came across an overturned truck in a ford. Staff Sgt Roxborough, with great flair organised the locals- the truck was removed and we went on our way. Tired and filthy we arrived in Quetta where we halted to signal the Embassy at Islamabad to ask for clearance to use the new route. In the telegraph office we came under the wing of a captain in the Pakistan Army who spoke excellent English. He drove us to his house, phoned the Embassy and then drove us to two British Majors who were attending the Quetta Staff College. The Majors and their families were very kind, accommodated and feeding all of us for two days.

Both expedition members and vehicles were in very good condition. Nearly everyone had diarrhoea at some stage, but thankfully nothing more serious. The tinned rations were adequate, if a little boring, we tried to vary the diet with plenty of fresh vegetables washed in 'pinkie' [potassium.] The main meal we had in the evening around 6 o'clock was always sufficient. For breakfast we alternated between porridge a la Cpl Briggs and bangers and beans a la Cpl Cowper. Lunch was healthy but not such a success, tinned fruit salad- because of the heat it was always very warm and now the sight of fruit salad makes me feel quite ill!

From Quetta we drove through intense heat of the desert, enjoying the flat land with an occasional oasis of intense green. The poor roads of Pakistan were a great contrast to the highways of Iran. Crossing the border at Qile Safed the Iranians searched the Landover's very thoroughly. Two days of almost continual driving brought us to Tehran. All the embassy staffs we came across on the journey were most helpful- in Tehran they permitted us to use the swimming pool and have a good rest in the embassy compound with no need for a guard.

Progressing westward we were again surprised by the begging children in Turkey, also by the dogs of the East, who all seemed to be closely related being big husky like creatures. On several occasions we came across them moving in packs of ten. Whilst camping one unpleasant night outside Kandahar we were surrounded by such a pack. In these areas it was necessary to have a guard, he had to throw stones to keep the howling beasts away.

Having crossed the Turkish border we took the new military route from Dogubayazit round the lovely snow-capped Mount Arrarat to Horasan. The route is to be recommended being far better and not much longer than the Tir road. However at one stage near the Russian border a photograph was taken, not particularly of the border and a very irate Turkish officer demanded that we destroy the film.

The expedition members now had the opportunity to do some sightseeing in Istanbul where even a taxi ride is an experience as the city is choked with vast ailing American cars from the 1950's. The drivers are magnificent; they pull out at full speed seeming to make a point on not looking to see if the way is clear! With the beautiful sight of the sun rising over the Bosphorous the expedition set off, glad and having crossed the 'Heeby Geeby Line.'

One of the things that struck us as we progressed westwards were the women. We had seen very few east of Istanbul and those were covered in long black shrouds with yashmaks across their faces. It amused us wondering how husbands knew their wives in a crowd- all being identical.

On to Thessalonica in Greece, through Yugoslavia and the magnificent scenery of Austria where the expedition experienced their first mechanical problem, a seized gearbox. It turned out to be less serious than it appeared and we progressed to the Autobahn to Paderborn. On Monday afternoon 5th September 1977 the expedition returned to Paderborn in excellent shape after travelling across Asia and reliving Regimental history. To the amazement of the expedition, as we entered Paderborn the Green Rover had its first problem, a trailer tyre puncture, - not a bad record for two months of almost continual driving over 13,400 miles.

Warrant Officer 2 Alan Kells MBE

I joined the Army as a boy soldier and served with the Queen's Royal Irish Hussars for 22 years. A cavalry soldier who never rode a horse I was always a tankman- first as a driver then tank commander and finally Squadron Sergeant Major.

Military Service - Main Dates
Jul 67 – Joined Army as a young soldier – initial training at Catterick Camp Yorkshire.
Jul 68 – Member of a British Army Tank Troop exchange trip to Fort Hood Texas.
Highlights:
• *We all became 'Honorary Texans' and received a certificate from the State of Texas.*
• *We received the Freedom of the City of Waco.*
• *Official visit to the NASA Space Centre in Houston.*
• *Official visit and Tour of the Alamo.*
1974-1977 – A sergeant instructor of the Permanent Staff at the Junior Leaders Regiment in Bovington, Dorset (since disbanded). Trained young 15, 16 & 17 year old adolescents prior to adult Army service.
1977 – Overland trip from Germany to Afghanistan in the Queen's Silver Jubilee Year.
1985-1988 – Sergeant Major in charge of forming a new Yeomanry Squadron (Cavalry) of the Territorial Army in Northumberland and to have it become 'Operational for Role' within 2 years. This was a huge task, but with 6 excellent and hand-picked senior and junior NCOs under my command and a regular Adjutant for muscle, we achieved the aim and took the Squadron to Germany for validation of role.

Misc
Mostly based in Germany as British Army of the Rhine (BAOR) as part of 'Cold War' Forces.
From Germany completed tours of:
• *Canada x4 (Battle group & Armoured warfare training)*
• *Cyprus x2 (Peacekeeping with UN Forces)*
• *Berlin x2 (British sector whilst the 'wall' was up)*
• *N Ireland (As search advisor to Unit).*

*Tank Commander in Chieftain
tank Paderborn, Germany
1974*

Interesting Facts:
- *Was a 'refuge collector' during Dustman's dispute in the Winter of Discontent.*
- *Was a 'fireman' during 1977 Firefighters strike.*
- *Was Quartermaster Sergeant in charge of HMP Rollestone (converted Army camp)
  during 1988 Prison Officers strike.*

*Many successful courses for Promotion, Trade training and Educational requirements
have been undertaken whilst serving in the Army. Other prominent courses undertaken
include:*
- *Joint Service Downhill Ski instructor's course.*
- *Hockey coaches course (County Level).*
- *Basic German language course.*

*After completing 22 years regular Army service I continue to work in the MOD as a Civil
Servant at Army Headquarters in Andover.*

*My career in the Army was a truly memorable time both on and off duty. I managed to
get the opportunity to visit many diverse and interesting parts of the world, as well as the sheer
pleasures of undertaking the jobs entrusted to me. These experiences will never be forgotten.*

*It is often said that behind every successful man there is a woman. In my case I owe
my wife so much. We married in 1972 after a courtship of only seeing each other when
home on leave from Germany; not forgetting traumas like the 8 week UK postal strike
in 1971 (no mobile phones or internet then and telephoning from UK to Germany was
nearly non-existent). Luckily we managed to get a married quarter in Germany and,
although there were no English TV channels and limited radio, we made the most of our
time overseas getting to know the country and making German friends (as well as our*

friends within the 'married families patch'). Sadly, work took me away a lot and shortly after our daughter was born in 1974, I was away for 6 months on a peacekeeping tour of Cyprus (even less communication for 6 months whilst on tour). We both know that 'today's marriages are much more likely to have marital problems, even with all the facilities and social media available.

Since leaving the Army

I have tried to keep active by keeping fit via my passion of skiing and mountaineering. It's not helped by the fact that I suffer from Asthma but, thankfully this is well controlled by the dedicated Consultant and his Team at Salisbury District Hospital who look after me. I therefore took it on myself to raise money for Salisbury Hospital Respiratory Unit and Asthma UK to help fellow sufferers.

To raise money I have taken on some very challenging treks. Not only have I raised £thousands, but it proves to my Consultant that those asthmatics (like me) can take on very physical activities at altitude, providing that their asthma is under control.

Every summer is spent trekking in the French Alps between 1500 & 3000m. The most physical trek's to date have been:

- *Oct/Nov 05 - Trek to Everest Base Camp.*
- *Jun/Jul 08 - Mont Blanc challenge.*
- *Sep 08 – Trek to top of Mount Etna, Sicily.*
- *Mar 11 – Grand Traverse, South Island, New Zealand.*
- *Aug 12 – Dents du Midi, Switzerland – ascent of Haute Cime.*
- *Jul 13 – Trek up and across Trient Glacier – ascent of Pointe d'Orny.*
- *Oct 13 – Trek Ben Nevis – CMD route ascent.*

Finally, I was honoured in Jan 09 with the award of MBE for Public and Voluntary Service. The public part was my work involvement at Army HQ in the Repatriation process of our fallen in both Iraq and Afghanistan. I was part of a 3 x person team responsible for arranging the repatriation process from Theatre to UK (although the other 2 members of the team have changed many times, I remain as continuity).

The civilian part of the honour was for my charity raising as previously mentioned.

CHAPTER 15

Desert Storm – First Gulf War 1990-1991
Simon Firth

"The Logistic Support of the British Forces in the Gulf was an absolutely gigantic accomplishment," General Sir Peter de la Billiere.

Operation Granby: The British Armies Contribution to the Liberation of Kuwait – 1990-1992

British Logistics for The First Gulf War
Introduction

In the early hours of 2 August 1990 The Kingdom of Kuwait was invaded by Iraq. That same evening the UN Security Council passed a resolution demanding that Saddam Hussein should withdraw his Army immediately. It was as early as the 7th August that the United States launched Desert Storm to support the Saudi Arabian Army should Saddam Hussein decide that he would invade that country.

On the evening of 15th September Tom King, the Secretary of State for Defence, announced that the UK Joint Force Headquarters was to be set up at High Wycombe and that 7th Armoured Brigade was to be deployed to Saudi Arabia.

This Chapter describes the immense logistic effort needed to support our forces deployed to the Gulf.

Formation of Joint Force Headquarters

On the 16 September the operational and the logistic staff began to assemble in the old Nuclear Bunker underground at High Wycombe. The tri Service Joint Force Headquarters (JFHQ) was under the command of Air Chief Marshal Sir Paddy Hine and Chief of Staff Air Marshal Dick Johns who later became the Chief of the Air Staff.

The Bunker was a relic of the cold war. Everything was underground and when sealed was completely self-contained. I remember arriving the first time and dropping down into the bowels of the earth and then walking along echoing concrete passages until arriving at my office in the Logistic area. The main working area was a large room with rows of workstations occupied by about 50 staff with the balance in smaller offices surrounding this main area. Each station had a computer screen linking it to the Gulf and to other logistic support units. Every Logistic Service was represented including the Engineers and a team to hire and direct commercial shipping.

My appointment at JFHQ was Assistant Chief of Staff, Land Logistics and Personnel. It was my task to form this Logistic and Personnel Staff, whose role would be to provide all the Logistics required to support and to sustain 7 Armoured Brigade and any other forces eventually deployed.

The Challenge

In 1990 the British Army had already suffered a series of cuts both in manpower and equipment. The Army had been concentrating most effort and equipment design on fighting on the North German Plain. The 15-20 years of pretty continuous cutting of budgets, slimming down on units and reducing our capability and capacity had had its effect. The front line units were sustained although on slim establishments. The logistics support and backup had been cut back in all Services not just the Army.

The other Army problem was that the 1 (Br) Corps in Germany was dictating much of our training and doctrine as well as tactics. In spite of Ireland, which was excellent for junior leaders, the armoured tactics and operational doctrine was based on a defensive battle in Germany with virtually every piece of equipment which we bought applied to the potential defensive battle in Germany. I suspect that it was right at the time, and certainly the tanks, armoured personnel carriers and crust of the Army operating in Germany was professional, efficient and very well trained. The difficulty was that the backup to provide support for extended operations just did not exist. There was a chronic shortage of spares, reserves, equipment, manpower, ammunition and, of course, the wherewithal to fight in the desert.

Fortunately we had 6 months to deploy and to make up some of the deficiencies.

In the lead up to the Gulf War every gun in Germany had their barrels taken away to provide reserves, every tank engine was taken out of the tanks, the ammunition we had to buy in from Italy and all sorts of places. We had to cannibalise infantry battalions to provide the manpower reserves to provide the proper war establishment and battle casualty replacements.

There was a chronic shortage of every kind of spare and other equipment needed in the Desert. Just a few examples; there was no desert kit or boots, the tanks weren't able to resist all anti-tank weapons and this was the same for the APC's [Armoured Personnel Carrier]. The tracks were particularly vulnerable.

The other major difficulty was that the power packs weren't geared for the sand so they were doing a 100 km before breaking down; on average the Warrior was a bit better than that.

The Lynx helicopters had only had about 38 spare engines and without filters could only manage about 10 hours flying. The Regimental Commander was instructed to keep flying to the minimum until we could obtain filters. Perhaps naturally he wanted to train his pilots both in flying in the desert but also operationally so this advice was ignored and in little over a day all his spare engines had gone and his helicopters had to be grounded.

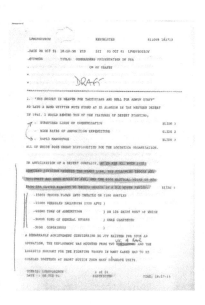

We rang the manufacturer who said «right we will accelerate production and the first one should be ready in early March»! Not much good to us. So we called for the Chairman or Chief Executive of ACME Filters, Westland and Rolls Royce for an immediate meeting. It was only as they arrived in their chauffeur driven cars with aides that we realised the level of help we could get. The attack date was very secret so we took them 4 floors down into the bunker, excluded the aides and gave them a Top Secret Briefing and asked for help. Miraculously the first 4 filters flew to the Gulf 48 hours later.

Early Deployment Planning
It was a challenging time as the Headquarters in the bunker became established. The Logistic area would be responsible for the provision into theatre of ordnance supplies, ammunition, transport which would include a large number of tank transporters – many taken up from trade, medical which was a particular challenge as we had decimated our medical forces and of course spares, recovery and workshop support as well as engineer support. Each team was backed up by its support Headquarters, most of which were at Andover.

Almost immediately I flew out to Saudi Arabia; to Riyadh initially, where the Americans thoughtfully provided a small Executive jet which enabled me to travel the long distances, particularly down to the well-developed port of Al Jubayl, without which this whole operation would have been extraordinarily difficult. The purpose of this early visit was to find out and identify some of the challenges that we would face when we deployed our forces. The Commander of the US Marines 1st Division met me and arranged for me to fly up to their defensive position near the border and to spend a couple of days in the desert. I also had a meeting with Major General 'Gus' Pagonis the charismatic Commander of the US Logistics.

On arrival near the border to visit the US marine Division I expected to find the ice cream machine going and air conditioning, but was completely wrong. They were a tough fit well trained organisation dug in and operating professionally with standing patrols and mobile patrols going right up to the border to give early warning of any incursion from Iraq or Kuwait. It was immediately apparent that water, fresh food and the very long lines of communications were obvious challenges, but also our lack of desert clothing, boots and other equipment. Although flat, it was a hard stony and rough terrain which did immense damage to vehicles and equipment, and was particularly damaging for armoured vehicles and also helicopters when they landed and took off through the sandstorms.

A short visit to Bahrain followed to establish medical facilities. Bahrain airport has two terminals a military terminal and a civil terminal. I landed at the military terminal but the people who were meeting me assumed I was arriving by a civil flight so they were at the civil terminal. It was a long walk in 90 degrees.

There followed several political visits including a rather formal visit to the Governor of the area where we exchanged gifts. He promised great support.

It was at this time that the Goodyear tyre factory in the town was requisitioned as a Hospital. Later, after removing the tyres and starting the process of building the Hospital I met the Matron and advance party who invited me to return for tea and to see the Hospital in operation. After the relief of Kuwait on a later visit we sat down in one of the wards, mercifully almost empty and had tea from a silver teapot poured with some ceremony and a great deal of relief.

I stayed during this first visit in a house in a civilian cantonment. Brits all live in these cantonments so they could live their lives reasonably normally. Women couldn't drive as it was quite strict Muslim area and there was no alcohol. On my second night there I got back really hot so as there was a pool went to have a swim. Somebody came up and said, "Lovely the Brits are here" and offered me a drink, a Pepsi Cola! I was very thirsty so I knocked it right back and saw the chap looking at me a bit strangely, however he filled it up again and I drank that very quickly. I suddenly realised I was completely pie-eyed as the drink was laced with their own alcohol, a type of moonshine that they produced. He must have assumed I realised what it was. I got up and I walked straight back inside! If I had stayed out in that sunshine for another two minutes I wouldn't have moved.

On return to the UK it was now even clearer that we had a very big problem; we needed to create the logistic support for an armoured force which was resilient and was able to operate over extended distances in the desert.

The newly formed Joint Force Headquarters (JFHQ) was nearly complete in their home underground. They were already grappling with some of the enormous challenges that the Logisticians were going to have to solve. I was an Infantryman with little logistic experience although a knowledge of what would be needed. However in the Logistic and Personnel Headquarters there were 120 specialised Staff Officers with years of experience in their speciality and a network of support behind them. They were a wonderful lot, completely dedicated to producing the very best service that they possibly could to those who were being deployed and were already way ahead with trying to solve some of the seemingly intractable problems.

Brigadier Firth and Captain Martin in the Bunker

I have to mention that Margaret Thatcher and her Government were completely supportive and money was not particularly the problem. However manpower was, and there was an irritating capping of numbers which made it extraordinarily difficult as new challenges appeared and we had to make detailed and endless cases for manpower if we wanted to have increased forces in the Gulf.

Chain of Command

It was at the end of September that General Peter de la Billiere was appointed as Commander of our Forces in the Gulf and came to JFHQ at High Wycombe on 5 October for an initial briefing prior to his deployment to his Headquarters which was being established in Riyadh alongside General Norman Schwarzkopf and the Coalition Headquarters.

The Battle Management Group at JFHQ had now been formed under the Chairmanship of Dick Johns and with 6 Members which met twice a day at 6 am and 4pm. The planning of the deployment and the move of aircraft and other facilities were the responsibility of this Management Group together with all support and personnel matters. This soon expanded to include operational oversight and planning.

The Members of the BMG could only miss one meeting and this restricted the time that you could be away unless in Theatre and here was a problem. Clare and

I had moved into the house in Codford that needed a fair amount of work which we were going to do together. I disappeared to the Bunker for 7 months leaving everything to her; every now and then I returned home often by helicopter for a very short visit. If I missed the four o'clock meeting I had to be back at six in the morning or if I missed the six o'clock one I had to be back by four. Sadly my interest in the detailed refurbishment and redecoration of the house could have been greater!

The BMG now got seriously to work. We discussed how to deploy and then support 7 Armoured Brigade and possibly in due course an Armoured Division in a desert environment and operating over long distances. Eventually the Logisticians were supporting the biggest deployment of British Forces since the 2nd World War, totalling over 45,000 individuals operating in a desert several thousand miles from their base and hundreds of miles into the desert.

Creating the Logistic Support

A considerable amount of midnight oil was burnt as we began to consider all the things which would be required to keep this force on the road and fighting. After all a tank without fuel or ammunition is just scrap metal. We had already examined the business of water and engineer teams had gone out to Saudi Arabia to start prospecting for water and to drill wells if needed. In addition 2 ships were taken up from trade (TUFT) which carried water and were based in Al Jubayl with similar arrangements initially for fuel.

However there were even more compelling problems such as obtaining desert clothing and boots, tanks which were only managing to do an average of 100 kilometres between breakdowns and the Warrior Armoured Personnel Carrier was only slightly better. Our medical services had been completely emasculated and Field Hospitals had to be created and deployed together with Field Surgical Teams. The distances in the desert were going to be so enormous that tanks could not approach the battle on tracks and a very large number of tanks transporters would be required with many hired in theatre with all the difficulties of local drivers. In addition there was a shortage of ammunition, of spares in all areas and of course shipping.

There remained very few British flagged ships and most had to be taken up from trade (TUFT). A particular challenge was to produce fresh food and a Field Bakery found in a museum was eventually refurbished and deployed and produced hot bread and rolls for most of our deployed force. Indeed Kate Adie used to come to the Field Bakery most days to have a shower and also to find fresh bread and rolls.

The build-up in the Gulf of ammunition, fuel, replacement power packs, and rations was monitored and reviewed daily. Fortunately Martin White had rented a large cold store at Al Jubyal and this was of enormous help in purchasing and supplying fresh food.

A difficult problem was the care of fatal casualties. For religious reasons they could not be buried in theatre as was our normal policy. Several refrigerated containers were rented and mercifully hardly used but allowed the fatalities to be held until after hostilities when they could be returned to UK with due ceremony.

Care of the wounded was an absolute priority. A system had to be devised to get casualties off the battlefield and back to the UK as rapidly as possible but with staging areas for those too ill to travel. Our medical services were desperately short and individual reservists were reluctant to volunteer unless compulsorily called up. The key to survival of the wounded would be Field Surgical Teams able to carry out lifesaving surgery as far forward as possible. We just did not have this capability.

A British Field Hospital close to the border with Iraq ready for early casualties with full surgical capabilities and helicopters.

Fortunately several countries including Romania and Canada offered field hospitals and others sent Field Surgical Teams which all helped to build a network of

Field Hospitals and medical support. This included a Field Hospital in the Goodyear factory and base Hospitals in Cyprus and Bahrain. Casualty evacuation helicopters were deployed to collect casualties often far forward and fly them rapidly to a field Hospital in the desert. Dedicated C130 medical evacuation planes could fly casualties from forward desert strips just behind the battlefield back to UK or Cyprus. Fortunately this was hardly tested.

There was the threat of chemical warfare and this led to the programme of inoculations. We borrowed excellent decontamination equipment and vehicles from the German Army.

Deployment Starts

In early October 1990 it was time for another extended visit to the Gulf starting at the Headquarters in Riyadh with a session with Peter de la Billiere and his staff before flying on to Al Jubayl to meet Brigadier Martin White who had established the Force Maintenance Area next to the docks. This competent professional and very sharp Logistician was our man in the Gulf and we enjoyed an extremely close and good relationship which helped enormously to provide all the support that was needed. It was our task to provide what he needed.

Throughout October 7 Armoured Brigade was arriving in theatre and it was quite emotional to see a British Landing Ship Tank unloading Challenger Tanks onto the dockside and seeing the professional reception arrangements which were being made. Marrying up the hardware with the manpower became difficult as the timings between those flying out and the tanks proved a little difficult, particularly as the armoured vehicles had to be up-armoured.

The RAF Transport Fleet was immensely impressive. They seemed to be working day and night and we were very fortunate that quite recently a number of Tri-Star's had been purchased which allowed a few passengers but a large area for freight. They flew vast tonnages of stores into the Gulf.

It was a surprise to discover that our armoured vehicles needed up armouring and this became a major task. Steel sheets were manufactured in the United Kingdom, flown out to the Gulf and a system was in place so that tanks and APCs on arrival went straight into a special REME Workshop to have these large sheets of metal attached to the sides to protect the tracks and give added protection to the hull.

There were other difficulties at that time because most units had been reduced to 60% of their strength, so they had to be reinforced to bring them up to a war fighting capability. In addition the War Maintenance Reserve had been reduced and had to be reconstituted together with a force of battle casualty replacements and also a Guard Force of 3 Infantry Battalions to create and be prepared to accept a very large number of prisoners. There can hardly have been a Battalion or an Armoured Regiment in the British Army that did not have soldiers in the Gulf.

In addition, as mentioned, the British Army of the Rhine was stripped of gun barrels, tank engines, spares and every conceivable type of support in order to create the back up for what was now to be 1st (UK) Armoured Division deployed in the Gulf. The Division was preparing for the offensive operations which now subsumed the defensive plans that had been developing.

Operations

In the initial stages of deployment 7 Armoured Brigade was training with the US Marines. They built up a marvellous relationship and had created common operational procedures.

General Peter de la Billiere was convinced that the British Golden Division should not be employed in a slogging battle directly north up the coast and into Kuwait but should take part in what was now developing into plans for a wide left hook across the desert approaching Kuwait from the west. General Norman Schwarzkopf was very reluctant to make changes so late in the day and it would have created some problems of deployment and assignment which naturally he was reluctant to solve at this late stage.

However, Peter de la Billiere with the full backing of Paddy Hine decided that he must press on with this case for reassignment. General Schwarzkopf expressed doubts as to whether our Division could support itself during an extended battle in the desert. The issue of this re-subordination was building to a climax and Peter de la Billiere asked that I and a small Logistic Team could brief Schwarzkopf's Force Commanders on our ability to sustain a Force travelling 300 to 500 miles through the desert.

We flew out overnight 12/13 December to present on 13 December. Phillip Taylorson and Peter Sharp accompanied me, both professional Logisticians. This small team would present to all of the component Commanders of the Coalition; a daunting task. During the flight we sat over a computer and spent the night working and re-working the facts and figures which were not particularly encouraging. One of the team was convinced that we should be honest and say that the Division could not support itself, while the other member of the team felt that the usual inventiveness of our forces would overcome any difficulties that they encountered. In the event we decided that we must be upbeat and rely on the usual ability and flexibility of the British Army to keep the Division supplied and moving.

We produced a few slides in American tonnes showing our requirements and how we would provide what was needed. The presentation demonstrated how fuel, water, ammunition, medical, resupply and technical support would be provided and even suggested that we might have more water available than we needed and could offer some of this to the American Forces! This impressive audience of senior coalition commanders were clearly doubtful to start with but the facts produced were persuasive. There were a few questions but the message was accepted and In due course General Schwarzkopf agreed that re-subordination could take place.

The British Team
Lieutenant General Sir Peter De La Billiere
Brigadier Simon Firth
Lieutenant Colonel Philip Taylorson
Major Peter Sharp
Presenting to:
General Norman Schwarzkopf - Commander in Chief Allied Forces

Listed:
Lieutenant General Calvin Waller - Deputy Commander in Chief Allied Forces
Major General Bob Johnston - Chief of Staff HQ Allied Forces
Major General Moore - Chief of Operations Allied Forces
Major General Starling - Chief of Logistics Allied Forces
Rear Admiral Sharp - Chief of Civil Liaison and Public Affairs Allied Forces
Lieutenant General John Yeosock - US Army Commander
Brigadier General Monroe - Chief of Logistics. US Army CENTAF
Lieutenant Chuck Horner - Commander of Coalition Air Forces
Colonel Tuder - Assistant Chief of Logistics US Army CENTAF
Colonel McClenahan -Deputy to Commanding General US US Marines Central
Command

In Peter de la Billiere's book 'Storm Command' he described the presentation as a
"brilliant exposition only 20 minutes long, of how to support the Division with our
own resources even though its supply line would be up to 400 miles long." In due
course 1st Armoured Division came under command V11 US Corps much to the
disappointment of 7 Armoured Brigade and the US Marine Corps.

Once this re-subordination had taken place Martin White started the process of
building a Forward Force maintenance Area 300 miles up the single supply route.
I made my last visit to ensure that we were providing everything that we could and
that it was working on the ground. The visit took me up into the desert to visit 7
Armoured Brigade and the Queen's Royal Irish Hussars. I was given a driver who
allegedly knew his way up the tap line MSR and into the operational area. After we
had been travelling north for a couple of hours I began to realise that we must be far
north and had missed the road west and might even be approaching the Iraqi border.
We eventually stopped at what seemed to be a Police Post, where some extremely
unfriendly Policemen took us into their tent, gave us tea, but were clearly unsure
what to do with us. I have never really found out where we had got to in the dark,
but certainly did not feel that we were amongst friends.

As expected morale was high in the Division and preparations well advanced.
Equipment was performing much better and maintenance extremely thorough. The
mean time between breakdowns was now 150 Kms but this still meant that if the full
Division was advancing an armoured vehicle would breakdown about every 50 Kms.
We needed to address this.

The War

We could not have managed this operation without nearly 6 months of preparation, but that time had allowed us to deploy all the forces, time to train in the desert and find weaknesses, improve reliability of equipment and put in place a complex and efficient logistic system including time to outload from Al Jubayl into the forward force maintenance area and beyond the stores, ammunition, fuel and everything that would be needed to support a hungry, thirsty and mobile Division as they crossed into Iraq, swung right and headed for Kuwait city.

In conjunction with Martin White we had invented a system of logistics, which had been described to Schwarzkopf at the briefing, of mobile support teams following our forces as they advanced. As one became depleted, then another moved forward to take its place, so that the armoured forces never had to stop and wait. Our wheeled support vehicles just could not keep up so we used the M453 tracked vehicles, borrowed from the Americans, to re-supply combat stores and to follow the combat forces closely. Following the visit to the Division we now arranged for the M453 to carry power packs directly behind the advancing Brigades and be able to come straight alongside a broken tank and change the power pack within minutes.

Again quoting from Peter de la Billiere's book Storm Command he says that:

"The reason for our success was the outstandingly high level of our logistic back up which had continuously expanded and adapted to meet every demand."

Martin White's able direction had developed this into an effective system to support a rapid advance northward and the move forward from a Forward Maintenance Area to Forward Bases as required. This included an enormous ammunition site, about 24,000 tonnes of ammunition, 3 million litres of fuel, the bakery which continued to provide fresh rations right into the middle of February, a long line of supply which was a round trip of about 500 miles with drivers and low loaders continuously moving up and down the tap line road which was our main supply route.

Our job - by sea, by air and by purchasing in theatre - was to make sure that Martin White had every facility that he needed and this was an enormous task with ships taken up from trade combined with the enormously heavy workload on RAF Transport Command.

I want to make special mention of the medical support which was developed with an early estimate of about 300 casualties dead and wounded each day of the battle in the initial phases. Fortunately casualties were very light and this comprehensive system was hardly used. In the first visit to Al Jubayl with the small team who were there already, we had identified the Goodyear Factory as an ideal place for a hospital but also devised a system of casualty evacuation helicopters which could take casualties back to an air strip in the desert and from there direct to Cyprus or to the United Kingdom.

War

The air war started just after midnight on 17th January with a coordinated and enormous assault on the Iraqi communications infrastructure and reserves and this continued right the way through until the start of the ground war. The purpose was to reduce the effectiveness of the Iraqi Army so that the ground forces could carry out their swing through Iraq and into Kuwait.

However just after midnight on night of 30th and 31st January a large Iraqi force stormed across the border through Khafji and threatened a serious breakthrough. The Coalition Forces mostly Arab were able to stop this attack and allow the Allied Air Forces to pick off the armoured vehicles and to defeat this incursion. However a large amount of artillery ammunition had been used and this made me wonder whether the amount that we had calculated to be needed per gun was sufficient.

The next morning we ordered a new ammunition ship to be taken up from trade, purchased additional ammunition from Italy which was picked up by the ship on its way to the Gulf, and this loaded ammunition ship arrived at Al Jubayl and came alongside just as the war ended. I am still waiting for the bill.

The Ground Attack

The ground war started at 04.00 on G day which was Sunday 24th February and in spite of the degradation of the Iraqi Forces in front of our advance, I always have a thought for the tank driver of the first tank to cross the border into Iraq and how he would have no idea what his reception might be or indeed the operations and fighting which he and his fellows might be about to encounter which could include chemical attack. It was just dawn and in the half-light the leading tank crossed the small ridge and slowly advanced down into the narrow lane which had been cleared in the minefield. Then accelerating up the slope and into Iraq and war. At that stage the outcome of the battle was completely unknown and there was also the threat of chemical and biological warfare.

However the Division had a rapid and successful advance to the edge of Kuwait city, cutting the Basra road with the only casualties being a blue on blue when an

American A10 attacked two Warriors of the 3rd Battalion the Royal Regiment of Fusiliers. Resistance was mercifully light but still active enough for our 2 Brigades to have to operate effectively and to fight their way forward including hand to hand fighting. They had the edge with night vision and with the range of their guns, and were therefore able to deal with resistance as it appeared.

The re-supply system worked miracles and kept the whole Division on the move. There was still considerable concern about the reliability of our armoured vehicles, the resupply of the power pack which weighed 6 tons was efficient enough to keep most vehicles operating, although there was a trail of broken down vehicles which had to be recovered, mended and put back into the battle line. 74 tank power packs were changed during the advance and it is to the credit of the arrangements and REME that only one tank was out of action at the end of the battle.

The logisticians worked in difficult conditions throughout this battle to keep our Division operating, fuelled up with plenty of ammunition and their vehicles moving. It also included the Lynx helicopters who were in action so that commanders at every level were never inhibited by inadequate logistic support. On conclusion of operations the Division had travelled 300 miles, knocked out over 60 main battle tanks and 90 armoured personnel carriers and 37 artillery pieces besides capturing 5000 prisoners. The prisoners were in a really poor state, both exhausted and often wounded, but were of course looked after well, fed and made as comfortable as can be in a prisoner of war camp. The total of Iraqi prisoners taken by the Coalition Forces was over 60,000.

Post War
Once hostilities were completed I was fortunate enough to fly to Saudi Arabia and Peter de la Billiere lent me his HS125 for a tour of parts of the battlefield and to visit our Logistic Units.

Martin White and his team were tired but also elated at having produced such an effective support system. Iraq seemed to be covered in a haze of oily smoke and on the ground covered with burnt out and half destroyed armoured vehicles. It was an extremely depressing sight. In one location there were piles of Iraqi ammunition and some of it was filled with chemical, which I am pleased to say, was never used.

Prior to the operations there was much discussion about inoculations for biological and chemical warfare and every soldier in theatre was offered a cocktail of inoculations and injections which many accepted. In the event neither biological nor chemical warfare was used.

There has been some questioning of the decision to stop operations at the time that they did and even some comment that our forces had defeated the Iraqi Army and could easily have gone straight on to Baghdad.

I think this would have been quite wrong. The United Nations Resolution gave legal power to relieve Kuwait and this was done. Towards the end of hostilities there were streams of refugees and military leaving Kuwait across the Mitla Ridge and onto the Basra Road. Our pilots were stacked above this road and quite unopposed were able to destroy vehicle after vehicle on the road. This became an extremely uncomfortable operation and it was a relief when operations ceased, even though the Republican Guard had not been completely destroyed.

In the bunker at High Wycombe there was considerable pleasure and joy at a job which had been well done. Logistics had not inhibited operations.

Clearing Up

It was all over very quickly but the recovery, repair and return of tons of ammunition and other stores was a major task. We also spent time and effort arranging for representatives of the National Army Museum to fly out to the Gulf and return with containers of Iraqi equipment.

We were visited by Her Majesty the Queen who came round the Logistic Operations Room. The computer system designed to connect people in the Gulf was operating and all the screens were on. When Her Majesty visited this room she was interested in this system of communications and looked over the shoulder of an operator at his screen. To my horror I saw what she was looking at. The operator had sent a message "Queen is just coming – must go" and the reply was "F*** off – pull the other one" or something which was pretty offensive. The Queen looked over his shoulder and saw the message but took it entirely in her stride and said to the Operator: "Will you tell your friend that We are here and wish him the best of good fortune for the future". She certainly captured all our hearts at that moment.

We were also visited by the Prime Minister John Major and he gave us a salutary lesson in the reality of military operations. During our brief we had made some comments about the lack of resilience in our forces, the shortage of manpower and some of the difficulties in managing both the equipment and our resupply system. He accepted all this and made copious notes, but at the end he said "Well we won didn't we."

I suppose that we must appreciate that we are an Insurance Policy and as with any Insurance Policy you pay the smallest premium. Of course this means that our leaders must rely on the initiative, drive and flexibility of our Armed Forces to rise to the occasion whatever the challenge and however difficult this might be.

Conclusion

There are often completely unexpected operations which need special efforts. The deployment of 1st Armoured Division to the desert for the Gulf War and the subsequent operations was sudden and a surprise. The Logistic support that was provided by so many people in extraordinary circumstances to a force operating on its own in the desert was certainly exceptional.

Commanders Presentation in USA on Operation Granby
Commander Transport and Movements HQ UKLF
Date 8th October 91

"The desert is heaven for tacticians and hell for Admin staff " so says a handwritten note found at El Alamein in the western desert in 1942.

I would remind you of the features of desert fighting;
  - Stretched lines of communication
  - High rates of ammunition expenditure
  - Rapid manoeuvre

All of which pose great difficulties for the logistics organisation.

In anticipation of desert conflict, by 25th Feb 91, when 1 (UK) Armoured Division crossed the start line, the following troops and equipment had been moved by air, and the 6000 Nautical miles by sea from the United Kingdom the Saudi Arabia in a six month period.

35000 TROOPS FLOWN INTO THEATRE ON 1100 SORTIES
15000 VEHICLES INCLUDING 2500 AFVS
46000 TONS OF AMMUNITION)
30000 TONS OF GENERAL STORES) on 126 ships most of which
were chartered.

5000 CONTAINERS)

A remarkable achievement considering no JTP existed for such an operation, the deployment was mounted from two UK and BAOR and the logistical support for the fighting troops in many cases had to be cobbled together at short notice from many disparate units.

We learn:

- *Two thirds of UK troops, some 6000 troops were deployed in the Gulf. In order to achieve this UK had to rely on 100 Territorial Army soldiers on six month engagements serving with the United Nations Forces in Cyprus.*
- *Some members of the T.A. in specialist fields, particularly in the Royal Army Transport Corps were called out. The majority of TA. soldiers including 496 MCLU who helped outload the US Ammunition Depot at Caerwent were volunteers who were doing annual camps or additional voluntary training days in support of the operation.*
- *Movement Controllers were at a premium and in order to release sufficient assets to deploy in the Gulf twenty TA Movement Controllers were employed in BAOR.*
- *17 Port and Maritime Regiment Royal Corp Transport provided port operators to assist with loading at Marchwood Military Port on Southampton Water & BAOR Ports as well as a major detachment at the port of Al Jubayl in Eastern Saudi Arabia.*
- *The arrival port in Saudi Arabia for the 1 (UK) Armoured Division meant Port Operators were working under the most arduous conditions- temperatures of 55 degrees were recorded on the tank decks on board ship.*
- *There was also a shortage of Specialist Vehicle Drivers, in particular HGV drivers which affected the tank transporter operations. Although this was eased in part by the use of the host nation low loaders this caused further difficulties because of the uncertain reliability of the local drivers. Vehicles often went missing or failed to appear for tasks at all. At one point during the Haj in Ramadan a dozen or so of our coaches disappeared overnight- they had gone to Mecca to make some extra cash!*
- *There was also a lack of sufficiently trained fuel tanker drivers. This was addressed by building a Bulk Fuel Installation.*
- *Ambulance Support was provided by the Ghurkha Transport Squadron from Hong Kong assuming the role of an Ambulance Squadron in the Gulf. The reason for this was that apart from troop ambulances on BAOR there is no regular ambulance unit in the British Army.*
- *Ninety percent of the RCT's transporters deployed in Saudi Arabia were tasked virtually non-stop for eight months. As well as all of the British armoured vehicles 7 Tank transporter regiment RCT were called upon to remove a large number of captured Iraqi vehicles.*

The RCT drove millions of miles with astonishingly few traffic accidents considering the conditions they were asked to operate in thousands of tons of stores and equipment were moved over thousands of miles. Fighting troops on the ground were given the right stores at the right time in order to carry out their tasks. RCT soldiers acquitted themselves particularly well in all phases of the operation- standards of leadership, training and professionalism prompted high praise from all quarters and enhanced the corps reputation.

Unlike the American Reserve Forces the UK Territorial Forces were not fully mobilised. Also unlike the American military the British forces use relatively few containers in peacetime and were not geared up to manage or handle large numbers efficiently. As an indication of the relative infancy in container operations, the British Forces deployed only three rough terrain container handlers compared with the one hundred deployed by the American Forces. We were unable to purchase any further container handling equipment in theatre and could only hire locally driven container handlers on a short term basis. The equipment was unreliable and could only be used in the port area. For long periods the handling of containers was a headache! The problem was solved by using other methods such as craneage, drops with its container flat tracks and HIK equipment. In early deployment the US Marines in Al Jubayl were most helpful and lent us some of their RCTHS .

Notes
JTP : *Joint Theatre Plan*
BAOR: *British Army of the Rhine.*
HIK: *Hooklift Interface Kit*
RCTHS: *Regimental Combat Team, Headquarters and Service Company [US Marines]*
Note: *Thanks to Colonel Richard H. Whaley (retired) US Army for American military terms.*

Logistic Facts and Figures
Moved into Theatre
1126 Flights
126 ships
35504 Pax
13500 Vehicle
48000 tonnes of ammunition
5000 ISO Containers

Units
3 Field Squadron R.E.
Moved 849,000 tonnes of earth
Dug 168,000 metres of ditching
Produced 26,000,000 litres of drinking water.

14 Sqn RE
In loaded 12,250,000 maps
10 Regt RCT
Delivered 24,000,000 litres of water
27 RCT
In one month [January 1991] covered 1,150,000 miles
24 [Airmobile] Field Ambulances
Administered 10,000 vaccinations – 25,000 injections.

The Desert Rats in the Gulf
DESERT STORM was the name given to the International operation to liberate Kuwait
from the occupying Iraqi forces in 1991. It began on 16th January with the biggest air
raid ever mounted. The air war continued for six weeks, and on 24th February DESERT
SWORD the land operation began.

Just 100 hours later, US President Bush called a ceasefire; Kuwait had been liberated and
the Iraqi Army had been driven out and crushed.

DESERT SABRE was the British Army's contribution to DESERT SWORD. The
35,000 troops of the 1st Armoured Division, The Desert Rats, played a key part in what
proved to be one of the swiftest and most impressive victories in recent military history.

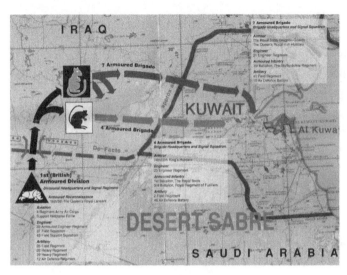

Desert Sabre Map

Brigadier Simon Firth CBE

Simon Firth was born into a military family in 1939. There was little discussion about a career. It was assumed that he would join the Army and the Gloucestershire Regiment. This seemed to be inevitable as his father had been in the Gloucestershire Regiment and had a most distinguished career and a quite extraordinary time during World War 2. He commanded the Royal Sussex in North Africa and then commanded 5 different Brigades on the way up through Italy, having landed at Salerno. He fought in Anzio where he replaced a wounded Commander and was also at Casino, Florence, Rome and most of the opposed river crossings.

Towards the end of the War he went to Greece to command the British Troops in that country during the Civil War and then to Berlin during the Berlin Airlift. Simon remembers being in Berlin after the war, aged about 7 to find a completely demolished city with all the food, coal and everything needed being flown into Berlin while the City was completely cut off by the Russians. He returned to Berlin with the Gloucestershire Regiment 25 years later to find a glass and steel city which had risen from these horrific ashes.

On Commissioning he joined the Gloucestershire Regiment, served in a variety of places including Germany and Cyprus where he met his wife Clare. They were then fortunate to have a posting to the 1st Battalion the Royal Canadian Regiment in London, Ontario for two and half very happy years before joining the Glosters in Berlin. After Staff College he spent a considerable amount of time in Northern Ireland. The Glosters *were deployed in Londonderry in 1969 as one of the first Battalions and this was followed by several tours in the Divis Flats and Lower Falls area of Belfast.*

He was Brigade Major of 3 Infantry Brigade responsible for the Headquarters commanding the eleven battalions guarding the Border. In 1977 he was appointed to Command 1st Bn the Gloucestershire Regiment in Ballykelly with responsibility for the notorious South Derry area.

Following command and a period of teaching at the Army Staff College, he went to the Ministry of Defence on the staff of the Quartermaster General and started learning something of the art of logistics and support and also the Defence Organisation Secretariat working for the Chief of the Defence Staff while the reorganisation of the Ministry of Defence took place. It was then the Royal College of Defence Studies followed by command of 49 Infantry Brigade, part of 2 Infantry Division with a NATO reinforcement role in support of the 1st British Corps in Germany.

Finally he became the Assistant Chief of Staff at Headquarters United Kingdom Land Forces in Wilton, responsible for logistics, personnel and Army quartering which led into his role in the Gulf War.

He retired in 1992. He then ran the Bath and West Showground for about 10 years. He was awarded for operations in Northern Ireland the GOC's Commendation, Mentioned in Dispatches, M.B.E., O.B.E and finally following the Gulf War the C.B.E.

CHAPTER 16

From the Common's to the Combat Zone - Iraq 2003
Andrew Murrison

I served for 18 years as a medical Officer in the Royal Navy during what is now almost affectionately known as the Cold War. When I left to become MP for the Wiltshire constituency of Westbury in June 2001 I thought my days in uniform would be confined to a rather jolly fortnight once a year on exercise as a reservist. I was wrong.

In March 2003 Tony Blair decided to commit the UK to a war in Iraq for reasons that have turned out to be spurious. The then Leader of the Opposition took my party through the lobby in support – without me.

Ironically, in September 2003 call up papers landed on my doormat in Warminster inviting me to report to the reserves mobilization centre at Chetwynd Barracks near Nottingham. I was delighted. We were in the throes of moving house, a process I detest, so my wife would have to manage the whole ghastly business without me. Hurrah!

It was the summer recess and the dreaded party conference season so the day job was not at its usual frenetic pace. MP colleagues kindly offered to plug gaps and, I understood, there was e-mail in Iraq that I could use to deal with anything urgent.

At Chetwynd barracks the quartermaster, an amused constituent, issued me with a whole load of stuff that hopefully is now in its final resting place, the loft. One of the more obvious signs of 'jointery' in the Armed Forces is that these days you are quite likely to find RN and RAF personnel decked out in green or desert combat gear looking like soldiers, unthinkable when I joined up in 1981.

Officers of a certain rank and doctors are issued, not with the workmanlike SA80 rifle, but with a 9mm Browning pistol. In Iraq this largely decorative item is seen as a status symbol. As a navy doctor I never had to handle small arms since they are rather frowned on in ships. After much patient coaching, I was reasonably confident that I would get through my deployment without provoking any disobliging 'blue-on-blue' incidents.

I have never enjoyed flying 'Crab-Air.' RAF trooping flights mean you have to sit facing the back, the stewardesses are invariably hirsute RAF corporals and no drinks trolley will call. It is best to take a relaxed view of departure and arrival times.

My arrival at the battlegroup HQ of 40 Regiment Royal Artillery at Az Zubayr port between Basra and Um Qasr provoked some merriment. I would have expected nothing else – a *Navy* doctor and a politician, what sport! The CO was a very able man called Lieutenant Colonel Richard Nugee. Richard observed upon my arrival that he learnt I was coming, not from Brigade, but from an altogether more reliable source, the Daily Telegraph.

40 Regiment RA was operating in its infantry role supported by detachments from other units. I sensed 'The Lowland Gunners' missed their guns but the current commitment to counter-insurgency operations has left the Army short of infantry. It is a tribute to its other arms that they are able to flex in the way they do.

Dr Andrew Murrison MP in Iraq 2003

Part of the battlegroup's job was to apprehend what were then called Former Regimen Extremists, later Former Regimen Loyalists. The British Army has some experience of picking up suspects from its operations in Northern Ireland. The '4 o'clock knock' is found to be the most effective since people are usually at home and at that time in the morning less likely to offer resistance. The prize was always the discovery of a high value suspect of the sort the Americans listed in their 'pack of cards.' During these early morning excursions into the small towns of southeast Iraq, the medical teams I was responsible for deployed forward to render assistance as required. Very much in the line of fire.

Detainees were questioned locally and either released or sent to the now controversial Theatre Internment Facility (TIF) at Um Qasr.

Undoubtedly the Army apprehended some very bad men and I suspect made Iraq a safer place. Those that criticise the robustness of operations from the comfort of their armchairs have very little appreciation of the environment at the time and seem to imagine that Basra in 2003 was like Bristol or Birmingham.

However, I did feel for the bulk of the detainees, some of whom I suspect were stitched up by informants trying to settle old scores or been the victims of intelligence of the quick and dirty variety. If I had been hauled out of my bed at 4am in front of my family, been obliged to crouch in the dirt for hours in the lee of an SA80 rifle and suffered the indignity of interrogation by an individual who had not modelled himself on Mary Poppins I think I would be a bit miffed. My heart and mind probably would not be well disposed towards my adversaries.

In truth I had to deal with relatively little trauma. Most of the cases that presented to my Regimental Aid Post were medical rather than surgical. Throughout history, disease has always been much more effective in degrading a fighting force than injury. Boring old gastroenteritis was my main problem.

An IT cabin had appeared at HQ for the use of off duty personnel. It was a pearl beyond value since it meant I could file my weekly column to the Wiltshire Times and deal with urgent constituency business. The column went swimmingly until the dead hand of the MOD's media people shut it down. I could file my copy but it would have to be censored by them – and censoring takes an awfully long time. I was not surprised when the MOD managed to turn the Iranian hostage crisis of March 2007 into an embarrassing media circus.

During my time in Iraq we were treated to two ministerial visits. I missed the first one. As I arrived at Shaibah military hospital, the Minister of State for the Armed Forces Adam Ingram was departing by helo in a frenzy of dust. He had apparently been promising the doctors and nurses shed loads of money for defence medicine. Never trust a politician.

Next up was the Secretary of State himself. Richard Nugee thought it would be fun to take me along to Geoff Hoon's briefing session at the Divisional HQ that had been set up in Saddam's garish palace overlooking the Shatt Al Arab in Basra. I am not sure if Geoff was pleased to see an adversary in uniform.

I watched my party's leadership debacle on Sky TV from Iraq with a growing sense of detachment and flew home in the dying days of the fratricide. Meeting up with battle-scared colleagues in the Commons, I felt a degree of shame at being absent from the Westminster field of battle at a particularly bloody stage in my party's evolution. Eventually, Michael Howard emerged the victor, unopposed, and began the difficult task of rebuilding the Conservative Party.

As a war-sceptic returning from active service in Iraq, I was in some demand by the media, a novel and gratifying experience for a backbencher. I had a good run touring the studios before being called in to have my horoscope read by the then Chief Whip. I was considered to be 'off message.' Maybe my stint back in uniform had re-injected some sense of discipline. I shut up and found myself on the front bench.

Did my experience in Iraq change my view of the wisdom of Tony Blair's great adventure? Not a bit of it. The cost in lives, in treasure and in the goodwill of people worldwide has been enormous. But my few weeks in Iraq did teach me one thing – the British Army is simply the best and we should all be extremely proud of it.

Sometimes in a democracy lions are led by donkeys.

Dr Andrew Murrison MP served in the Royal Navy from 1981-2000 leaving as a Surgeon Commander. A reservist, he deployed to Iraq in 2003 during Operation TELIC II. He was a Shadow Defence Minister before the 2010 General Election and was appointed Minister for International Security Strategy in September 2012. He is the Conservative MP for south west Wiltshire and the Prime Minister's special representative for the Centenary Commemoration of the First World War.